WRITING & ILLUMINATING, AND LETTERING

A SCRIPTORIUM

*This drawing (about two-fifths of the linear size
of the original) is made from a photograph of a
miniature painted in an old MS. (written in 1456
at the Hague by Jean Mielot, Secretary to Philip
the Good, Duke of Burgundy), now in the Paris
National Library (MS. Fonds français 9,198).*

*It depicts Jean Mielot himself, writing upon a
scroll (said to be his "Miracles of Our Lady").
His parchment appears to be held steady by a
weight and also by (? the knife or filler in) his left
hand—compare fig. 41 in this book. Above there
is a sort of reading desk, holding MSS. for
copying or reference.*

WRITING & ILLUMIN-ATING, & LETTERING

BY EDWARD JOHNSTON, C.B.E.,
WITH DIAGRAMS AND ILLUS-
TRATIONS BY THE AUTHOR
AND NOEL ROOKE

PITMAN · LONDON
PENTALIC CORPORATION · NEW YORK

PITMAN PUBLISHING LIMITED
39 Parker Street, London WC2B 5PB

Associated Companies

Copp Clark Ltd, Toronto · Pitman Publishing Co. SA
(Pty) Ltd, Johannesburg · Pitman Publishing New
Zealand Ltd, Wellington · Pitman Publishing Pty Ltd,
Melbourne · Sir Isaac Pitman Ltd, Nairobi

Published simultaneously in the USA by Pentalic
Corporation, 132 West 22 St., New York, N.Y. 10011.

© Barbara Johnston & Priscilla Roworth 1977

First published in Great Britain 1906
32nd Impression 1975
First published in paperback 1977

UK ISBN 0 273 01064 6

Reproduced and printed by photolithography
in Great Britain at The Pitman Press, Bath

EDWARD JOHNSTON
A Biographical Note by Noel Rooke

Edward Johnston was by nature a student but partly owing to poor health, he never went to school; instead, he taught himself. This confirmed his natural independence in speculation and his scrupulous care for truthfulness in statement; he corrected and recorrected his conclusions himself. His first interests were physics, electricity and mathematics, to which was later added literature. Dominating these was a passion to discover the truth, whole and unadulterated, about all that interested him, and about what he was doing. His interests became vehicles in which he journeyed in search of truth; his life became a pursuit.

Poor health stopped an early attempt at a profession—medicine—which he was studying at Edinburgh University. He had been attracted by lettering from childhood, when he was made to write out texts in colour. From the age of about sixteen he attempted illuminated manuscripts but there was no help to be had from outside himself, to show him how to do it worthily. Penmanship had decayed, even the methods of shaping, and still more of using any but a narrow pen had been lost; narrow pens were pressed to make strokes bulge. Textbooks stated that any letter with a stem wider than could be made with a narrow pen should be drawn in outline and the space filled in with a brush. He had set himself to solve the riddle of the sphinx. He did not know it, but William Morris, and, later, Harry Cowlishaw, had both tried some experiments with penmanship, but passed on to other work. Starting from zero, alone, he rediscovered the lost methods and began to use them.

v

An introduction to Cowlishaw brought him to W. R. Lethaby, principal of the Central School of Arts and Crafts, "the one man in the world who could have helped me" as he afterwards said. That was the turning point in his life. Lethaby, who had a gift for divining students' potentialities, decided, after only one meeting with Johnston, to put him in charge of the "illuminating" class he was to start. He sent Johnston to study at the British Museum and arranged that Sir Sydney Cockerell should show him the manuscripts which he would recommend for his study. Cockerell laid stress on the Caroline and the Winchester hands of the tenth and eleventh centuries, on which Johnston later based his "foundational hand". Johnston studied them with the scrutiny of which only he was capable. The fact that after seven years of testing he should use six of them, Plates V, VII, VIII, IX, X, XI, to illustrate this book shows the wisdom of Cockerell's choice. Plates XIII, XIX, XX, and XXI are from manuscripts in Cockerell's possession which he allowed Johnston to study. To the end of his life Johnston valued Cockerell's severe criticism more highly than any other.

In 1899 Lethaby offered Johnston a class at the L.C.C. Central School of Arts and Crafts in which to teach his new discoveries. His first students included the youthful Eric Gill, the more mature Graily Hewitt—both of whom later contributed to this book—and the world-famous Cobden-Sanderson. Though the class occupied only two-and-a-half hours a week, Johnston spent ten times as long in preparing for it. A member of this class myself, I watched active and enquiring minds, such as Gill's and Cobden-Sanderson's, stretched to racing speeds in endeavouring to keep up with him. The teaching was mainly individual, with some seminar work, and blackboard talks. This book is a crystallisation of the teaching of those evenings. Two years later Lethaby asked Johnston to take a class at the Royal College of Art. As the students there were less advanced, had a more uniform background, and were six times as numerous, individual teaching was greatly restricted. However, Johnston was steadily perfecting his blackboard lectures.

Two years later he married. We are all immeasurably indebted to Mrs Johnston for what she was to him.

About the same time, Lethaby asked him to write this book, as one of a series by teachers at the Central School. It became his main work for more than three years, cutting out everything else but a little teaching. He wrote it in two years and spent the third in rewriting, shortening it by one half to its present length. This was a practical necessity but I regretted it.

Up to now his activity had been canalised, firstly into discovery, then into learning what to teach, and lastly, into writing this book. When he had finished the book he was free as never before, and his formal penmanship seemed to develop more in six months than in the preceding six years. The immediate developments were published in his portfolio, *Manuscript and Inscription Letters*. This, I think, should be studied together with this book, because it shows what had been passing through his mind while he was correcting the final proofs of the book and is, to me, almost a part of it. In 1929 he began another work on calligraphy, *Formal Penmanship*, to try to pass on what he had learnt since 1906, but this was left unfinished at his death. It was subsequently edited by Heather Child and is published by Pentalic Corporation of New York.

From 1906, Johnston's influence was great, but deep rather than wide. At first it seemed more immediately effective in subjects in which he would not have sought to interfere. For example, as a scribe he would not have ventured to design type: at most he would have co-operated by discussing essentials of letter forms with the punch-cutters who would shape the metal. At that time, Germany was beginning to abandon Gothic blackletter in favour of renaissance Roman forms, and was looking for a lead. An attempt to persuade Johnston to teach in Germany had not been successful; instead a gifted German student, Miss Anna Simons—who afterwards translated this book into German—had been sent to his classes in London and she was already back in Germany teaching Johnston's methods. Some of her German students did not have Johnston's scruples and designed printing type which, while having the imperfections resulting from penmen dictating to metal workers, struck a note which had immense influence, first in Germany, then in America, and finally in France and England. This early connection with Germany gave Johnston one lasting friend, Count Kessler, for whose Cranach Press he later co-operated with the punch-cutters, Prince and George Friend, to produce two typefaces.

He accepted a commission from a company which later became part of London Transport, to draw an alphabet for use by photo-litho-transfer on their drawn and lithographed posters. This "Underground Blockletter" of 1916 was for their own use only and was not available elsewhere. It created so much admiration that the Germans produced three block types (Cable, Erbar and Futura) which have had very wide and extensive use. Such is its popularity in America that Cable has perhaps been used more than any other display type ever made. In 1928 Eric Gill's "Gill sans" made a much finer block letter available in general use. It is second only to the "Johnston" from which it is derived, and has become the most widely used display type in Britain.

There is another subject on which Johnston had a paramount influence, although it was not his main subject: everyday handwriting. A steadily increasing number of people all over the world are being influenced by the attention he drew to semi-formal hands in Chapter XV. Johnston's main work, however, was neither in printing nor in ordinary handwriting, but in formal penmanship, from which the other two had originated. He always maintained the distinction between handwriting and formal penmanship. Formal penmanship remains intrinsically and potentially more important than either of its derivatives and it was through this that Johnston inspired first himself, then others.

For more than half his working life he wrote in round hands or hands slightly compressed. He wrote with a clarity and a directness which had not been attained for hundreds of years. In his last twenty years he developed some highly compressed hands, which had the advantages of Gothic blackletter and retained the advantages of curved strokes in round letters such as o and e. These hands are most definitely not for ordinary purposes, but are unsurpassed when the intention is deliberately to delay the process of reading in order to gather subtle overtones from the text. They command the enthusiasm of expert scribes, but are liable to greater abuse than the rounder letters.

Johnston did not approve of students writing "for practice"; he insisted that learning must be from making actual things. In his own work he did not believe in writing a trial "to see how it looks"; his results could not be achieved as the sum of a series of "mock-ups". Instead, after long thought, calculation and preparation, lasting if need be for days or weeks, he would write the actual thing, right off, at speed. If he was not satisfied he would do it again, sometimes two or three times, but each attempt was *intended* to be the final one. The cause of failure would have been defective execution, not defective planning.

His execution was a blend of deliberation and speed; the higher the speed, the greater the deliberation. His work might perhaps appear to invite direct imitation, for he shows definite methods and principles and offers standards. But the appearance would be misleading, for the value of all he did depended on the quality of the particular thought he gave to each job, as well as to his general insight. It is not easy to offer a clue to this; it is perhaps better to try to suggest how he had forged and tempered the edge of his mind.

His daughter, Miss Bridget Johnston, has rightly said that the importance of religion in his life can hardly be over-emphasised, but it was not of a usual kind. For him all work was a combination of prayer and praise; it made him feel ill to see work badly done. His active obedience to the two commandments, love of God and love of man, was qualified only when he met contempt for, or subtle disregard of truth. There are, he believed, three main approaches to Truth: Religion, Science and Art, and that creation is the outstanding function of the artist and craftsman, which distinguishes him from the religious or scientific man; that a craftsman's work could be described in the three stages of "embodying, animating and inspiring"; and that the craftsman's creations "inspire the craftsman, embody his idea and give it material life". But in a book for craftsmen, such as this, the order should be as in

ix

Genesis II, 7, "And the Lord God formed man of the dust of the ground and breathed into his nostrils the breath of life and man became a living soul." The craftsman must see, as God did, in Genesis, that his work is good; until he has set the seal of his own approval upon it, it will not be complete. From the very beginning of his working life Johnston said that the idea which had inspired him had been "*to make living letters with a formal pen*".

He held that in all work Truth must be sought; beauty is an ultimate grace which will be conferred upon the craftsman's work if it is well done. A search for beauty or an attempt to capture it will fail, like an attempt to pursue happiness. If truth has been served the result will be beauty. For him praise by work and the search for truth was life. The intensity of his belief had such a hold on him, and had such results in him, that it was possible to say, as Sir Francis Meynell did, "He was one of the few really great men of our time".

Note: The last paragraph but one is a paraphrase of a paper contributed by Bridget Johnston to a meeting of the Society of Scribes on November 10, 1945. This was printed under the title of *Tributes to Edward Johnston* at Maidstone College of Art, 1948.

AUTHOR'S PREFACE

THE arts of WRITING, ILLUMINATING, & LETTERING offer a wide field for the ingenious and careful craftsman and open the way to a number of delightful occupations. Beyond their many uses—some of which are referred to below —they have a very great educational value. This has long been recognized in the teaching of elementary design, and the practice of designing Alphabets and Inscriptions is now common in most Schools of Art. Much would be gained by substituting, generally, WRITING for *designing*, because *writing* being the medium by which our letters have been evolved, the use of the pen—essentially *the* letter-making tool—gives a practical insight into the construction of letters attainable in no other way. The most important use of letters is in the making of books, and the foundations of typography and book decoration may be mastered —as they were laid—by the planning, writing, and illuminating of MSS. in book form. Of this a modern printer, Mr. T. J. Cobden-Sanderson, says:

" In the making of the Written Book, ... the adjustment of letter to letter, of word to word, of picture to text and of text to picture, and of the whole to the subject-matter and to the page, admits of great nicety and perfection. The type is fluid, and the letters and words, picture, text, and page are conceived of as one and are all executed by one hand, or by several hands all working together without intermediation on one identical page and with a view to one identical effect. In the Printed Book this adjustment is more difficult. . . . . . . Yet in the making of the printed book, as in the making of the written book, this adjustment is essential, and should be specially borne in mind, and Calligraphy and immediate decoration by hand and the unity which should be inseparably associated therewith would serve as an admirable discipline to that end." (*And see p.* 332 *below*.)

And though calligraphy is a means to many ends, a fine MS. has a beauty of its own that—if two arts may be compared—surpasses that of the finest printing. This in itself would justify the transcribing and preservation of much good literature in this beautiful form (besides the preparation of "Illuminated Addresses," Service Books, Heraldic and other MSS.) and make the practice of formal writing desirable. And furthermore as the old-fashioned notion *that a legible hand is a mark of bad breeding* dies out, it may be that our current handwriting will take legibility and beauty from such practice. And even the strict utilitarian could not fail to value the benefits that might some day come to men, if children learnt to appreciate beauty of form in their letters, and in their writing the beauty of carefulness.

Of the practice of ILLUMINATING—properly associated with writing—it may be observed that, among various ways of acquiring *a knowledge of the elements of design & decoration* it is one of the most simple and complete. Moreover, a fine illumination or miniature has a beauty of its own that may surpass the finest printed book-decoration. And pictures in books may be as desirable as pictures on the wall—even though like the beautiful household gods of the Japanese they are kept in safe hiding and displayed only now and then.

Magnificent as are the dreams of a fine Decoration based on lettering, the innumerable practical applications of LETTERING itself (see Chap. XVI) make the study of *Letter-Craft* not only desirable but imperative. And perhaps I may here be permitted to quote from *The Athenæum* of Feb. 3, 1906, which says of "the new school of scribes and designers of inscriptions"—

"These have attacked the problem of applied design in one of its simplest and most universal applications, and they have already done a great deal to establish a standard by which we shall be bound to revise all printed and written lettering. If once the principles they have established could gain currency, what a load of ugliness would be lifted from modern civilization! If once the names of streets and houses, and, let us hope, even the announcements of advertisers, were executed in beautifully designed and well-spaced letters, the eye would become so accustomed to good proportion in these simple and obvious things that it would insist on a similar gratification in more complex and difficult matters."

Yet *Ordinary Writing* and even scribbling has had, and still might have, a good influence on the art of the Letter maker, and at least the common use of pen, ink, & paper makes it a simple matter for any one to essay a formal or 'book' hand. A broad nib cut to give clean thick and thin strokes (without appreciable variation of pressure) will teach any one who cares to learn, very clearly and certainly. And though much practice goes to the making of a perfect MS., it is easier than people suppose to make really beautiful things by taking a little pains. As "copy book" hands simple, primitive pen-forms — such as the Uncial & Half-Uncial (pp. 4, 36)—afford the best training and permit the cultivation of the freedom which is essential in writing; they prepare the way for the mastery of the most practical characters—the ROMAN CAPITAL, roman small-letter, & *Italic*—and the ultimate development of a lively and personal penmanship.

MODERN
DEVELOP-
MENT OF
WRITING
&
ILLUMI-
NATING

Developing, or rather *re*-developing, an art involves *the tracing in one's own experience of a process resembling its past development*. And it is by such a course that we, who wish to revive Writing & Illuminating, may *renew* them, evolving new methods and traditions for ourselves, till at length we attain a modern and beautiful technique. And if we would be more than amateurs, we must study and practise *the making of beautiful THINGS* and thereby gain experience of Tools, Materials, and Methods. For it is certain that we must teach ourselves how to make beautiful things, and must have some notion of the aim and bent of our work, *of what we seek and what we do*.

Early illuminated MSS. and printed books with woodcuts (or good facsimiles) may be studied with advantage by the would-be Illuminator, and he should if possible learn to draw from hedgerows and from country gardens. In his practice he should begin as a scribe making MS. books and then decorating them with simple pen & colour work. We may pass most naturally from writing to the decoration of writing, by the making and placing of *initial letters*. For in seeking first a fine *effectiveness* we may put readableness before "looks" and, generally, make a text to read smoothly, broken only by its natural division into paragraphs, chapters, and the like. But these divisions, suggesting that a pause in reading is desirable, suggest also that a mark is required—as in music—indicating the "rest": this a large capital does most effectively.

A technical division of illumination into *Colour-work*, *Pen-work*, and *Draughtsmanship* is convenient (see Chap. XI). Though these are properly combined in practice, it is suggested that, at first, it will be helpful to think of their effects as distinct so that we may attain quite definitely some mastery of pure, bright colours & simple colour effects, of pen flourishing and ornament, and of drawing (whether plain or coloured) that will go decoratively with writing or printing. This distinction makes it easier to devise definite schemes of illumination that will be within our power to carry out at any stage of our development. And while the penman inevitably gains some power of pen decoration it is well for him as an illuminator to practise in bright colours and gold; for illumination may be as brilliant and splendid in its own way as stained glass, enamels, and jewellery are in theirs.[1] At first, at any rate, hues that have the least suspicion of being dull or weak are to be avoided as though they were plainly "muddy" or "washed-out." The more definite we make our work the more definitely will our materials instruct us; and such service must precede mastery.

Referring again to good LETTERING: the second part of this book deals with some of its *Qualities*, *Forms*—the Roman Capitals & their important pen-derivatives—and *Uses*. It is written largely from

---

[1] See Chap. XVI, "Of Colour" in *Stained Glass Work* by C. W. Whall, in this Series, and the illuminator might profit by the suggestion (*ibid.*, p. 198) of playing with a home-made kaleidoscope.

the penman's point of view,[1] but a chapter on inscriptions in stone has been added and various types and modes of letter making are discussed. The essential qualities of Lettering are *legibility*, *beauty*, and *character*, and these are to be found in numberless inscriptions and writings of the last two thousand years. But since the traditions of the early scribes and printers and carvers have decayed, we have become so used to inferior forms and arrangements that we hardly realize how poor the bulk of modern lettering really is. In the recent "revival" of printing and book decoration, many attempts have been made to design fine alphabets and beautiful books —in a number of cases with notable success. But the study of Palæography and Typography has hitherto been confined to a few specialists, and these attempts to make "decorative" books often shew a vagueness of intention which weakens their interest, and an ignorance of *Letter-craft* which makes the poorest, ordinary printing seem pleasant by comparison. The development of Letters was a purely natural process in the course of which distinct and characteristic types were evolved and some knowledge of how these came into being will help us in understanding their anatomy and distinguishing good and bad forms. A comparatively little study of old manuscripts and inscriptions will make clear much of the beauty and method of the early work. And we may accustom ourselves to good lettering by carefully studying such examples as we can find, and acquire a practical knowledge of it by copying from them with a pen or chisel or other letter-making

---

[1] Dealing with the practical and theoretical knowledge of letter-making and arrangement which may be gained most effectively by the use of the pen.

tool. A conscientious endeavour to make our letter-ing readable, and models[1] and methods chosen to that end, will keep our work straight: and after all the problem before us is fairly simple—*To make good letters and to arrange them well.* To make good letters is not necessarily to "design" them —they have been designed long ago—but it is to take the best letters we can find, and to acquire them and make them our own. To arrange letters well requires no great art, but it requires a work-ing knowledge of letter-forms and of the reason-able methods of grouping these forms to suit every circumstance.

Generally this book has been planned as a sort of "guide" to models and methods for Letter-crafts-men and Students—more particularly for those who cannot see the actual processes of Writing, Illumi-nating, &c. carried out, and who may not have access to collections of MSS. Much of, if not all, the explanation is of the most obvious, but that, I hope, gives it more nearly the value of a practical demonstration. In describing methods and processes I have generally used the present tense—saying that they "*are*—": this is to be taken as meaning that they *are* so in early MSS. and inscriptions, and in the practice of the modern school of scribes who found their work on them.

Regarding the copying of early work (see pp. 161, 287, &c.), it is contended that to revive an art one must begin at the beginning, and that, in an honest attempt to achieve a simple end, one may lawfully

---

[1] In making choice of a model we seek an essentially legible character, remembering that our personal view of legibility is apt to favour custom and use unduly, for a quite bad, familiar writing may seem to us more readable than one that is far clearer in itself but unfamiliar.

follow a method[1] without imitating a style. We have an excellent precedent in the Italian scribes who went back 300 years for a model and gave us the Roman small-letter as a result (see p. 13). The beginner's attitude is largely, and necessarily, imitative, and at this time we should have much to hope from a school of Artist-Beginners who would make good construction the only novelty in their work. We have almost as much—or as *little*—to be afraid of in Originality as in Imitation, and our best attitude towards this problem is that of the Irishman with a difficulty—"to look it boldly in the face and pass on"—*making an honest attempt to achieve a simple end*. Perhaps we trouble too much about what we "ought to do" & "do": it is of greater moment *to know what we are doing & trying to do*. In so far as tradition fails to bound or guide us we must think for ourselves and in practice make methods and rules for ourselves: endeavouring that our work should *be effective* rather than have "a fine effect" —or *be*, rather than appear, good—and following our craft rather than making it follow us. For all things—materials, tools, methods—are waiting to serve us and we have only to find the "spell" that will set the whole universe a-making for us.

Endeavouring to attain this freedom we may make our Rules and Methods serve us (see p. 187),

---

[1] Much remains to be found out and done in the matter of improving tools & materials & processes, and it would be preferable that the rediscovery of simple, old methods should precede new & complex inventions. We still find the Quill— for its substance & for shaping it and keeping it sharp—is a better tool than a modern gold or metal pen (see p. 26). The old parchment, paper, ink, gilding-size & colours are all much better than those now obtainable (see pp. 17, 133, 139, 144–145). I should greatly appreciate any advice from illuminators and letter-craftsmen as to materials and methods, and should endeavour to make such information available to others—.E. J.

knowing that such Rules are only *Guides* and that Methods are suggested by the work itself: from first to last our necessary equipment consists in good models, good tools, & a good will. Within the limits of our craft we cannot have too much freedom; for too much fitting & planning makes the work lifeless, and it is conceivable that in the finest work the Rules are concealed, and that, for example, a MS. might be most beautiful without ruled lines and methodical arrangement (see p. 307). But the more clearly we realize our limitations the more practical our work. And it is rather as a stimulus to definite thought— not as an embodiment of hard and fast rules—that various methodical plans & tables of comparison & analysis are given in this book. It is well to recognize at once, the fact that mere taking to pieces, or analysing, followed by "putting together," is only a means of becoming acquainted with the mechanism of construction, and will not reproduce the original beauty of a thing: it is an education for work, but all work which is honest and straightforward has a beauty and freshness of its own.

The commercial prospects of the student of Writing & Illuminating—or, indeed, of any Art or Craft—are somewhat problematical, depending largely on his efficiency & opportunities. There is a fairly steady demand for Illuminated Addresses; but the independent craftsman would have to establish himself by *useful* practice, and by seizing opportunities, and by doing his work well. Only an attempt to do practical work will raise practical problems, and therefore *useful practice is the making of real or definite things.* In the special conditions attaching to work which the craftsman is commissioned to do for another person, there is a great advantage.

And the beginner by setting himself specific tasks (for example: making a MS. book for a specific purpose—see p. 66) should give reality to his work. As a craftsman in Lettering he might get work in some of the directions mentioned in pp. 301–5.

Although the demand for good work is at present limited, the production of good work will inevitably create a demand; and, finally, the value of Quality is always recognized—sooner or later, but inevitably —and whatever "practical" reasons we may hear urged in favour of *Quantity*, the value of Quality is gaining recognition every day in commerce and even in art, and there or here, sooner or later we shall know that *we can afford the best*.

EDWARD JOHNSTON

My thanks are due to Mr. T. J. Cobden-Sanderson, to Mr Emery Walker, and to Mr. George Allen for quotations: to Mr. Graily Hewitt, to Mr. Douglas Cockerell, to Mr. A. E. R. Gill, to Mr. C. M. Firth, and to Mr. G. Loumyer, for special contributions on gilding, binding, and inscription-cutting: to Mr. S. C. Cockerell for several of the plates: to Mr. W. H. Cowlishaw, to the Rev. Dr. T. K. Abbott, to Dr. F. S. Kenyon of the New Palæographical Society, to the Vicar of Holy Trinity Church, Hastings, to the Secretary of the Board of Education, S. Kensington, to Mr. H. Yates Thompson, to Mr. G. H. Powell, and to others, for permission to reproduce photographs, &c. and to Mr. Noel Rooke and Mr. Godfrey J. Hogg for assistance with the illustrations and many other matters: I should like moreover, to acknowledge my indebtedness to Mr. W. R. Lethaby and Mr. S. C. Cockerell for encouragement and advice in years past.
E. J.

ADDENDA & CORRIGENDA

P. 17. Beginners practising *large* writing may more easily use a *thin, or diluted, ink:* in *small* writing this does not show up the faults with sufficient clearness.

P. 25. Quills often have a sort of *skin* (which tends to make a ragged nib); this should be scraped off the back.

Pp. 29 & 39. Until the simple pen-stroke forms are mastered, the pen should be used without appreciable pressure. With practice one gains *sleight of hand* (pp. 51, 275), and slightly changing pressures & quick movements on to the *corners*, or points, of the nib are used. The forms in the best MSS. shew such variations; *e.g.* the Uncials in fig. 5 appear to have been made with varying pressure (perhaps with a soft reed) & their fine finishing-strokes with the nib-point (*comp.* forms in fig. 146). *Versals* likewise shew varying, and sometimes uncertain, structures that suggest a form consisting of strokes other than definite pen strokes.

P. 30. An ordinary strong nib may be *sharpened* several times, before it is re-cut, by paring it underneath (fig. *a*). The extra fine nib

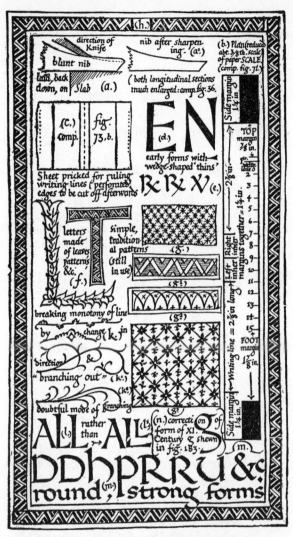

FIGS. *a* to *n*, illustrating Addenda & Corrigenda.

(p. 25), which is recommended for all fine
and careful work, must be re-cut every
time.

P. 65. The plan of a paper scale is shewn in
fig. *b*.

P. 75. The dots for lines were often pricked
through the edges of the book-sheet,
which were cut off after ruling (fig. *c*).

P. 84. The spread or *wedge-shaped* thin stroke,
sometimes very strongly marked, is
common in early forms (fig. *d*).

P. 110. *y* & *R*: better (pen) forms of these are
shewn in fig. *e*.

P. 174. Ornamental Letter forms may *consist of*
flourishes, patterns, leaves, flowers, &c.
(see fig. *f*).

Pp. 181–183. *Diapering* generally means the varie-
gation, figuring, or flowering, of a plain
or patterned surface, with a finer pattern
(see fig. 191*a*). Some diagrams of simple
patterns (*g*–*g*² from modern *cantagalli*
ware) are shewn in fig. *g*. Note: the
more solid penwork line-fillings in figs.
87, 126, make effective framing borders
(see fig. *h*).

Pp. 185–186. Note: the principle of breaking
straight or long lines, mentioned in
regard to background edges (p. 158),
and illustrated in the line-finishings (fig.
126) and flourishes (fig. 79), is related
to *branching out* and is re-creative, whereas the prolonged line is tiresome (see figs.
k, *k*¹, & *comp. k*²).

P. 213. The B & D should be *round-shouldered*—
see note to p. 246 below.

P. 224. It is sometimes better to make narrow forms than to combine wide ones—example fig. *l*.

Pp. 234–239. ⎱ The large types — "Old Face" (founded on Caslon Type) and "Old French" (modern) respectively —are used in these pages as reference or index letters (not as models).
Pp. 244–252. ⎰

P. 244. Generally *round-shouldered* letters have finer and more stable forms than square-shouldered, and generally emphasis should be laid on the *strong, thick stroke running obliquely down from left to right* (\\), while the weak, thin stroke (/) is rather to be avoided (see fig. *m*). The writing used in the diagrams in this book, considered as a formal hand, shews a little too much of the thin stroke (see p. 421).

P. 288. Commonly letters are made more slender in proportion as they are made larger, and it is generally not desirable (or possible) in practical work to have exactly similar proportions in large and small lettering.

P. 289. g from fig. 173 inaccurate—*comp.* fig. 173 & see fig. *n*.

P. 295. Ornamental letters: see note to p. 174 above.

P. 417. A small writing is often the most practical —in the matter of speed in reading and less bulk in the MS., besides speed in the writing of it—but it is more difficult for the beginner to write it well and it is apt to lose some of the virtues of formal penmanship (see Fine-pen writing, pp. 25, 52, 275, 288, 418).

P. 421. Oblique thin stroke: see note to p. 244 above.

CONTENTS

PART I

WRITING & ILLUMINATING

CHAPTER I

THE DEVELOPMENT OF WRITING

CHAPTER II

ACQUIRING A FORMAL HAND: (1) TOOLS

CHAPTER III

ACQUIRING A FORMAL HAND: (2) METHODS

XXV

CHAPTER IX

LAYING & BURNISHING GOLD

CHAPTER X

THE USE OF GOLD & COLOURS IN INITIAL LETTERS & SIMPLE ILLUMINATION

CHAPTER XI

A THEORY OF ILLUMINATION

CHAPTER XII

THE DEVELOPMENT OF ILLUMINATION

CHAPTER XIII

" DESIGN " IN ILLUMINATION

PART II

LETTERING

CHAPTER XIV

GOOD LETTERING—SOME METHODS OF CON-
STRUCTION & ARRANGEMENT

CHAPTER XV

THE ROMAN ALPHABET & ITS DERIVATIVES

APPENDIX A

CHAPTER XVI

SPECIAL SUBJECTS

APPENDIX B

CHAPTER XVII

INSCRIPTIONS IN STONE
(*By A. E. R. Gill*)

APPENDIX C

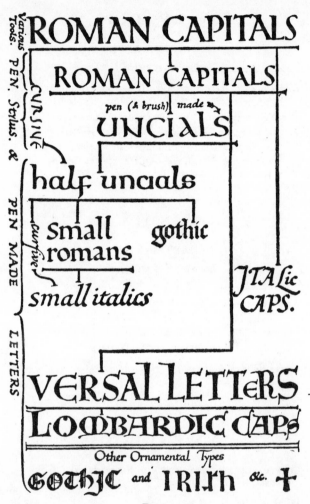

FIG. I

xxx

PART I

WRITING & ILLUMINATING

CHAPTER I

THE DEVELOPMENT OF WRITING

NEARLY every type of letter with which we are familiar is derived from the Roman Capitals, and has come to us through the medium, or been modified by the influence, of the pen. And, therefore, in trying to revive good Lettering, we cannot do better than make a practical study of the best pen-forms, and learn at the same time to appreciate the forms of their magnificent arche-types as preserved in the monumental Roman inscriptions.

The development and the relations of the principal types of letters are briefly set out in the accompanying "family tree"—fig. 1. When the student has learnt to cut and handle a pen, he can trace this development practically by trying to copy a few words from each example given below.

I

THE ROMAN ALPHABET.—The Alphabet, as we know it, begins with the ROMAN CAPITALS[1] (see fig. 2). Their fine monumental forms were evolved by the use of the chisel—

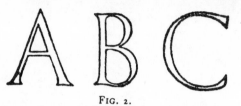

FIG. 2.

probably under the influence of writing—and had reached full development about 2000 years ago (see Plates I, II, and Chapter XV).

FORMAL WRITING—the "*book-hand*" or professional writing of the scribes—comes of the careful writing of the Roman Capitals (see also *footnote*, p. 4, on the beginnings of fine penmanship). It was the—

"*literary hand*, used in the production of exactly written MSS., and therefore a hand of comparatively limited use. By its side, and of course of far more extensive and general use, was the *cursive hand* of the time "[2]

---

[1] "The alphabet which we use at the present day . . . . is directly derived from the Roman alphabet: the Roman, from a local form of the Greek; the Greek, from the Phœnician. . . ."
It had been supposed that the Phœnician came from the Egyptian hieratic, but "*Recent discoveries prove the existence, in very remote times, in all quarters of the Mediterranean and in Egypt, of symbols resembling certain alphabetical signs and preceding even the Egyptian hieroglyphics. The early origin of our alphabet therefore still remains to be worked out.*"—*Sir Edward Maunde Thompson, "Greek and Latin Palæography," 3rd edition* (1906), pp. 1. 321.
[2] Ibid. .p. 196.

2

In early *cursive writing*—the running-hand or ordinary writing of the people—

"The Letters are nothing more than the old Roman letters written with speed, and thus undergoing certain modifications in their forms, which eventually developed into the *minuscule hand*."[1] (See fig. 3.)

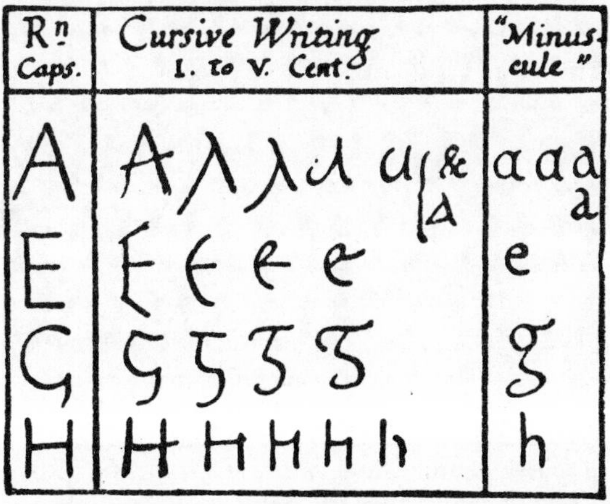

R^n Caps.	Cursive Writing 1. to V. Cent.	"Minus-cule"
A	A λ λ ͐ u ᷓ & ᴀ	a a ɑ ɑ
E	Ɛ Ɛ Ɛ ᴄ	e
Ƈ	ϛ 5 ϛ 5	ᵹ
H	H H H h h h	h

FIG. 3.

Here it is sufficient to trace the history of the *formal* Latin "hands," but the continual, modifying influence exerted on them by the ordinary *cursive* writing should be borne in mind. Notable results of this influence are seen in *Half-Uncials* and *Italics*.

SQUARE CAPITALS were formal, pen-made Roman Capitals, of the monumental type: they were used (perhaps from the *second*) till about the

---

[1] "G. & L. Palæography," p. 204. (Minuscules = "small." letters," not capitals: *conf.* printer's "lower-case." *Half-Uncials are sometimes distinguished as "round minuscules,"* p. 266, *below.*)

end of the *fifth* century for important books (see Plate III).

RUSTIC CAPITALS were probably a variety of the " Square Capitals," and were in use till about the end of the *fifth* century (fig. 4; see also p. 261).

FIG. 4.—Æneid, on vellum, third or fourth century.

ROMAN UNCIALS were fully developed by the fourth century, and were used from the fifth till the eighth century for the finest books (fig. 5).

Uncials are true pen-forms[1]—more quickly written than the " Square," and clearer than the " Rustic " Capitals — having the characteristic, simple strokes and beautiful, rounded shapes which flow from the rightly handled reed or quill. The

---

[1] It is possible that their forms were influenced by the use of the brush in painting up public notices and the like. The introduction of the use of vellum—a perfect writing material—in the making of books, undoubtedly led to a great advance in the formality and finish of the book-hands (especially of the Uncial character); practically, it may be said to mark the beginning of *penmanship* as a "fine" art. This development may be assigned to the time between the first and the third centuries (palæographical dates before the fifth century must generally be regarded as approximate).

4

INOMI

CONFITEB

INDIRE

INEOQ

JUSTITI

JUSTIFICA

CUSTO

NONMEĈ

FIG. 5.—Psalter, fifth century.

typical Uncial letters are the round D, E, H, M, U (or V), and A and Q (see p. 264).

ROMAN HALF-UNCIALS—or *Semi-Uncials* —(fig. 6) were mixed *Uncial* and *Cursive* forms adopted by the scribes for ease and quickness in writing. Their evolution marks the formal change from *Capitals* to " *Small-Letters*."

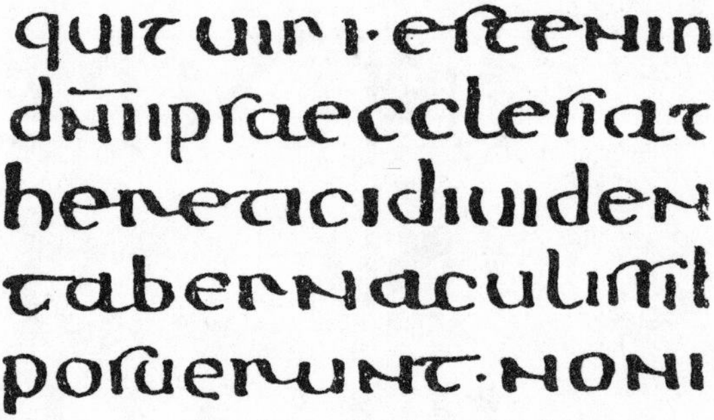

FIG. 6.—S. Augustine: probably French sixth century.

They were first used as a book-hand for the less important books about the beginning of the sixth century.

IRISH HALF-UNCIALS were founded on the Roman Half-Uncials (probably brought to Ireland by Roman missionaries in the sixth century). As a beautiful writing, they attained in the seventh century a degree of perfection since unrivalled (see Plate VI).

They developed in the eighth and ninth centuries into a " pointed " writing, which became the Irish national hand.

ENGLISH HALF-UNCIALS (fig. 7) were modelled on the Irish Half-Uncials in the seventh

6

century. They also developed in the eighth and
ninth centuries into a " pointed " writing.

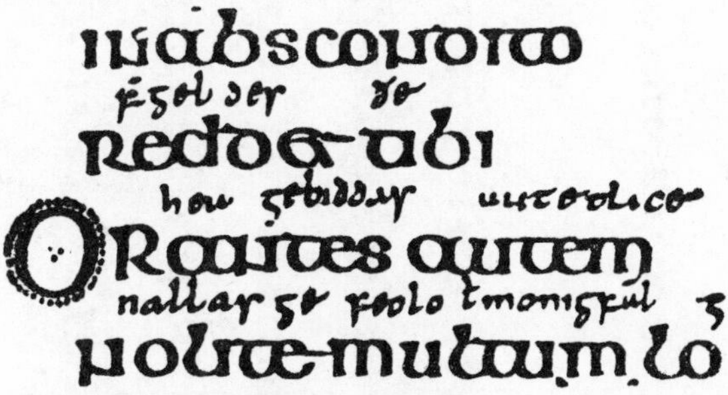

FIG. 7.—"Durham Book": Lindisfarne, about A.D. 700.
(See also Plate VII.)

*CAROLINE (or CARLOVINGIAN) WRIT-
ING.*—While English and Irish writing thus came
from Roman Half-Uncial, the Continental hands
were much influenced by the rougher Roman Cursive, and were comparatively poor till near the end
of the eighth century.

" The period of Charlemagne is an epoch in the history
of the handwritings of Western Europe. With the revival
of learning naturally came a reform of the writing in which
the works of literature were to be made known. A decree
of the year 789 called for the revision of church books;
and this work naturally brought with it a great activity in
the writing schools of the chief monastic centres of
France. And in none was there greater activity than at
Tours, where, under the rule of Alcuin of York, who
was abbot of St. Martin's from 796 to 804, was specially
developed the exact hand which has received the name
of the Caroline Minuscule."[1]

---

[1] "Greek and Latin Palæography," p. 233.

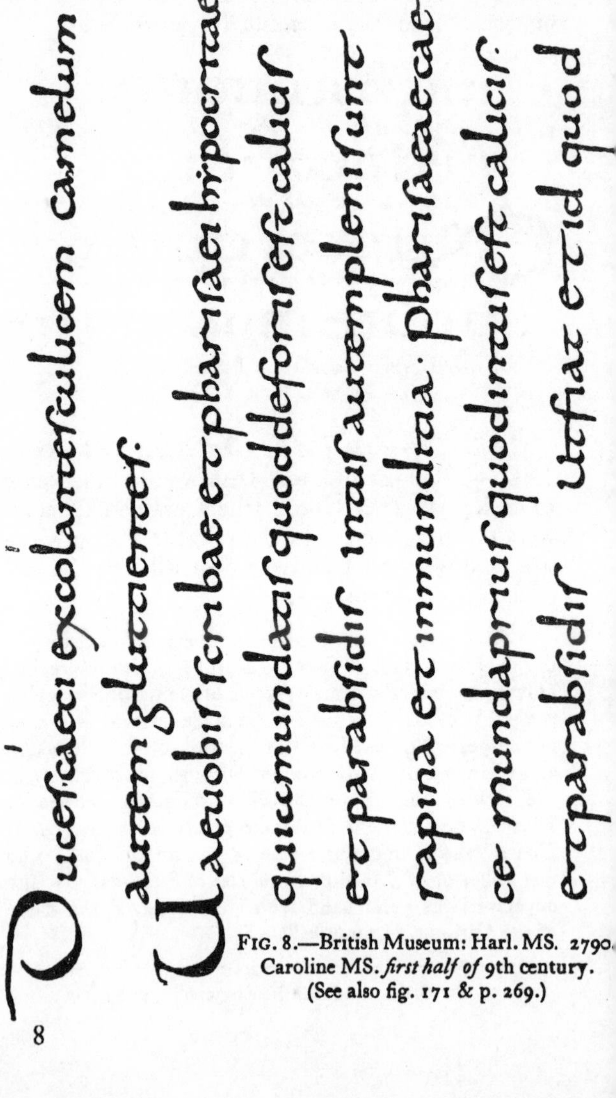

FIG. 8.—British Museum: Harl. MS. 2790. Caroline MS. *first half of* 9th century. (See also fig. 171 & p. 269.)

The influence of the Caroline hands (see fig. 8) presently spread throughout Europe. The letters in our modern copy-books may be regarded as their direct, though degenerate, descendants.

SLANTED-PEN or TILTED WRITING. —The forms of the letters in early writing indicate an easily held pen—slanted away from the right shoulder. The slanted pen naturally produced *oblique* thick strokes and thin strokes, and the thick curves were " tilted " (see fig. 9).

In the highly finished hands—used from the sixth to the eighth centuries—such as the later Uncials and the Roman, Irish, and English Half-Uncials, the pen was manipulated or cut so that the thin strokes were approximately horizontal, and the thick strokes vertical (fig. 10). The earlier and easier practice came into fashion again in the eighth and ninth centuries, and the round Irish and English hands became " pointed " as a result of slanting the pen.

The alteration in widths and directions of pen strokes, due to the use of the " slanted pen," had these effects on the half-uncial forms (see fig. 11):—

1. *The thin strokes taking an oblique (upward) direction* (*a*) (giving a sharp angle with the verticals (*d, a*)) led to angularity and narrower forms (*a¹*), and a marked contrast between thick and thin strokes—due to the abrupt change from one to the other (*a²*).

2. *The thick strokes becoming oblique* (*b*) caused a thickening of the curves below on the left (*b¹*), and above on the right (*b²*), which gave heavy shoulders and feet.

3. *The horizontal strokes becoming thicker* (*c*) gave stronger and less elegant forms.

9

SQVARE
RVSTIC *
UNCIAL

" Slanted pen ":
giving oblique
strokes & " tilted " O letters.

FIG. 9.

romɑn
UNC ial
, late.
IRISH
ençlish

pen held | OR | obliquely cut nib
Straight

" Straight pen " giving
horizontal thin strokes,
vertical thicks , & O round, upright letters.

FIG. 10.

10

4. *The vertical strokes becoming thinner (d)* (with oblique or pointed ends—not square ended) increased the tendency to narrow letters.

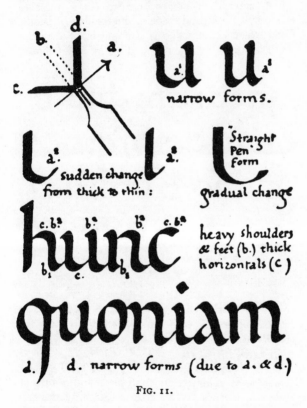

narrow forms.

sudden change from thick to thin :

Straight Pen form

gradual change

heavy shoulders & feet (b.) thick horizontals (c)

d. narrow forms (due to a. & d.)

FIG. 11.

It is to be noted that the Caroline letters—though written with a "slanted pen"—kept the open, round appearance of the earlier forms.

11

TENTH, ELEVENTH, AND TWELFTH
CENTURY WRITING.—The easy use of the
slanted pen, and the lateral compression of the letters
which naturally followed, resulted in a valuable
economy of time and space in the making of books.
This lateral compression is strongly marked in the
tenth century (see fig. 12), and in the eleventh and

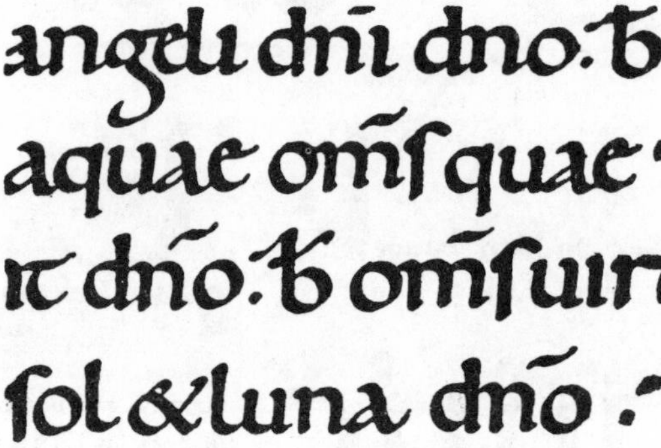

FIG. 12.—Psalter: English tenth century.
(See also Plate VIII.)

twelfth centuries it caused curves to give place to
angles, and writing to become "*Gothic*" in character
(see Plate XI.).

THIRTEENTH, FOURTEENTH, AND
FIFTEENTH CENTURY WRITING.—The
tendency to compression continued, and a further
economy of space was effected in the thirteenth and
fourteenth centuries by the general use of much
smaller writing (see fig. 13). In the fifteenth century writing grew larger and taller again, but the
letters had steadily become narrower, more angular,

12

and stiffer, till the written page consisted of rows of
perpendicular thick strokes with heads and feet con-
nected by oblique hair-lines—which often look as
if they had been dashed in after with a fine pen—
all made with an almost mechanical precision (see
Plate XVII).

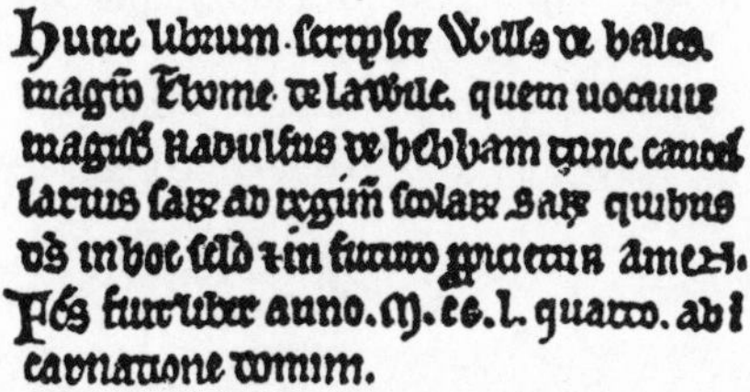

FIG. 13.—*Colophon* of English MS., dated 1254.

ITALIAN WRITING.—In Italy alone the
roundness of the earlier hands was preserved, and
though in course of time the letters were affected by
the "Gothic" tendency, they never lost the curved
forms or acquired the extreme angularity which is
seen in the writings of Northern Europe (compare
Plates X and XI).

At the time of the Renaissance the Italian scribes
remodelled their "hands" on the beautiful Italian
writing of the eleventh and twelfth centuries (see
Plates X and XVIII, XIX, XX). The early
Italian printers followed after the scribes and
modelled their types on these round clear letters.
And thus the fifteenth century Italian formal writing
became the foundation of the "*Roman*" *small letters*,
which have superseded all others for the printing
of books.

13

ITALICS.—The *Roman Letters*, together with the cursive hand of the time, gave rise to "*Italic*" letters (see fig. 1, & pp. 275, 280, 419).

ORNAMENTAL LETTERS originated in the simple written forms, which were developed for special purposes, and were made larger or written in colour (see Versals, &c., figs. 1, 189).

Their first object was to mark important words, or the beginnings of verses, chapters, or books. As *Initial Letters* they were much modified and embellished, and so gave rise to the art of *Illumination* (see pp. 79, 80).

CHAPTER II

ACQUIRING A FORMAL HAND: (1) TOOLS

Acquiring a Formal Hand: Tools, &c.—The Desk— Paper & Ink—Pens: *The Reed: The Quill*—Of Quills generally—Pen-knife, Cutting-slab, &c.

ACQUIRING A FORMAL HAND: TOOLS, &C.

The simplest way of learning how to make letters is to acquire a fine formal hand. To this end a legible and beautiful writing (see p. 36) should be chosen, and be carefully copied with a properly cut pen.

For learning to write, the following tools and materials are required:—

Desk.
Writing-paper.
Ink and *filler*.

Pens (Reed and Quill) with "*springs*."
Pen-knife, sharpening-stone, and *cutting-slab*.
Magnifying glass.
Two-foot (preferably *three-foot*) rule, and pencil.
Linen pen-wiper.

THE DESK

An ordinary desk or drawing-board can be used,
but the best desk is made by hinging a drawing-

FIG. 14.

board (" Imperial " size) to the edge of a table.
The board may be raised and supported at any
desired angle by a hinged support, or by a *round*

tin set under it (fig. 14). For a more portable desk two drawing-boards may be similarly hinged together and placed on a table (fig. 15).

FIG. 15.

A tape or string is tightly stretched — horizontally — across the desk to hold the writing-paper (which, as a rule, is not pinned on). The lower part of the writing-paper is held and protected by a piece of stout paper or vellum fixed tightly, with drawing-pins,

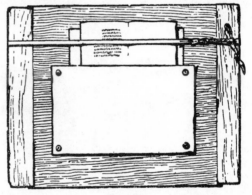

FIG. 16.

across and over it (fig. 16). Under the writing-paper there should be a *"writing-pad,"* consisting of one

16

or two sheets of blotting-paper, or some other suitable substance.[1]

It is a good plan to have the lower, front edge of the desk bevelled or rounded, so that the tail part of a deep sheet, which may hang below the table, does not become accidentally creased by being pressed against it. A curved piece of cardboard fixed on the edge will answer the same purpose.

PAPER & INK

For "practice" any smooth—not glazed—paper will do. For careful work a smooth, very fine-grained *hand-made* paper is best (pp. 69, 77).

Stick Indian ink is best, and a *good-quality stick* is worth paying for; the necessary rubbing down on a slab is well worth the trouble. We can ourselves *control* the thickness, colour, and state of this ink, and safely add to it, e.g. vermilion and yellow ochre (to make a deep brown), or gum-water (to prevent *spreading* on porous writing surfaces).

Jet black is the normal hue; it will also test the quality of the writing; it shows up all the faults; *pale* or *tinted* inks rather conceal the faults, and lend a false appearance of excellence (p. 286). A thin ink greatly adds to the ease of writing (see p. xxi); too thick inks do not flow freely enough.

A brush is used (*in left hand*) for filling the pen.

PENS

A Reed or Cane pen is best for very large writing —over half an inch in height—and therefore it is

---

[1] Some Eastern scribes use a "pad" of *fur*. This, or a piece of springy cloth, or other elastic substance, would probably be helpful, and experiments should be made in this direction.

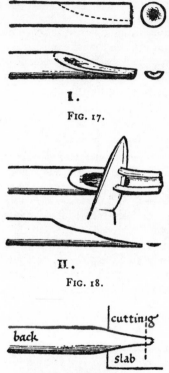

I.

FIG. 17.

II.

FIG. 18.

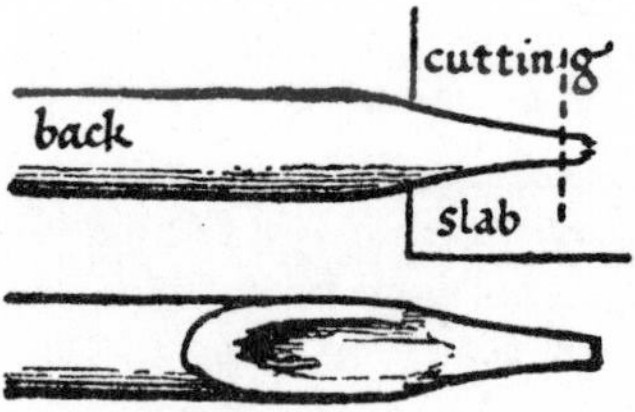

back

cutting

slab

III.

FIG. 19.

of great use in study-
ing pen strokes and
forms.

A Quill is best
for smaller writing,
and is used for all
ordinary MS. work
(pp. 20–26).

The REED[1] pen
should be about 8
inches long.

I. One end is cut
off obliquely (fig.
17).

II. The soft in-
side part is shaved
away by means of a
knife laid flat against
it, leaving the hard
outer shell (fig. 18).

III. The nib is
laid, back up, on
the slab (p. 27), and
— the knife - blade
being vertical—the
tip is cut off at right
angles to the shaft
(fig. 19).

IV. A short
longitudinal slit
(*a–b*) is made by

---

[1] The ordinary "Reed pen" of the artists' colourman is
rather soft and weak for formal writing. The reeds used by
the native scribes in India and Egypt, and some of the harder
English reeds, are excellent. A fine, hollow cane also makes
a very good pen.

inserting the knife-
blade in the middle
of the tip (fig. 20).

V. A pencil or
brush - handle is
held under the
nib, and is gently
twitched upwards
to lengthen the
slit (fig. 21). An
ordinary reed
should have a slit
about ¾ inch long.
A very stiff pen
may have in addi-
tion a slit on either
side of the centre.

The left thumb
nail is pressed
against the back
of the pen—about
1 inch from the
tip—to prevent it
splitting too far up
(see also fig. 27).

VI. The nib is
laid, back up, on
the slab, and —
the knife-blade
being vertical—the
tip is cut off at an
angle of about 70°
to the shaft, remov-
ing the first rough
slit *a–b* (fig. 22).

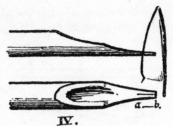

FIG. 20.

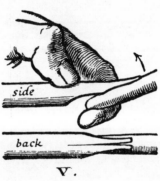

FIG. 21.

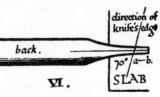

FIG. 22.

19

VII. A strip of thin metal (very thin tin, or clock spring with the "temper" taken out by heating and slowly cooling) is cut the width of the nib and about 2 inches long. This is folded into a *"spring"* (fig. 23).

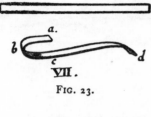

VII.

FIG. 23.

VIII. The *spring* is inserted into the pen (fig. 24).

The loop *a b c* is "sprung" into place, and holds the spring in the right position. The loop *c d*, which should be rather flat, holds the ink in the pen. The point *d* should be about ⅛ inch from the end of the nib.

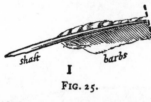

VIII.

FIG. 24.

THE QUILL.—A Turkey's Quill is strong, and suitable for general writing. As supplied by the stationers it consists of a complete wing-feather, about 12 inches long, having the quill part cut for ordinary use. For careful writing it should be re-made thus:—

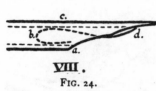

I

FIG. 25.

I. The quill should be cut down to 7 or 8 inches (fig. 25); the long feather if left is apt to be in the way.

II. The "barbs" or filaments of the feather are stripped off the shaft (fig. 26).

20

III. The nib already has a slit usually about ¼ inch long. This is sufficient in a fairly pliant

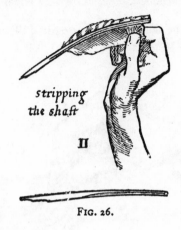

stripping the shaft

II

FIG. 26.

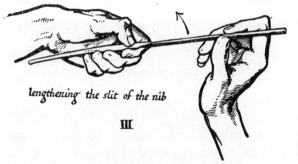

lengthening the slit of the nib

III

FIG. 27.

pen; in a very stiff pen (see p. 26) the slit may be lengthened to ⅜ inch. This may be done with care by holding a *half-nib* between the forefinger and

21

thumb of each hand, but the safest way is to *twitch* the slit open (fig. 27), using the end of another pen (or a brush-handle) as explained under *Reed*, V (see p. 19).

IV. The sides of the nib are pared till the width across the tip is rather less than the width desired[1] (fig. 28).

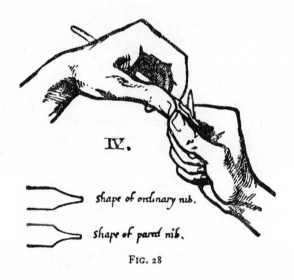

IV.

shape of ordinary nib.

shape of pared nib.

FIG. 28

V. The nib is laid, back up, on the glass slab, and the extreme tip is cut off obliquely to the slit, the knife blade being slightly sloped, and its edge forming an angle of about 70° with the line of the shaft (fig. 29; *for extra sharp nib* see fig. 36).

---

[1] The width of the cut nib corresponds exactly with the width of the thickest stroke which the pen will make in writing.

The shaft rests lightly in the left hand (not *gripped* and not pressed down on slab at all), and the knife blade is entered with a steady pressure.

If the nib is then not wide enough it may be cut again; if too wide, the sides may be pared down.

Cut very little at a time off the tip of the nib; a heavy cut is apt to force the pen out of shape and spoil the edge of the nib.

VI. The nib should then be examined with the magnifying glass. Hold the pen, back down, over a sheet of white paper, and see that the ends of the two half-nibs are in the same straight line *a–b* (fig. 30).

The nib should have an oblique chisel-shaped tip, very sharply cut (fig. 31).

A magnifying glass is necessary for examining a fine pen; a coarse pen may be held up against

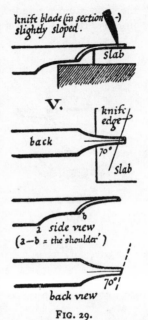

FIG. 29.

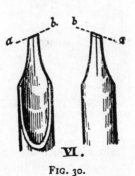

FIG. 30.

23

the light from a window—a finger-tip being held
just over the nib to direct the eye (fig. 32).

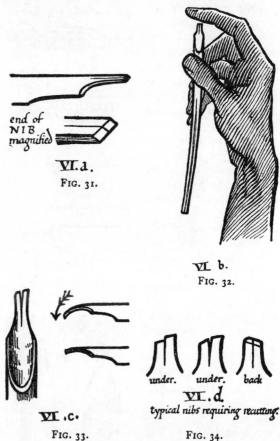

end of
NIB
magnified

VI.a.

FIG. 31.

VI b.

FIG. 32.

VI .c.

FIG. 33.

under.   under.   back

VI .d

typical nibs requiring recutting.

FIG. 34.

A nib in which the slit does not quite close may be
bent down to bring the two parts together (fig. 33).

Uneven or blunt nibs (fig. 34) must be carefully re-cut.

VII. The *Spring* (see *Reed*, VII.) (about $\frac{3}{32}$ inch by $1\frac{1}{2}$ inch) is placed so that the point is about $\frac{1}{16}$ inch from the end of the nib. The long loop should be made rather flat to hold plenty of ink (A, fig. 35)—neither too much curved (B: this holds only a drop), nor quite flat (C: this draws the ink up and away from the nib).

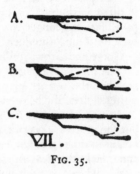

FIG. 35.

OF QUILLS GENERALLY

For ordinary use the nib may be cut with a fairly steep angle, as shown (magnified) at *a*, fig. 36.

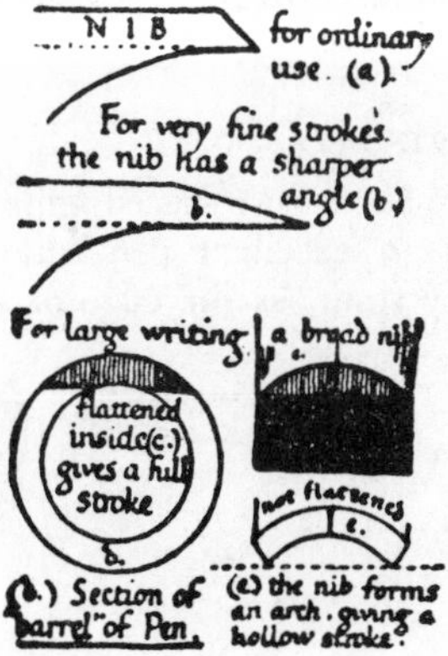

But it is better for all careful work and fine, sharp writing that the angle be made very sharp: the knife blade is laid back (much flatter than is shown in fig. 29) and the quill is cut quite thin; the knife blade is then held vertical and the extreme tip of the nib is cut off sharp and true (*b*, fig. 36).

For large writing, the curved inside of the quill is pared *flat* (*c*, *d*, fig. 36)

FIG. 36.

25

to give full strokes. If the nib be left curved and hollow underneath (*e*), it is apt to make hollow strokes.

The pen may be made more *pliant* by scraping it till it is thinner, or by cutting the "shoulder" (*a–b*, fig. 29) longer, or *stiffer* by cutting the nib back until the "shoulder" is short.

Goose and Crow Quills (see p. 138).

The main advantages of a quill over a metal pen are that the former may be shaped exactly as the writer desires, and be re-cut when it becomes blunt.

A metal pen may be sharpened on an oilstone, but the process takes so much longer that there is no saving in time: it is not easily cut to the exact shape, and it lacks the pleasant elasticity of the quill.

A gold pen is probably the best substitute for a quill, and if it were possible to have a sharp, "chisel-edged" *iridium* tip on the gold nib, it would be an extremely convenient form of pen. A "fountain pen" might be used with thin ink.

PEN-KNIFE, CUTTING-SLAB, &c.

THE KNIFE.—Quill makers use a special knife. A surgical scalpel makes an excellent pen-knife. The blade should be fairly stout, as the edge of a

section
of blade

FIG. 37.

thin blade is easily damaged. It should be ground only on the right side of the blade and tapered to a point (fig. 37) and be kept very sharp.

THE SLAB.—A piece of glass (preferably white) may be used for fine quills; hard wood, bone, or celluloid for reed and cane pens.

SHARPENING STONE.—An "India" (coarse) & a "Turkey" (fine) stone. Use thin *lubricating* oil.

MAGNIFYING GLASS.—A magnifying glass (about 1 inch in diameter) is necessary for examining fine pen nibs to see if they are "true." A "pocket" glass is the most suitable for general use, and for the analysis of small writing, &c.

RULE.—A 2, or 3-foot wood rule having brass strips let in to protect the edges, or a metal rule.

LINEN PEN-WIPER.—A piece of an old *linen* handkerchief may be used to keep the pen clean.

CHAPTER III

ACQUIRING A FORMAL HAND: (2) METHODS

Position of the Desk—The Writing Level—Use of the Pen—Holding the Pen—Filling the Pen, &c.

POSITION OF THE DESK

Always write at a slope. This enables you to sit up comfortably at your work, and to see the MS. clearly as though it were on an easel—and, by the resulting horizontal position of the pen, the ink is kept under control. It may be seen from ancient pictures that this was the method of the scribes (see *Frontispiece*). Never write on a flat table; it causes the writer to stoop, the MS. is seen foreshortened and the ink flows out of the pen too rapidly.

The slope of the desk may be about, or rather less than, 45° to begin with: as the hand becomes accustomed to it, it may be raised to about 60° (fig. 38).

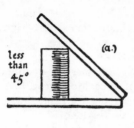

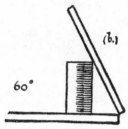

less
than
45°

(a.)

(b.)

60°

FIG. 38.

The "heel" of the right hand may be tired at first, but it soon grows used to the position. A rest for the left arm, if necessary, can be attached to the left side of the board.

Lighting. The desk is placed very near to a window, so that a strong light falls on it from the left. Direct sunlight may be cut off by fixing a sheet of thin white paper in the window. *Careful work should be done by daylight.* Work done by artificial light always appears faulty and unsatisfactory when viewed by day.

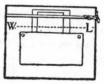

W------------------L

FIG. 39.

THE WRITING LEVEL

Each penman will find for himself the *writing level* along which his pen will move most naturally and conveniently (see figs. 39 and 16). The *paper guard* should be pinned on about 1 inch below the writing level: the *tape* is

fixed across about 3 inches above the guard. In the
case of very large writing the space between the tape
and the guard is greater, and in the case of a very
small MS. it is less.

The writing level is kept constant. When one line
has been written, the writing paper—which is placed
behind the tape and the guard—is pulled up for
another line.

USE OF THE PEN

For the practical study of pen-forms use a cane
or a reed pen—or a quill cut very broad—giving a
broad, firm, thick stroke. It is the chisel edge (p. 23)
of the nib which gives the "clean cut" thick and
thin strokes and the graduated curved strokes
characteristic of good writing (fig. 40).

FIG. 40.

Therefore, *let the nib glide about on the surface with
the least possible pressure,* making natural pen-strokes
the thickness of which is only varied by the different

29

directions in which the nib moves (see *Addenda*, p. xxi).

It is very important that the nib be cut "sharp," and as often as its edge wears blunt it must be re-sharpened. It is impossible to make "clean cut" strokes with a blunt pen (see *Addenda*, p. xxiii).

When the nib is cut back, the "shoulder" should be cut back to preserve the elasticity of the pen (p. 26).

HOLDING THE PEN

THE HAND holds the pen lightly and easily. A good method is to loop the thumb and forefinger over, and slightly gripping, the shaft of the pen, and support the shaft from below with the second finger. The third and fourth fingers are tucked, out of the way, into the palm (figs. 41, 45).

The pen should be so lightly held that *the act of writing should draw the edge of the nib into perfect contact with the paper, both the half-nibs touching the surface.* (To make sure that the contact is perfect, make experimental thick strokes on a scrap of paper—pinned at the right-hand side of the desk—and see that they are "true," *i.e.* that they are of even width, with "clean cut" edges and ends.) The writer should be able to feel what the nib is doing. If the pen be gripped stiffly the edge of the nib cannot be felt on the paper; and it will inevitably be forced out of shape and prematurely blunted.

A thin slip of bone—a "folder" or the handle of the pen-knife will do—is commonly held in the left hand to keep the paper flat and steady (see fig. 41).

THE CUSTOMARY MANNER. — The ancient scribe probably held his pen in the manner most convenient to himself; and we, in order to write with freedom, should hold the pen in the way to which, by long use, we have been accus-

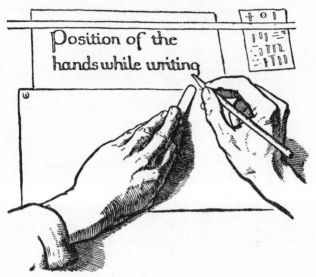

Fig. 41.

tomed; *provided that, for writing an upright round-hand, the pen be so manipulated and cut as to make fine horizontal thin strokes and clean vertical thick strokes* (see fig. 40, & *footnote,* p. 268).

SLANTED SHAFT, &c.—Most people are accustomed to holding a pen slanted away from the right shoulder. The nib therefore is cut at an

31

oblique angle[1] to the shaft, so that, while the shaft is slanted, *the edge of the nib is parallel with the horizontal line of the paper*, and will therefore produce a horizontal thin stroke and a vertical thick stroke. For example: if the shaft is held slanted at an angle of 70° with the horizontal, the nib is cut at an angle of 70° with the shaft (fig. 42). The angle of the nib with the shaft may vary from 90° (at right angles) to about 70°, according to the slant at which the shaft is held (fig. 43).

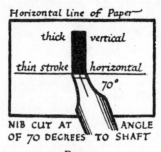

NIB CUT AT ANGLE OF 70 DEGREES TO SHAFT

FIG. 42.

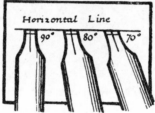

NIBS CUT AT VARIOUS ANGLES

FIG. 43.

If the writer prefers an extremely slanted shaft, to cut the nib correspondingly obliquely would weaken it, so it is better to counteract the slant by slightly tilting the paper (fig. 44).

To produce the *horizontal thin stroke*, therefore:

> *The slant at which the shaft is held,*
> *The angle at which the nib is cut*, and
> *The tilt which may be given to the paper:*

---

[1] If the edge of the nib were cut at right angles to the shaft, obviously the horizontal stroke would not be thin, and the true thick and thin strokes would be oblique (see "*slanted pen*" *writing*—figs. 9 & 11).

32

must be so adjusted, one to another, that the chisel edge of the nib is parallel to the horizontal line of the paper. Before writing, make trial strokes on a scrap of paper to see that this is so: the vertical thick strokes should be square ended and the full width of the nib, the horizontal strokes as fine as possible.

TILTED PAPER

FIG. 44.

HORIZONTAL SHAFT, &c.—The pen shaft is held approximately horizontal. This will

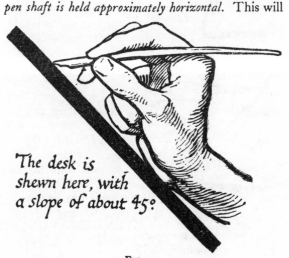

The desk is shewn here, with a slope of about 45°

FIG. 45.

be found the natural position for it when the slope

33

of the desk is about 50° or 60°. It gives complete control of the ink in the pen, which can be made to run faster or slower by slightly elevating or depressing the shaft (fig. 45).

normal
(a.)

board lowered:
pen elevated.
(b.)

board raised:
pen depressed
(c.)

FIG. 46.

The writing-board may be slightly lowered or raised with the object of elevating or depressing the pen shaft (fig. 46 & p. 84).

The pen makes a considerable angle with the writing surface, so that the ink, which is held in the hollow of the nib, comes in contact with the paper at the very extremity of the nib, making very fine strokes (*a*, fig. 47).

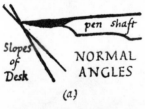

pen shaft

Slopes
of
Desk

NORMAL
ANGLES

(a)

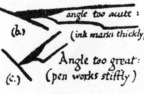

angle too acute :
(ink marks thickly)
(b)

Angle too great :
(pen works stiffly)
(c.)

FIG. 47.

The spring is adjusted carefully, the tip being approximately $\frac{1}{16}$ inch from the tip of the nib. The nearer the spring is to the end of the nib, the faster the ink flows. The loop must be kept flattish in order to hold the ink well (see figs. 35, 48).

34

It is convenient to stand the ink, &c., beside the desk on the left, and for this purpose a little cup-shaped bracket or clip may be attached to the edge of the writing-board. The filling-brush stands in the ink dish or pot of colour (p. 142), and is taken up in the left hand; the pen, retained in the right hand, being brought over to the left to be filled.

Improved forms of springs are shown in fig.

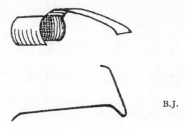

B.J.

FIG. 48. OUTER AND INNER SPRINGS.

48; but springs seem to be necessary only under difficult conditions such as writing on the flat or on a flattish desk, or on a difficult writing surface, or when using a very broad nib (requiring a great deal of ink).

When the pen, the ink, and the writing surface are all working well the ink is repelled from all but the track which is laid down by the broad, sharp Edge of the Nib, as it makes its clear-cut strokes. As the pen-shaft is nearly horizontal the ink is under the writer's control and the nib may be filled to dripping-point (without a Spring). I usually *pile* the ink up on the back of my nib (with the brush).

In careful work the pen should be tried, on a

35

scrap of paper, almost every time it is filled (to see that the ink is flowing rightly).

The nib is kept clean. A carbon ink (p. 17), through gradual evaporation, is apt to clog the nib (especially in hot weather); therefore, every now and then, the nib may be wiped on the back of the left forefinger or the spring may be taken out and the whole thoroughly cleaned. It is impossible to write well with a dirty pen.

CHAPTER IV

ACQUIRING A FORMAL HAND: (3) MODELS

Models—Notes on Construction: Script I.—Coupling the Letters—Spacing: Letters, Words, & Lines—Uncial Capitals: Script II.—Numerals & Punctuation Marks—Of *Copying* MSS. Generally.

MODELS

THE best training is found in the practice of an *upright round-hand* (p. 266). Having mastered such a writing, the penman can acquire any other hands— sloping or angular—with comparative ease (p. 287).

The English Half-Uncial writing in Plate VII. is an excellent model. Those who have sufficient time to spare for the careful study of this, or any other legible and beautiful round-hand, should obtain access to the MSS. in a museum, or procure good *facsimiles* (see Plates at end of Book, & p. 352).

Those who have not sufficient time for a careful and thorough study of an early MS. will find it easier to begin with a simplified and modernised writing, such as Script I. (fig. 49).

abcdefghilm nnopqrrsaux

"Durham Book" hand (copy).

abcdefghijklm nopqrstuvxyz :

Modernized Half-Uncial (I.).

Fig. 49.

Before copying a hand it is well to examine carefully the manuscript from which it is taken: observe its general appearance: note the character and mode of the ruling, and the sizes and relative proportions of page, text, margins, and ornaments. With regard to the actual forms of the letters and the mode of their arrangement, such a method of analysis as the following will be found useful, as an aid to accuracy in copying, and definiteness in self-criticism.

A METHOD OF ANALYSIS		EXAMPLE: Analysis of Script I. (as in fig. 50).
1. THE WRITING	general character:	*Modernised Half-Uncial.*
(Ruling)	Double or single lines, &c. (see pp. 268, 269):	*Double lines (see figs. 59, 65).*
Letters	round or angular:	*round.*
	upright or sloping:	*upright.*
	coupled or separate:	*coupled.*
2. THIN STROKES:	horizontal or oblique (see figs. 10, 9):	*horizontal.*
3. THICK STROKES:	heavy, medium, or light (see fig. 183):	*medium.*
4. "HEADS" & "FEET":	character (see fig. 145):	*solid, triangular, &c.*
5. STEMS (*ascending & descending*):	short, medium, or long (see fig. 183):	*medium.*
6. SPACING (*Letters, Words, Lines*):	close or wide (see fig. 154):	*fairly close (see figs. 54, 55).*
7. ARRANGEMENT:	in mass (of equal lines), or in column (of unequal lines) (see fig. 154):	*in mass of equal lines (see fig. 66). [It is, however, very suitable for unequal lines: cf. Pl. vii.]*
8. MEASUREMENTS (*& proportions see pp. 324, 327*):	width of thick stroke (see p. 49):	$l =$ *about $\frac{3}{32}''$ wide.*
	height of *o* and *d* (see pp. 48, 50):	$o =$,, $\frac{3}{8}''$ *high.* $d =$,, $\frac{11}{16}''$ *high.*
	writing lines, distance apart (see p. 48):	*Lines $1''$ apart.*
9. COMPONENT PARTS:	number and forms (see pp. 41, 47, 50):	*a has 3 strokes.* *b ,, 3 ,,* *c ,, 2 ,,* *and so on (see fig. 51).*

The pen generally is held so as to give approximately horizontal thin strokes (see p. 32), but in making **v** (**w**, **y**), **x**, parts of **z**, &c., it may be "slanted." In figs. 51 and 57 these forms are marked with a small diagonal cross ✕ (see also p. xxiii).

Most of the strokes begin as *down-strokes*, but at the *end* of a *down-stroke*, when the ink is flowing freely, the stroke may be continued in an upward direction (as in *coupling-strokes*, &c., the *feet* of letters, the thin stroke of **x**, and, if preferred, in making the last stroke of **g**, **s**, and **y**).

While the ink is still wet in a *down-stroke*, the nib may be replaced on it and be pushed *up*ward and outward to form the round arch in **b**, **h**, **m**, **n**, **p**, and **r**. This stroke, reversed, is also used for the top of **t** (For making these up-strokes, see fig. 51).

The thin finishing-strokes of **j** (fig. 50), & **F**, **G**, **J**, **N** (fig. 56), are made with the point of the nib. —*See Addenda*, p. xxi.

NOTE.—The forms +o in ✕ in fig. 51 contain all the principal strokes in this alphabet, and are therefore useful for early practice.

COUPLING THE LETTERS

These letters are joined together by means of their *coupling-strokes*, which for this purpose may be slightly drawn out, and forward, from the naturally round forms of the letters (see **c**, **e**, &c., fig. 52 & fig. 59).

The *coupling-strokes* are finishing strokes—and as such are akin to *serifs* (p. 208)—growing out of or added to such stems as need "finishing." Coupling enables *beginners* to write faster and with more

39

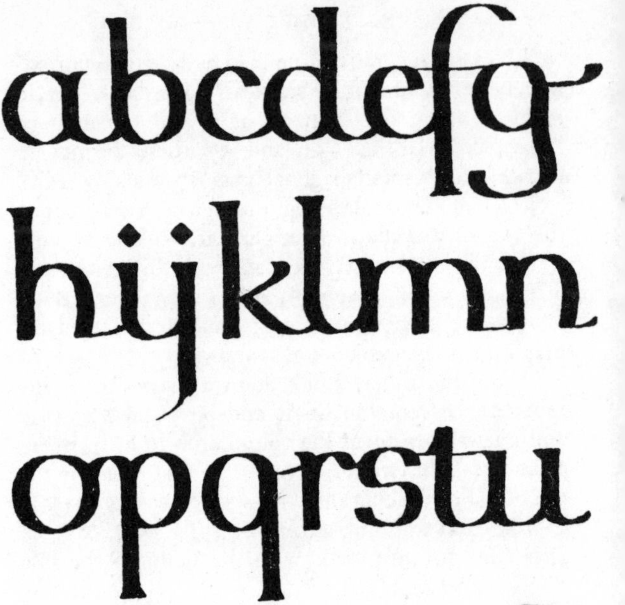

abcdefg

hijklmn

opqrstu

vuwxyz&

?:.df,wyz

Modern. Half-Uncial. I.

MCM
IV

FIG. 50.

40

+ o i n x

normal position ("Straight pen"). **m. & n.**

c c c e t m

x = "Slanted pen".

o r s u u v z

& y b d l h k l

(g. s. & y. tail strokes may be carried)
up

f g j p q y

coup-
ling
Strokes

"feet"   bows

2.

3.

1.

x.

ip

t.

FIG. 51.

freedom, the concluding or " coupling " stroke not
being *slowed down*, but written with a dash, which

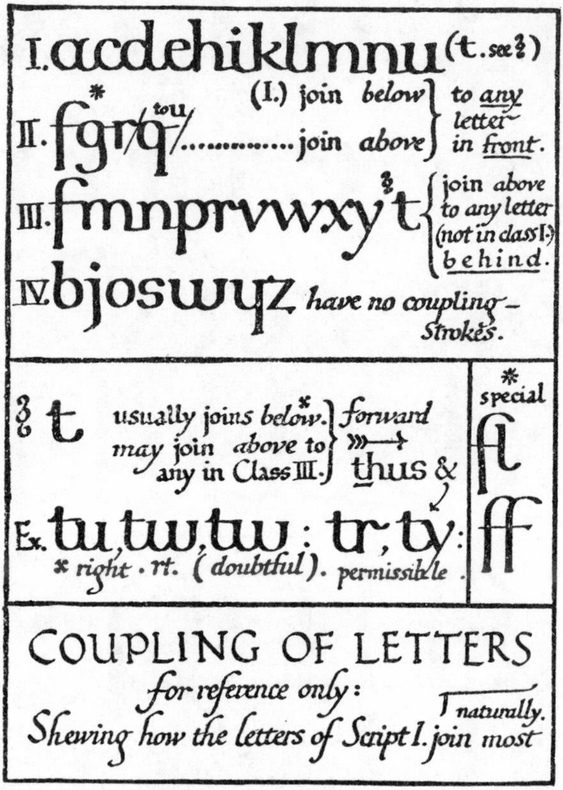

I. acdehiklmnu (t. see ?)

(I.) join *below* to *any* letter in front.

II. fgrq/.............. join *above*

III. fmnprvwxy t { join above to any letter (not in class I.) behind.

IV. bjoswyz have no coupling Strokes.

t usually joins below. may join *above* to any in Class III. } forward ⟫⟶ thus &

special fl

Ex. tu, tw, tw : tr, ty :
* right . rt. (doubtful). permissible.

ff

COUPLING OF LETTERS
for reference only :
Shewing how the letters of Script I. join most naturally.

FIG. 52.

is covered by the first stroke of the succeeding letter.
It keeps the individual words more distinct, and

42

therefore permits closer spacing of the text. It should be observed, however, that, excepting the Irish Half-Uncial forms where coupling is a characteristic, all the most formal manuscripts are *structurally uncoupled* (see Plates VIII, X, XXI, & *comp. opp.* tendency in Plate XII). The freer and more *cursive* the hand, the greater is the tendency to join and run letters together, as in ordinary writing.

It is preferable to couple letters below, if possible. Couplings above are sometimes apt to confuse the reading; for example, the cross-bar of **t** (though the most natural coupling for the scribe to use—see *petatis*, Plate VII) should generally be made to pass over or fall short of the succeeding letter (fig. 52).

SPACING: LETTERS, WORDS, & LINES

The letters of a word are fitted together so that there is a general effect of evenness. This evenness is only to be attained by practice: it is characteristic of rapid skilful writing, and cannot be produced satisfactorily by any system of measurement while the writer's hand is still slow and uncertain. It is worth noting, however, that the white interspaces vary slightly, while the actual distances between the letters vary considerably, according to whether the adjacent strokes curve (or slant) away or are perpendicular (figs. 53, 152).

It is sufficient for the beginner to take care that two curved letters are made very near each other, and that two straight strokes are spaced well apart.

If the curves are too far apart there will be spots of light, and, where several heavy stems are made too close together, "blots" of dark, marring the evenness of the page.

43

Words are kept as close as is compatible with

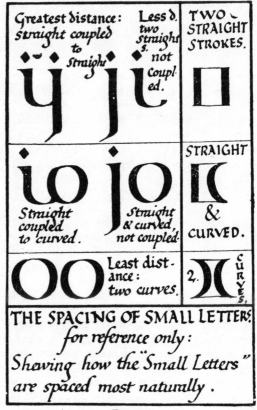

FIG. 53.

legibility. The average space between two words is
less than the width of the letter o (fig. 54).

44

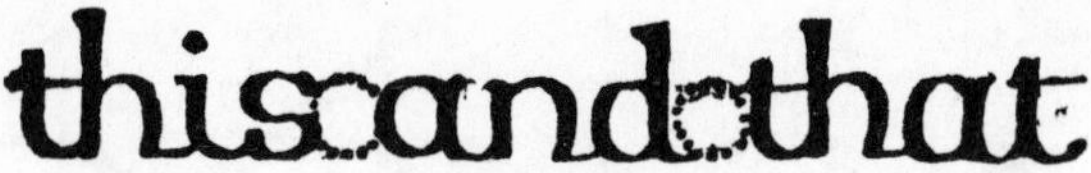

thiscandothat

FIG. 54.

The Lines in *massed writing* (see p. 226) are kept as close together as is compatible with legibility. The usual distance apart of the *writing-lines* is *about* three times the height of the letter **o** (see also p. 291).

The *descending strokes* of the upper line must " clear " the *ascending strokes* of the lower line.

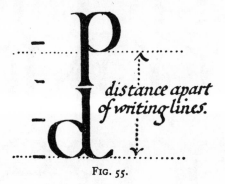

FIG. 55.

Interlocking of these strokes may be avoided by the experimental placing of **p** over **d** (fig. 55).

UNCIAL CAPITALS: SCRIPT II

These *modernised Uncials* (see fig. 56, & p. 264) are intended to go with Script I, and their analysis and mode of construction are almost identical with those of Script I (see pp. 38, 39).

45

ABCDE
FGHIJK
LMNO
PQRST
&ɯ UVXYZ

MCMIV.   Uncials.   II

FIG. 56.

46

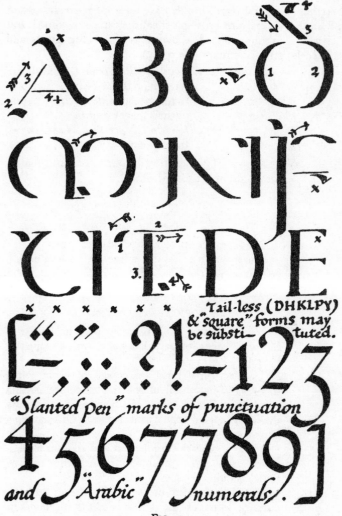

ABECO
MDNIJ
UILDE

Tail-less (DHKLPY)
& "square" forms may
be substi—   tuted.

["·,·;·:·…·?·!·] = 123
"Slanted pen" marks of punctuation
4567789]
and "Arabic" numerals.

FIG. 57.

Grouping: Uncials have no *coupling-strokes;* when several are used together, they are not joined, but evenly grouped, allowing as before for curves and straight strokes (see p. 43).

Spacing: (a) *When used with Script I*, Uncials are written on the same lines, and have to follow the same spacing (in spite of their longer stems).

(b) *When Uncials are used by themselves*, their spacing may be wider (p. 261).

NOTE.—The height of *Uncial* o is about equal to the height of the *Half-Uncial* d.

NUMERALS & PUNCTUATION MARKS

(See fig. 57.)

These are best made with a " slanted " pen (fig. 9).

When writing " Arabic numerals," 1 and 0 may be made *on the line*, **2468** *ascending*, and 3579 *descending*.

OF *COPYING* MSS. GENERALLY

When copying a MS. it is best to choose a complete page—or part of a page—to be copied in facsimile.

Two or three lines are copied to begin with; then the composition of the individual letters and words is studied by means of a large pen; and finally the whole page is copied in facsimile. (Of *practising*, see pp. 51, 52.)

Make a general examination and analysis as suggested at p. 37. Accurate measurements will be found helpful.

Take the heights of the o and the d, and the distance apart of the writing-lines with dividers.

The width of the thick stroke is best found by making experimental thick strokes—the *full width* of the pen nib—on a scrap of paper: cut the paper in half across the thick strokes, and place the cut edge on the *thickest* strokes in the original MS., you will then find whether the pen nib should be cut wider or narrower.

The direction of the *thickest* strokes is approximately at right angles to the direction of the thin strokes; which commonly approaches the horizontal in early round hands, and is oblique in other hands (see figs. 9 and 10). The positions both of these strokes in the model, and of your pen, determine the angle of the nib. Therefore, *cut the nib across at such an angle to the shaft of the pen that, when you hold the pen naturally, the direction of the thin strokes which it makes on the writing paper will coincide with the direction of the thin strokes in the model;* but

    (*a*) The way in which the shaft is held,
    (*b*) The angle at which the nib is cut,
    (*c*) The position of the writing paper,

may all be slightly varied, so that the direction of the thin strokes can be followed exactly (see p. 32).

The writing paper is cut and ruled exactly in accordance with the model; and the heights of the letters and the widths of the thick strokes in the copy agree as nearly as possible with those in the original. It is therefore a good test for accuracy—*when a few lines of writing have been copied*—to measure and compare their *lengths*. If they correspond with their originals, it goes far to prove the copy a good one.

Before copying more of the page, the construction of the letters should be carefully studied. The number and the forms of pen-strokes in each letter are found by examination—with a magnifying glass if necessary—and by the experimental putting together of strokes, to form a similar letter. For this a large pen, such as a reed, is useful, and it is a good plan to write individual letters and words exactly two, three, or four times their *height* in the model: both the pen nib and the individual letters are made correspondingly two, three, or four times as *wide* as in the original.

It is particularly important, in copying, to preserve accurately the proportion of the *thick stroke* to the *height and width* of a letter (see p. 288). These are conveniently measured by the pen nib itself, or by the estimated width of the thick stroke; thus, in the writing shown in fig. 50, the *width* of the o is approximately *five*, and the *height* approximately *four*, times the width of the thick stroke.

Not only must the copier ascertain what the forms are like and what are their proportions, but he must try to find out *how they were made*. This is of the greatest importance, for the manner of making a letter, or even a single stroke, affects its form and character with a definite tendency (see p. 378 & fig. 172). And this becomes more marked the faster the writing. An apparently right form may yet be wrongly—if slowly—made; but in rapid writing, a wrong manner of handling the pen will inevitably produce wrong forms. As the real virtue of penmanship is attained only when we can write quickly, it is well worth training the hand from the beginning in the proper manner.

Patient and careful examination should be made of the changing pen-strokes, and of the mode in which they join—to form letters—and begin and end—to form "heads" and "feet." This, accompanied

by practical experiments in cutting and handling the
pen, will bring out details of the utmost technical
value. A certain amount of legitimate "faking"
(p. 210), play of the pen, and sleight of hand (p. 275),
may be found, but, in the main, the regular, natural,
thick and *thin* strokes of the pen, and the orderly
arrangement of the writing, give to a manuscript its
beauty and character.

Then having cut the nib rightly, you may, in a
sense, *let the pen do the writing*, while you merely
follow the strokes of the model, and you will, in
course of time, have the pleasure of seeing the same
beautiful writing—in the very manner of the ancient
scribes—growing under your own hand.

CHAPTER V

ACQUIRING A FORMAL HAND: (4) PRACTICE

Practice—Scripts I. & II.—Arranging & Ruling a
   Single Sheet—Problem I (a Sheet of Prose)—
   Problem II (a Sheet of Poetry)—Spacing &
   Planning Manuscript.

PRACTICE

IN acquiring a formal writing the penman should
have two paper books constantly in hand: one for
the study of the forms of letters, the other for both
the letters and their arrangement. The first should
contain large and very carefully made writing—with
perhaps only one word to the line; the second should

have smaller and quicker writing, neatly arranged on the pages, with four or five words to the line. (See MS. Books, Chap. VI.)

A broad nib is used in preference to a narrow one, so that the characteristics of true pen-work are brought out and the faults made clear. A fine, light handwriting is often very pretty, but it is certain to mislead the novice in penmanship (see p. 288).

Having acquired a formal hand the penman may modify and alter it, taking care that the changes are compatible, and that they do not impair its legibility or beauty. Such letters as are obsolete he replaces by legible forms akin to them in feeling, and, the style of the selected type becoming very naturally and almost unconsciously modified by personal use, he at length attains an appropriate and modern Formal-Handwriting. The process of "forming" a hand requires time and practice: it resembles the passage of "Copy-book" into "Running" hand, familiar to us all (see p. 287).

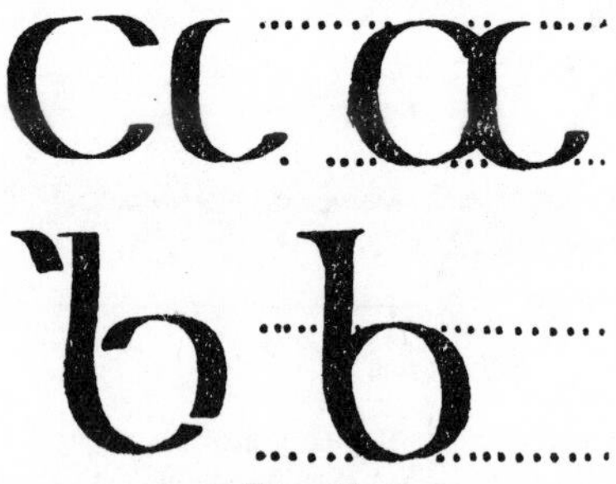

FIG. 58.

SCRIPTS I & II

Having cut the nib of a reed or large quill to the exact width required for the thick stroke, copy the component strokes of the letter α (Script I), and

52

FIG. 59.

FIG. 60.

the whole alphabet in this way several times (fig.
58). Next join the letters together (see p. 39) to

form words—writing always between ruled lines
(fig. 59 & p. 376).

Script II is similarly practised: the letters are
grouped (p. 48) to form words (fig. 60).

Next make a neat page of large writing, and,
if possible, write such a page every day. The more
definite and methodical practice is, the better.
" Practising " *anyhow*, on scraps of paper, does more
harm than good.

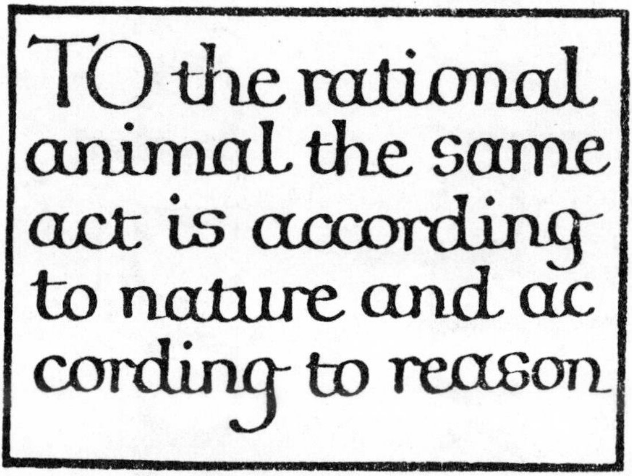

FIG. 61.

ARRANGING & RULING A SINGLE SHEET

The *size* of an inscription is commonly settled
before the arrangement of the text is planned out,
being determined by considerations of its future
position and office, or by custom and use (see
pp. 66–9 & 317).

54

The proportions of the writing, spacing, and margins will likewise properly *settle themselves* (see pp. 229, 69, 73), but where the size of the sheet only is fixed, we have, broadly speaking, to decide between "large" writing with "small" margins (fig. 61), and "small" writing with "large" margins (fig. 62).

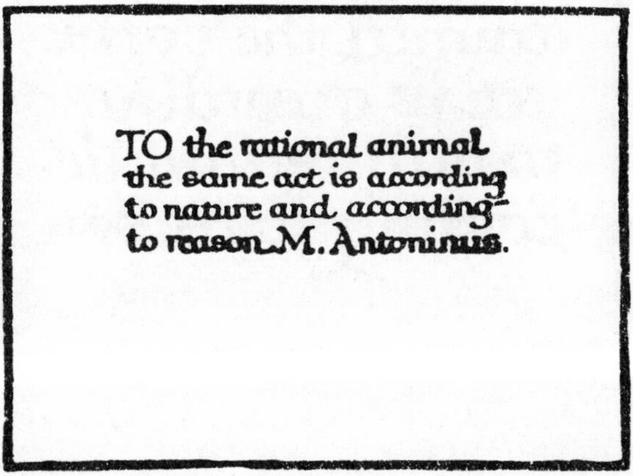

FIG. 62.

Generally a compromise is arrived at and the proportions are more evenly balanced (fig. 63).

Ruling (see also pp. 222, 65).—The mode of ruling *marginal lines* and *writing lines* is shown in fig. 65. The ruling should be light, but firm and accurate. A fine pen, or hard pencil, or a blunt point may be used. Where the *writing lines* are double (as for *round* hands, p. 268), it is best to have a double ruling point (see fig. 77). Two hard pencils firmly

55

lashed together make a convenient tool for large
work: the distance between the points is easily
adjusted by means of a small wedge.

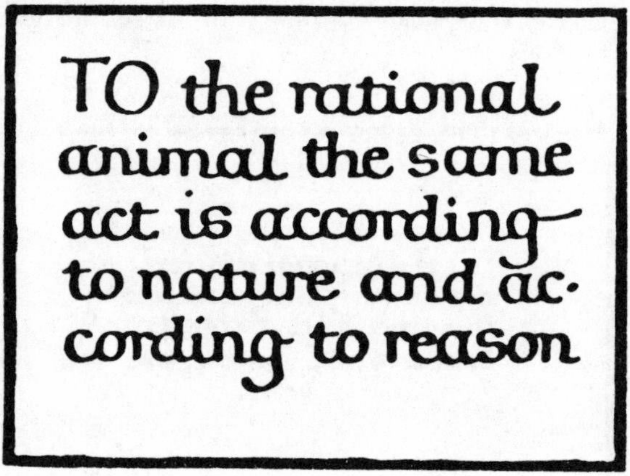

TO the rational
animal the same
act is according
to nature and ac-
cording to reason

FIG. 63.

PROBLEM I (A SHEET OF PROSE)

*To write out the Pater noster (50 words) in a formal
round-hand (arranged in "mass" of equal lines) on a
sheet of "foolscap" (i.e. 17 inches high and 13½ inches
wide).*

If the size of the writing be considered of the
first importance, a few words are written out in a
script chosen to suit the subject, the space, &c.,
and these are measured to find the area which the
whole text so written would occupy (fig. 64). The
size of the script is then modified, if necessary, to
suit the available area.

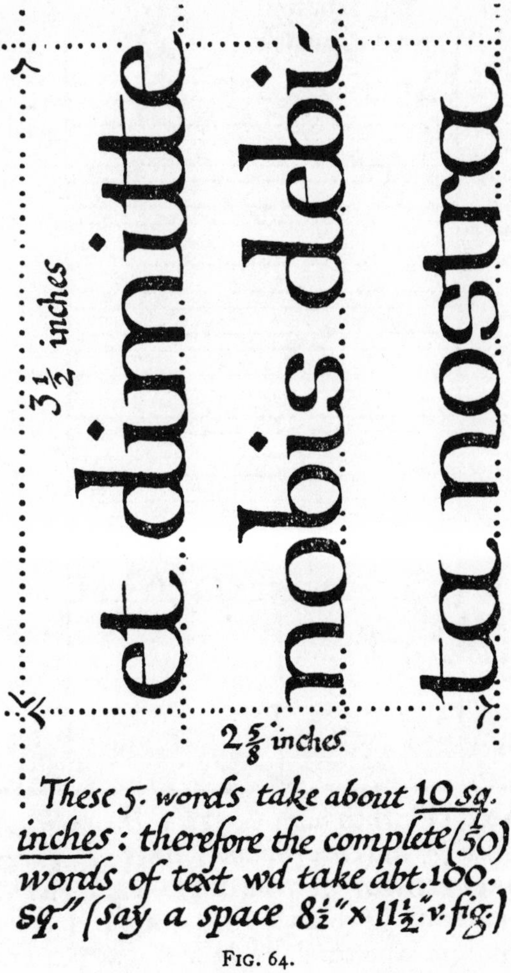

3½ inches

et dimitte

nobis debi

ta nostra

2⅝ inches.

*These 5. words take about 10 sq.
inches : therefore the complete (50)
words of text wd take abt. 100.
sq." (say a space 8½" × 11½". v. fig.)*

FIG. 64.

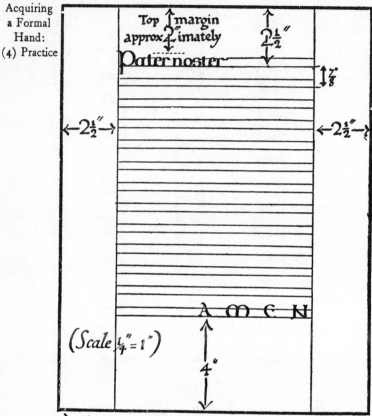

Top margin
approximately

Pater noster

$2\frac{1}{2}''$

$1\frac{7}{8}''$

$\leftarrow 2\frac{1}{2}'' \rightarrow$

$\leftarrow 2\frac{1}{2}'' \rightarrow$

$(Scale \ \frac{1}{4}'' = 1'')$

A M E N

$4''$

A sheet 17 inches high & $13\frac{1}{2}$ inches wide (f cap.)
Ruled with thirteen (double) lines — $\frac{5}{16}''$ gauge —
distance between WRITING-LINES = $\frac{7}{8}$ inch: v. $\updownarrow$:
Side margins, $2\frac{1}{2}''$(each): Foot margin, 4 inches:
Top margin approx. 2 in. ($2\frac{1}{2}''$ to 1st WRITING-LINE)

FIG. 65.

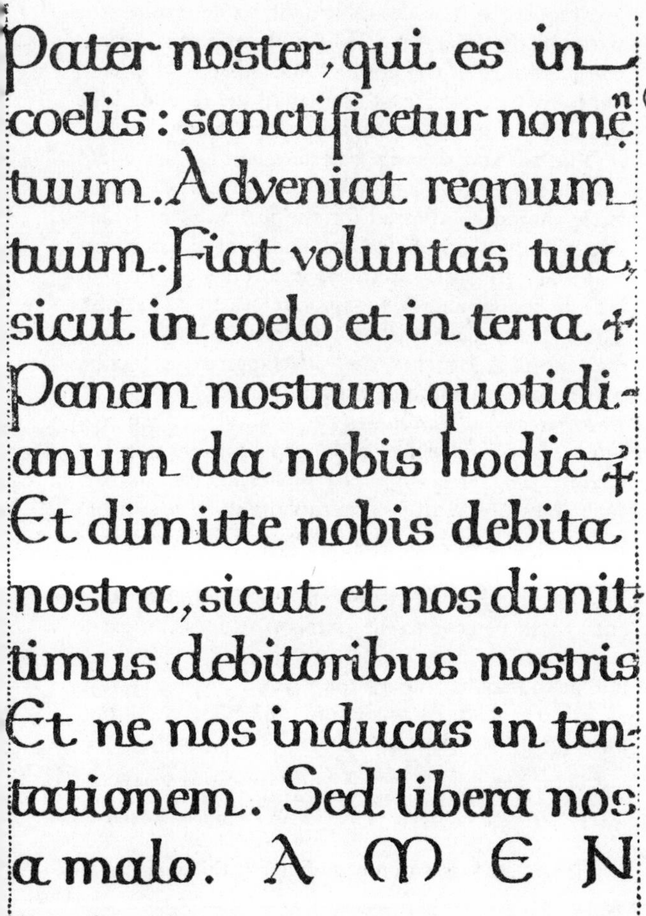

Pater noster, qui es in
coelis : sanctificetur nome[n]
tuum. Adveniat regnum
tuum. Fiat voluntas tua,
sicut in coelo et in terra. ✝
Panem nostrum quotidi-
anum da nobis hodie. ✝
Et dimitte nobis debita
nostra, sicut et nos dimit-
timus debitoribus nostris
Et ne nos inducas in ten-
tationem. Sed libera nos
a malo. A M E N

FIG. 66.

59

Frequently it is desirable first to determine the sizes of the margins. These depend on various considerations of the position and office of the MS., but more particularly on the size of the sheet and the character of its future environment[1] (see p. 315).

The *top* and *side margins* may be of equal width —or the *top* may be a little less (see *a*, fig. 70). Ample space should be allowed for the *foot margin*, which is generally about twice the width of the *top*, but may vary in different cases, according as the text falls short of or encroaches upon it (see pp. 316, 306). For a plain *foolscap* sheet: *sides* (each) $2\frac{1}{2}$ inches, *top* (approx.) 2 inches, and *foot* (approx.) 4 inches, may be taken as suitable margins (fig. 65).

The width of the sheet ($13\frac{1}{2}$ inches) less the two *side margins* ($2\frac{1}{2}$ inches each) gives *the length of the writing lines* ($13\frac{1}{2} - 5 = 8\frac{1}{2}$ inches). One or two such lines are written experimentally in a suitable script (say, $\frac{5}{16}$ inch), and *the average number of words per line* (four) is found.

The number of words in the complete text (fifty) will determine the number of lines: an extra line or so may be allowed for safety $\left(\dfrac{50}{4} = 12\frac{1}{2}, \text{ say,}\right.$ *thirteen*). The spacing of these is calculated

$\frac{5}{16}$ in. writing requires about $\frac{7}{8}$ in. (close) spacing (p. 45):
Thirteen lines at $\frac{7}{8}$ in. gives $11\frac{3}{8}$ in. — *depth of text*:
$11\frac{3}{8}$ in. from 17 in. leaves $5\frac{5}{8}$ in.[2] for *head* and *foot margins*

—and if the space is not sufficient, the writing is

---

[1] For example, a *framed* sheet does not require such wide margins as a similar sheet *un*framed.

[2] Really about 6 inches, because the top line of writing will not occupy its full $\frac{7}{8}$ inch, the unused part of which adds to the top margin (see fig. 65).

made a little smaller. If, on the other hand, the marginal depth left over were excessive, the writing *might* be made a little larger in order to fill up the space.

PROBLEM II (A SHEET OF POETRY)

To write out "*He that is down, needs fear no fall,*" *in a formal round-hand on a sheet of foolscap* (i.e. 17 *inches high* × 13½ *inches wide*).

Here there are three verses of four lines each: these with two space lines, left between the verses, give a total of fourteen lines (fig. 67).

A poem has a given number of lines of various lengths, and only very strong reason or necessity can justify our altering its proper form (*e.g.* by breaking up the lines) in order to make a mass of equal lines. Such theoretical margins as are possible in the treatment of prose can therefore seldom be observed in writing out a poem, and, unless the height or the width of the sheet can be altered, there is apt to be an excess of margin in one or the other direction. When such excess margin is obviously unavoidable, no objection can be made to its appearance. *Poetry may conveniently be treated as "fine writing"* (see p. 227).

If the size of the writing be considered of the first importance, several of the *longer lines* (*e.g.* the first and the eleventh in the poem given) are written on a piece of paper in the size of writing preferred (say, ¼ inch). By laying this paper on the given sheet, it is seen whether such lines would allow of sufficient *side margins*. (If they would not, the writing may be made smaller.)

The height of the writing (¼ inch) must allow of the full number of lines (fourteen) being properly

61

He that is down, needs fear no fall
He that is low, no pride :
He that is humble, ever shall
Have God to be his guide.

I am content with what I have,
Little be it or much :   I crave,
And, Lord, contentment still I
Because thou savest such.

Fulness to such a burden is,
That go on pilgrimage :
Here little, and hereafter bliss,
Is best from age to age

FIG. 67.

spaced on the sheet (17 inches) with sufficient *head* and *foot margins*. This is calculated—

¼ in. writing requires approximately ¾ in. spacing (p. 45):
Fourteen lines at ¾ in. gives 10½ in. ═ *depth of text:*
10½ in. from 17 in. leaves 6½ in. for *head* and *foot margins.*

—and if the space were not sufficient, the lines might be made a little closer, or the writing a little smaller (or, if necessary, the blank lines might be left out between the verses; p. 89).

The Sizes of the Margins.—It will be seen that the above method is primarily for settling *a length of line* which will allow of sufficient side margins. The process can be reversed; if necessary, the side margins are made of a given width, thus determining the exact length of the line, *the size of writing* which this line allows being found experimentally.

NOTE.—The *extra* long lines may slightly encroach on the right-hand margin: the effect of this is balanced by the falling short of other lines.

SPACING & PLANNING MANUSCRIPT

In penmanship great nicety of spacing and arrangement is possible. The *ascending* and *descending* strokes may be shortened or drawn out, the spaces between letters and words may be slightly increased or decreased, the lines may be written near or far apart, and the letters may be written with a broader or narrower nib.

Elaborate spacing and planning, however, should not be attempted at first, and straightforward, undesigned work is often the best. The student is apt to waste time writing out an elaborate draft in order to ascertain how to space the matter. This is a mistake, because if written well, it is a waste of good writing on a mere draft; if written ill, it is bad practice. The briefer experiments and calculations are, the better, though the simplest problem always requires for its solution a calculation or *process of guess and trial* (such as suggested in the preceding pages). Practice will make people very good *guessers*, and the best work of all is done when the worker guesses rightly, and follows his guesses with the actual work, itself the trial and proof of accuracy.

CHAPTER VI

MANUSCRIPT BOOKS [1]

MS. Books: Tools & Materials—Methods & Proportions—The Size & Shape of the Book—The Widths of the Margins—The Size of the Writing, &c.—Ruling—MS. Books: General Remarks.

MS. BOOKS: TOOLS & MATERIALS

Manuscript
Books

The making of manuscript books, based on a study of the early MSS., offers the best training to the scribe and illuminator in *writing, lettering, rubricating, gilding, illuminating initials and borders, and miniature painting,* and is the best means of mastering the foundations of Book Typography and Decoration.

Materials, &c. for MS. Books; Paper (see pp. 17, 69, 77, 281); *Vellum and Parchment* and *Pounce* (see pp. 76, 133, 139–41).—Cut a small sheet the

---

[1] MS. Books are further considered in Chap. XVI.

size of a page of the book, and clip the long edge between two flat pieces of wood (holding it as it would be if bound). If the page will bend over and stay down by its own weight, it is thin enough (R) fig. 68); if it stands up (W), it is too stiff.

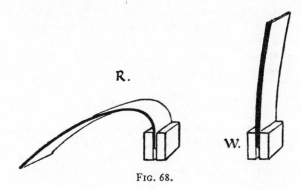

R.

W.

FIG. 68.

Cutting Sheets.—A frame or template (the size of the sheet desired) is used by parchment makers. It is useful for cutting out the sheets for a common size of parchment book. They are cut on the end-grain of wood, or on card or glass.

Folding.—A *Folder*, as used by bookbinders (or a bone paper-knife), is useful, and also a *Set or T-Square* for testing right angles, &c. The fold and the top edge of each book-sheet are commonly squared by proper folding.

Ruling, &c. (see p. 307).—For marking distances of lines, a carefully prepared paper[1] scale (p. xxiii) or a pattern & an awl (p. 75), or a *"star-wheel"*—

---

[1] The *direct* use of a thick wood or metal scale may lead to inaccuracy.

65

having regular intervals between the spikes—may be used. Or the ruling—of the writing lines—may be simplified by using a stout card frame (internally the size of the text-column) with strips glued across it: for a common size of book this might be made in stout tin or other metal. The lines are commonly ruled with a *ruling stylus* (see figs. 72, 77), or a sort of *"rake"* may be made to rule six lines at once.

Writing, Colouring, Gilding, Binding (Chaps. II, X, IX, XVI).

METHODS & PROPORTIONS

Having to make a manuscript book for a specific purpose, the scribe formulates in his mind a general plan of the work, and decides approximately the respective sizes of page and of writing which seem most suitable.

He endeavours to fashion the book in accord with its use, and therefore allows the (most suitable) material, the subject-matter and the office of the book, and the way in which it will be read and handled, to determine as far as is possible the proportions of its parts, and its treatment as a whole.

Its *material* may be vellum, parchment, or paper, on which a variety of pens, brushes, and other tools, with inks, colours, and metal foils, may be employed. Its *office* may be "useful" or "ornamental"; its contents may be long or short, weighty or light, and of greater or less worth; it may be for public or for private use; and the book may be intended to be placed on a lectern, to be held in the hand, or to be carried in a coat pocket.

In following out such natural indications, the

practised craftsman relies greatly on his working
methods, preferring a direct mode of treatment to
one which is too ingenious or subtle. In deciding
a doubtful point, a common-sense of proportion is
a sufficient guide, and one may generally assume
that great works are best " writ large," and that
large letters read best on an ample page, and *vice
versa*.

The main proportions which have to be considered are interdependent, and follow one another
in their natural order (see p. 220), thus—

1. *The size and shape of the book.*
2. *The widths of the margins.*
3. *The size of the writing*, &c.

And the methodical scribe makes his books of certain
definite and regular sizes, each size having corresponding and regular proportions of margins and
writing. Though these may greatly depend on individual taste and experience, it is suggested that—like
all good designs—they should be allowed as far as
possible to *settle and arrange themselves*.

THE SIZE & SHAPE OF THE BOOK

A book is thought of by the scribe chiefly as an
open book, and the width and height of its pages
are chosen with a view to its convenient shape and
pleasant appearance when open. The most econo-
mical sizes into which a suitable sheet of paper can
be folded (or a skin of parchment can be cut) may
commonly be allowed to decide these proportions.

When a printer is about to print a book he chooses
a sheet of paper which will fold into a suitable shape
and size. If the sheet be folded once to form two

67

leaves, the book is called a *folio* (fig. 69); folded again to form a "*section*" of four leaves—a *quarto* (4to)

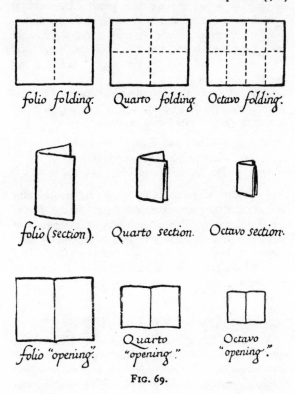

folio folding.　　*Quarto folding.*　　*Octavo folding.*

folio (section).　　*Quarto section.*　　*Octavo section.*

folio "opening".　　*Quarto "opening."*　　*Octavo "opening."*

FIG. 69.

or folded a third time to form a *section* of eight leaves —an *octavo* (8vo).[1] The book is made up of a

---

[1] The two, four, eight (or more) pages are printed on both sides of the sheet before it is folded. Two or more sheets are generally folded and put together to form a folio "*section*."

number of sections sewn on to strings or tapes (see
p. 311).

The penman will find that, besides saving time
and labour, it conduces to good work if he keep to
certain regular sizes for "large," "medium," and
"small" books; and, if the ordinary sheets of paper
which he uses will fold in convenient *folio, quarto,*
and *octavo* sizes, it is well that he make these his
standards for paper books.

Paper being made in sheets of various dimensions,
by folding a large or a small sheet, a "large" or
"small" folio—4to, 8vo—can be obtained.

It may be noted that the length and the width
of sheets of paper[1] are very commonly *about as* 9 *is
to* 7. And therefore, when the sheet is folded for
folio or *octavo*, the proportions are roughly about
$7 : 4\frac{1}{2}$, which are very good proportions for a page
of a book. It is obvious that a narrow ("*upright*")
book is easier to handle and more pleasant in appearance (when open) than an album or "*oblong*" shape
of book (*b* and *c*, fig. 70).

THE WIDTHS OF THE MARGINS

Margins are necessary in order to isolate and
frame a text: thus they contribute to its legibility
and beauty. It is better that they be wide rather
than narrow (see p. 72, & NOTE, p. 229); but
excessively wide margins are often neither covenient
nor pleasing (see p. 188).

The "page" or column of text should be in
such proportion to the page of the book, and be
placed on it in such a way as to leave adequate

---

[1] Such as *Foolscap* ($17'' \times 13\frac{1}{2}''$), *Crown* ($20'' \times 15''$), *Demy*
$22\frac{1}{2}'' \times 17\frac{1}{2}''$), *Royal* ($25'' \times 20''$), &c.

margins on every side. A narrow column of text is generally best, for short lines are easiest to write and to read, and do not tire the hand, *or the eye*, in passing from one line to the next. For this reason the text is often divided into two or more columns

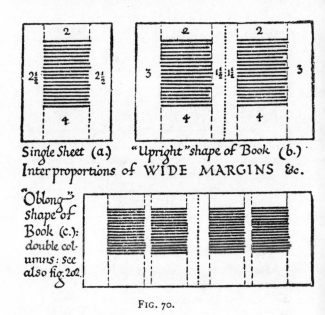

Single Sheet (a.)   "Upright" shape of Book (b.)
Inter proportions of WIDE MARGINS &c.

"Oblong" shape of Book (c.): double columns: see also fig. 202.

FIG. 70.

when the page is wide, or the writing is very small *in comparison*.

The exact proportion of margin to text in a given page depends on circumstances, and is largely a matter of taste (ex. fig. 71 & note 2, *b*, p. 220). But just as it is advantageous generally to keep to certain

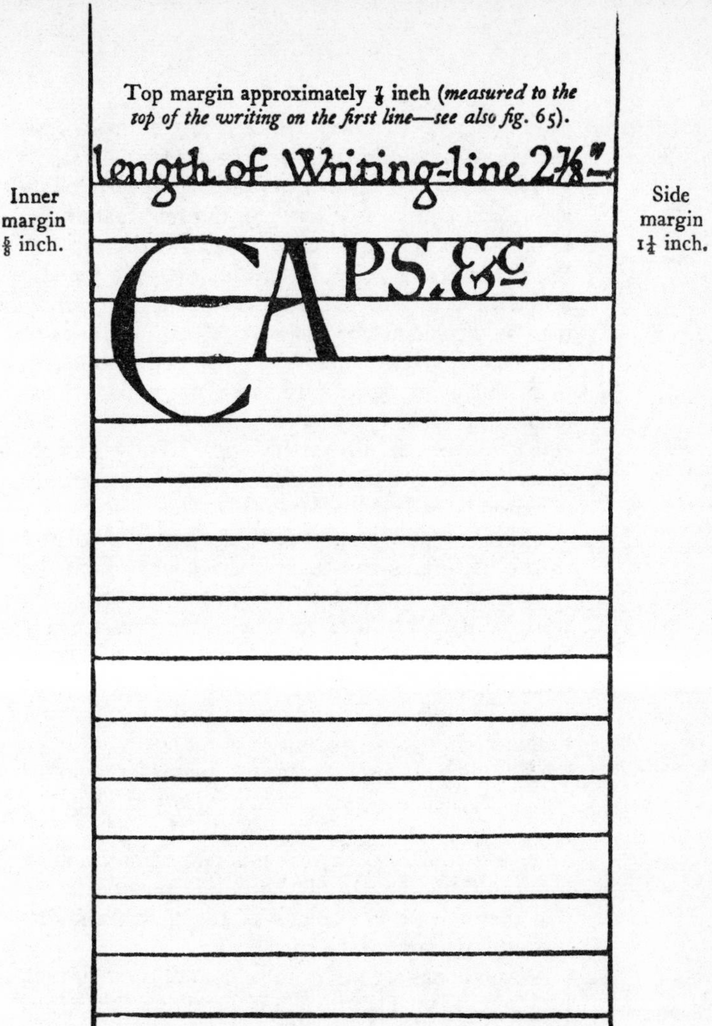

Top margin approximately ⅞ inch (*measured to the top of the writing on the first line—see also fig. 65*).

length of Writing-line 2⅞"

Inner margin ⅝ inch.

Side margin 1¼ inch.

CAPS.&c

FIG. 71.—Diagram showing the ruling of a (*Recto*) page 4¾ inches × 7¼ inches as for a manuscript book (allowing five or six words to the *Writing-line*). There are fifteen Writing-lines, the *Line-space* being ⅜ inch.

The proportions of large CAPITALS, shown above, are set by the Line-space (*footnote*, p. 187).

The Foot margin is 1¾ inch.

sizes of pages, it is well to keep to certain—*corre-sponding*—sizes of margins for regular use.

The proportions of the margins to each other follow a sort of tradition (see fig. 70), the foot margin (4) usually being twice as wide as that at the top (2), the side margins generally greater than the top and less than the foot. The two pages of an *opening* may be viewed as one sheet having two columns of text; and the two inner margins, which combine to form an interspace, are therefore made narrow (about 1½ each), so that together they are about equal to one side margin (fig. 70). These proportions (1½ : 2 : 3 : 4) approximate to the proportions common in early MSS.

Sufficient and proportional margins add greatly to the usefulness and beauty of a book. That the writers and illuminators used them when books were read and valued in a way we can scarcely realise now, shows that such things are not, as some might suppose, a matter of affectation. Besides the natural fitness of the common proportions commends them: a deep foot margin is a foundation to the whole, and gives a spare piece for the reader to hold,[1] and wide side margins rest the eyes and keep the text from "*running off the page*" at the end of each line; and (the *two*) narrow inner margins combine to separate the pages sufficiently, but not too far, so that they form two "columns" together, *framed* by the outer margins of the open book.

When books are meant to be bound, from $\frac{1}{16}$ inch to $\frac{1}{8}$ inch extra margin should be allowed *all round* the page for the cutting down and binding. The

---

[1] In Oriental books, which are sometimes held by their top margins, the *top* is deepest.

binding is apt to encroach on the inner margins,
especially in vellum books, which do not open
fully; in order, therefore, that the inner margins
may keep their proper width, an extra width of $\frac{1}{8}$
to $\frac{1}{4}$ inch (according to the stiffness of the material)
is allowed.

THE SIZE OF THE WRITING, &C.

The shape, size, and margins of the page (already
settled) together determine the length of the *writing-
line* (see fig. 71); and the *size of the writing* should
be such as will allow a reasonable number of words
to that line.[1]

Eight or nine words to the line is a common
proportion in ordinary printed books, and may be
taken by the scribe as his ordinary *maximum*. Lines
having very many words are difficult to read.

On the other hand, lines of only two or three
words each are generally tiresome, though they
may be allowed in special cases of *fine writing* (see
p. 226), where it is less necessary to economise space
or time, and the effect of an even mass is not desired.
But in any case where there is an attempt to make
the right-hand edge of the text approximately even,
at least four or five words to the line are necessary;
the scribe may therefore take four words per line as
his ordinary *minimum*.

We may say generally, then, that *an ordinary
manuscript book should contain between four and eight
words (or between 25 and 50 letter-spaces) to the
line.*

---

[1] If the average number of words be previously fixed—as in a
poem (see p. 61)—that will practically determine the size of the
writing.

73

The exact size of the writing allowed in a given case may be found by a process of guess and trial, but this is seldom necessary for the practical scribe who uses regular sizes for regular occasions.

The line spacing.—The size of the letter determines approximately the distance apart of the writing-lines (see pp. 45, 291). Much depends on whether the *ascending* and *descending* letters are long or short (see fig. 154).

The number of writing-lines to the page equals the number of times that the *line-space* is contained in the *text-column* (*i.e.* the height of the page less the top and foot margins)—allowing for the top line not requiring a full space (see fig. 71). Any fractional space left over may be added to the foot margin, or, if nearly equal to one line-space, a little may be taken from the margins to complete it.

The Large Capitals are commonly *one*, *two*, or *more* of the line-spaces in height (fig. 71, & p. 94).

RULING

Having folded and cut the large sheet of paper into small (book) sheets of the size determined on, take one of these as a pattern and rule it throughout as if it were to be used in the book.

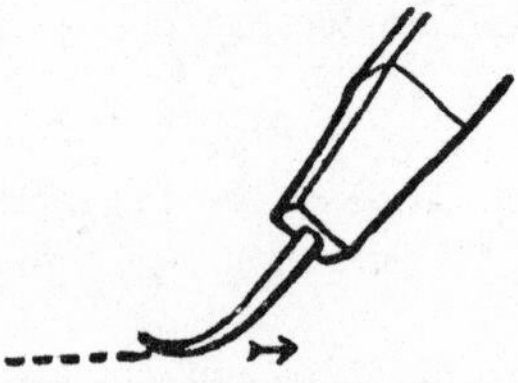

The ruling stylus has a blunt point, which indents the paper, but does not scratch it. A stout pin bent to a claw shape and held in a piece of wood does very well (fig. 72).

FIG. 72.

74

Under the writing paper there should be a "pad"
of ordinary paper (or blotting paper).

The marginal lines are ruled from head to foot of
each leaf (*a*, fig. 73). Besides being a guide for the
writing, they give an appearance of straightness and
strength to the written page.[1]

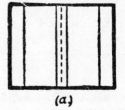 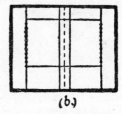

(*a*)   (*b*)

Fig. 73.

The writing lines are ruled across, between the
marginal lines, their places
having been indicated by
equidistant dots (*b*, fig. 73).

A dozen or more of the
small sheets of the book are
piled together on a board
*with their top edges exactly
coinciding*, and the pattern
sheet is accurately placed on
the top of the pile. The pile
of sheets may be fixed by a
narrow piece of wood placed
across and screwed down (fig.
74). (See *Addenda*, p. xxiii.)

The writing line dots are

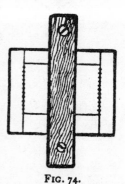

Fig. 74.

---

[1] They are often ruled double (see p. 307), and sometimes the
top and foot lines are ruled from edge to edge of the sheet.

pricked through all the sheets by means of a fine
awl or needle set in a wooden handle (fig. 75).

See also methods of ruling WITHOUT PRICKING
pp. 65–6.

FIG. 75.

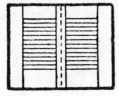

FIG. 76.

FIG. 77.

The writing lines are ruled
as in fig. 76 (sometimes across
the narrow inner margins).

For double writing lines a
double-ruling stylus may be
made of two pins fixed in a
wooden handle at the exact
width of the *writing gauge*
(fig. 77).

MS. BOOKS—GENERAL REMARKS

Sections (p. 68).—A *section*, or "gathering," commonly consists of four book-sheets, folded in half
into eight leaves (*i.e.* sixteen *pages*), but *three* or
even *two* sheets are sufficient when they are extra
thick, and *five* or *six* may be used when extra thin.
Parchment sheets should have their smooth sides so
placed together that each "opening" of the book
has both its pages rough or both smooth and the
pages are *pounced* after they are ruled (see p. 140).

Before the writing is begun the pages of the

76

section are numbered on the inner marginal line, about ½ inch or so below the footline. This will prevent mistakes.

Fly-leaves.—One or more leaves of the first and last sections in a book are left blank (besides the extra sheet or section (p. 310) which is used in the binding—attached to the cover). A book of any size or importance ought to have at least three fly-leaves at the beginning, and three or four at the end. These extra leaves protect the manuscript, and, in a sense, constitute *margins* for the whole body of the text. They may also be used to make thin books thicker, for the sake of the binding. At the end of Service books, or other books likely to be of permanent interest, additional fly-leaves should be provided for notes and annotations (see pp. 308, 310).

Rough or Smooth Edges.—The rough "Deckle" edges of hand-made paper are inconvenient in a book of any thickness, and should be trimmed off after folding, though they may be left in the case of very thin books. The deckle edge should not occur at the top of the page, as it would there be a trap for dust, and because it is important that the tops of pages should all be level. The top edge or head of a book is often cut and gilt in order to keep out the dust—this is called "*Library gilt.*" It is more suitable, however, that *all* the edges be gilt.

The Top Margins throughout the book are kept quite level. Any irregularity at the top of a page catches the eye at once, while slight differences at the side, or considerable differences at the foot, may occur without spoiling the appearance of the margins. All measurements for marginal and writing lines, &c., are therefore made from the *fold* of the

77

book-sheet and from the top edge, which is cut at right angles to the fold.

Regular Writing.—In writing one page it is a good plan to have its fellow page, or a similarly written one, fixed on the desk beside it as a pattern. This will save the beginner from a very common error—writing larger or smaller (which of course spoils the look of the pages).

Initial Page.—The text of a book commonly begins on a *recto*, or right hand, page (see p. 329).

CHAPTER VII

VERSAL LETTERS & COLOURED CAPITALS

Development of Versals—General Analysis of Versals—Notes on Construction of Versals—Spacing & Arrangement of Versals.

DEVELOPMENT OF VERSALS

THE earliest books consisted of a number of lines of continuous writing in capital letters. There were seldom any divisions of the text—into paragraphs, chapters, or the like—or even of one word from another; nor were important words distinguished by larger initials. The first division of paragraphs was made by a slight break in the text and a mark; later, the first letter of the first complete line of the new paragraph was placed in the margin and written larger. When "small-letters" were evolved, capitals ceased to be used for the body of the text, and became distinguishing letters for headings and important words.

The capitals written at the beginnings of books, chapters, and paragraphs grew larger and more ornamental, and at length were made in colour and decorated with pen flourishes. Such letters, used to mark the beginnings of verses, paragraphs, &c., have been called "Versals."[1]

In modern printing and ordinary writing the first line of a paragraph is generally *indented* (*a*, fig. 78),

FIG. 78.

but the earlier method of employing a special mark or letter (*b* or *c*) is more effective, and it might very well be used, even in modern printed books, for fine editions. Affording a legitimate opening for illumination and book-ornament, it was (and *is*) the natural method for the penman, who, starting with these useful capitals, by flourishing them—in their

---

[1] Though Versals may generally be regarded as *paragraph marking letters*, it is convenient to apply the term to the Versal type of letter (the early *Illuminator's Pen-capital*)—*e.g.* "a heading in Versal letters" (see fig. 91).

FIG. 79.
(*13th century*.)

own colour, or by dotting, outlining, or ornamenting them, with a contrasting colour (see fig. 79, from an old MS.), evolved the *Illuminated Initial*.

Types of Versal Letters (examples: Plates IX, X, XI, XII, and figs. 1, 78 to 94, 150, 161, 165, 166, 189). — The earlier Versals had very simple and beautiful pen shapes, and are the best models for the modern penman to follow. After the fourteenth century they were often fattened and vulgarised and overdone with ornament. In this way they not only lost their typical forms; but their "essential forms" —as letters derived from the Roman Alphabet — became much disguised and confounded (see fig. 128).

1. The LETTERS: — Essentially *Pen-made* and *Compound*—i.e. Built-up of Double Strokes and filled in—they exaggerate *the Contrast of Thick & Thin Strokes* natural to *Simple* Pen Writing. They are (Commonly Coloured) Roman Capitals with a "Gothic" Character and of great Variety (cf. figs. 166 & 79), using both "Round" & "Square" Forms of D, E, H, &c., and Short & Fat, or Medium, or Tall & Slender, Letters. (Commonly made one or more *Writing-Line-Spaces* High—v. figs. 71, 166.)

2. STEMS and Heavy Limbs: — Commonly Curved-in on either side of Stem. *The Stem-Waist* may measure from two to many Nib's-Widths across. Curved and other Heavy Parts match the Weight of the Stems.

3. Thin ARMS, &c.: — *Full width*, Single Pen Stroke, with free end Built-up (figs. 81 & 80).

4. SERIFS and Terminals: — Commonly Pen's Thinnest *Hair Stroke*, Long and slightly Curved, sometimes Ornamented (v. *Head Strokes & Serifs* of h & I, & *Tail Ornaments* of I & Q, fig. 79).

5. ARRANGING & Spacing: — *Singly*, set in Text or Margin or part in both (fig. 86):
In Words, Commonly One *Writing-Line-Space* apart (figs. 92, 166).

6. COMPONENT PARTS: —
A has approx. 10 strokes & filling.
B   ,,   8   ,,   ,,
C   ,,   8   ,,   ,,
and so on (see fig. 81).

81

AABBCCD
DEEFGGH
hIJKKLM
MMNOPP
QQQRR
SSTTTU
V
WWXXYYZ

" VERSAL" LETTERS 1904. MSS.

freely copied from XI·XII·and XIII Cent[y].
I K W WY y are made to match +.
For facsimiles see plates IX,X,XI,& XII

FIG. 80.

A small pen & a long slit — for Versals.

approximate
proportion of
Versal pen nib } to { "Small
PEN } — writing"
— NIB.

(a.)

A B C E D J

M N S T O

Component parts or pen strokes (b.)

A B C E

ends
made
with hori-
zontal
pen }

top of E
&c. }
top of
C &c. }

First
stage of
construct-
ion: to be
filled in.

(c.)

position
of pen in
making
horizontal —
strokes.

}

Position of
pen in

mak ing
hori zon-
tal curves.

1.

3.

3.

4

1. 2.

(d.) & ends E, C &c

(e.)

2.

(f.) (g.) (h.)

4.

order of making
stems and serifs:
(f.) serifs first
(g. & h.) serifs added.

b R Q (i.)

the thick part stops

&c. In making
these; the thin tail
may project but
at a balance.

FIG. 81.

83

(See figs. 80, 81, 85, 165)

Versal Letters are properly *built-up* (p. 255) with
true pen-strokes (*b*, fig. 81). Drawn or painted,
they acquire a different character (p. 256). Their
office being to mark important parts of the text,
they are generally distinguished by colour and freedom of form—tending to curves and flourishes.

The pen has an extra long slit ($\frac{1}{2}$ inch to $\frac{3}{4}$ inch),
and the *writing-board* may be lowered (see fig. 46, *b*)
to permit of the thick, liquid colour running out
freely. The nib is of the ordinary shape (but not
too oblique), and generally rather less in width
than the nib used for the accompanying text (*a*,
fig. 81. See also p. 257 and *especially* fig. 165).

The outlining strokes are quickly written and
immediately filled in, each letter being loaded well
with the colour, which thereafter dries evenly, with
a slightly raised "flat" surface. The liquid colour
should be fairly thick (see *Colours*, p. 142).

"*Gothic lettering*" is a term used for "Blackletter" and related types, as distinguished from
"Roman" types. "Gothic" capitals tend to roundness, the small-letters to angularity, but in each
the abrupt change from thick to thin strokes, and
the resulting contrast of stroke, are characteristics
—the outcome of penwork.[1] Versals, though primarily Roman letters,[2] have this contrast strongly
marked; *the ends of the thinner strokes spread* (see
p. xxiii), *and the heavy parts are crossed by thin serifs.*

The early Versals approaching the "Roman

---

[1] The pen, in direct proportion to the breadth of the nib,
tends to give a "Gothic" character to *all* letter forms.
[2] See Plate 5 in "Manuscript & Inscription Letters."

84

Letter" (p. 258) make excellent models, the later ornate "Lombardic" type (p. xxx) is not so safe. Versals are capable of great variety, and the "round" or "square" **D, E, H, M,** and **W** may be used at pleasure.

The Stems curve in slightly on either side. When they are very tall the mid part may be quite straight, imperceptibly curving out towards the ends (*b*, fig. 82). This gives an effect of curvature throughout the length, while keeping the letter graceful and straight. The head of a stem (especially of an *ascender*) may with advantage be made slightly wider than the foot (fig. 83). *This applies generally to all kinds of built-up capitals.*

FIG. 83.

FIG. 82.

The *stem width* may be nearly the same in Versals of different heights (*a*, fig. 84): generally the letters tend to become *more slender in proportion* as the letters grow taller (*b*). Very large Versals (or initials) are often made with a hollow stem to avoid a heavy appearance (L, fig. 84).

85

FIG. 84.

The Serifs are long and slightly curved in ornamental forms (fig. 79): shorter, and nearly straight in stiffer forms (fig. 166). In many cases the serifs appear to have been written *first*, the stems being added between them (*f*, fig. 81)—in old MSS. the stems often show ragged ends crossing the serifs. Sometimes the serif appears to have been *added to the stem in two pieces*, half on either side springing from the corners of the stem (*g*). The safest way seems to be the *complete finishing stroke added to, and forming sharp angles with*, the stem (*h*).

Arms or Branches.—Width of nib at start, and built-up at free end. (Pen horizontal, figs. 81, 165).

86

The Bows or Curves of Versals (and of *built-up*
letters generally) are best begun with the *inside stroke*

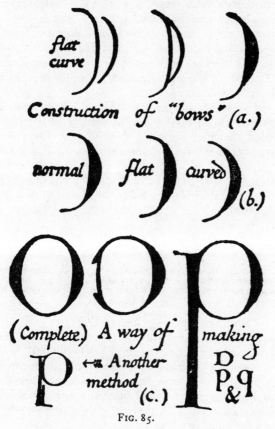

Fig. 85.

—a rather flat curve: and finished with the outer
stroke—a pronounced curve (*a*, fig. 85). This

preserves the continuity of the interior curve, together with the clean contrast of the thick and thin strokes (see *inside shapes*, p. 217). The normal form may be flattened or curved a little (*b*), but *exaggeration* in either direction produces a degraded form. Part round letters, as **D**, **P**, and **Q**, may be begun with *a complete inner oval,* or *a nearly completed* **O** (to which the stem is added); this preserves their interior symmetry (*c*).

The beauty and quality of Versal letters depends very much on their freedom; *touching-up* or trimming after they are made is apt to spoil them; and when good letters are made with a free hand, minute roughnesses, which are due to their quick construction, may be regarded as shewing a *good* rather than a bad form of *care-less* workmanship (see (*c*) fig. 164).

SPACING & ARRANGEMENT OF VERSALS

(Allowing for the special treatment of Versals called for by the extreme freedom and elasticity of their pen forms, the following remarks apply *generally to the spacing and arrangement of coloured capitals in written pages*.)

Versals accompanying Small Text are generally *dropped* below the writing-line, so that their tops are level with the tops of the small letters (fig. 86).

Sizes of Versals.—Letters which are of the same importance—*i.e.* serve the same purpose—are usually of like size and form throughout; and the more important a letter, the more it tends to be elaborated and decorated (see figs. 90, 92).

Special words in Text marked by Versals.—Where coloured capitals are used throughout the text (fig. 92), the colours are usually varied (pp. 100, 151).

Line beginnings marked by Versals.—Where every line of a page begins with a coloured capital, the majority of the forms are kept rather plain (see (5) p. 102). They may be effectively treated as a *band* of simple or variegated colour (p. 102). This is a common treatment for a list of names or a poem; sometimes, especially if there are many lines, *simple-written* capitals (p. 261) may be used instead of Versals.

Verses or Paragraphs may be marked by Versals *set in the text (a),* or *part in margin, part in text (b),* or *wholly in the margin (c,* fig. 86). The marginal capital is the simplest, and it has the advantage of leaving the page of text entire; it may, however, sometimes be desirable *to break the continuity* by an inset capital, especially in cases of closely written text, or of *stanzas not spaced apart* (see p. 104).

The first word of a paragraph, which is begun with a Versal, is often completed in *simple-written* capitals of the same colour as the text (*a,* fig. 86).

Various ways of marking Paragraphs.—(*a*) The paragraph marks ❡, ¶, preferably coloured, may be used instead of (or even *with*) Versals (*comp.* fig. 95); (*b*) by one word or line (or several words or lines) of *simple-written* (or built-up) capitals in black or colour (see fig. 93); (*c*) by some suitable *ornament* (see fig. 87); (*d*) in many cases it is well to have spaces between the paragraphs or verses (see p. 104).

Line-Finishings at the ends of Verses, &c. (pp. 171, 411), *may be made with the Versal pens and colours.*

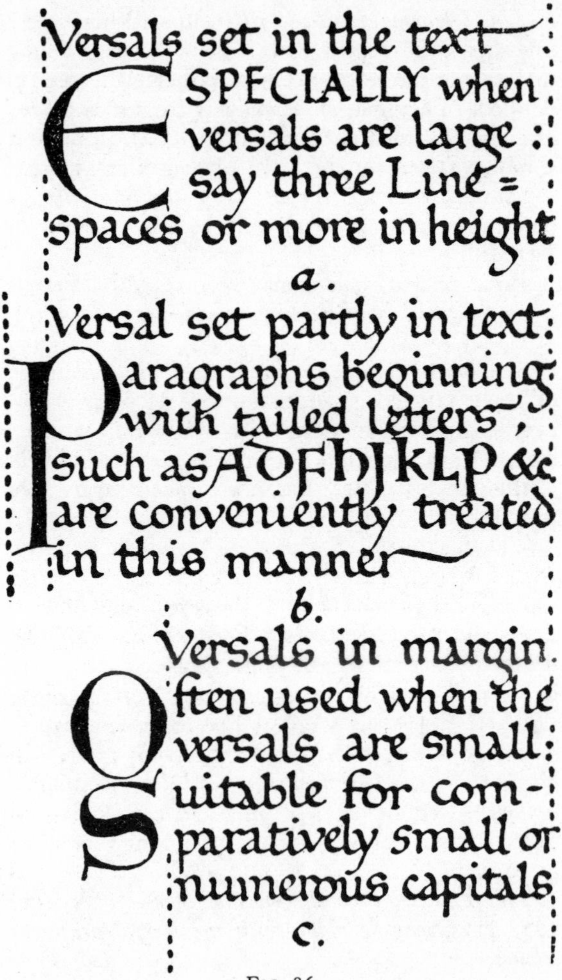

Versals set in the text—
ESPECIALLY when
versals are large :
say three Line =
spaces or more in height
a.

Versal set partly in text
Paragraphs beginning
with tailed letters,
such as A O F H J K L P &c
are conveniently treated
in this manner—
b.

Versals in margin
Often used when the
versals are small :
Suitable for com—
paratively small or
numerous capitals
c.

FIG. 86.

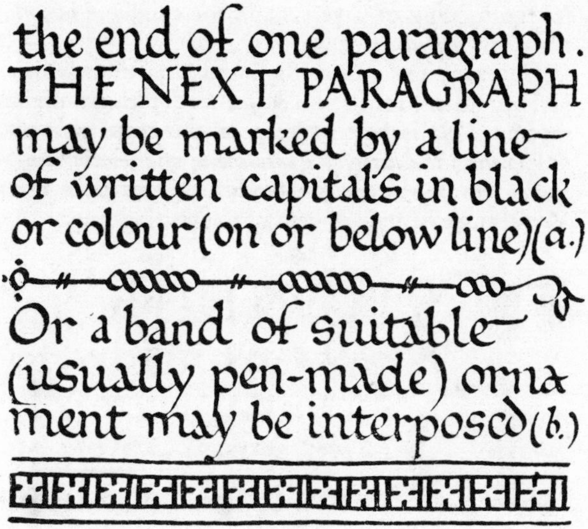

the end of one paragraph.
THE NEXT PARAGRAPH
may be marked by a line
of written capitals in black
or colour (on or below line)(a.)

Or a band of suitable
(usually pen-made) orna
ment may be interposed(b.)

FIG. 87.

To mark Chapters (or even Books), extra large
Versals (fig. 88) may be used, in lieu of more elaborate initials. Smaller Versals may be grouped round
about, beside or inside initials (p. 174 & fig. 92).

Headings and Pages in Capitals (see also pp. 94,
98).—Each line of capitals is generally kept uniform throughout its length,[1] though different lines
vary in size and colour (see fig. 89). If it be possible
it is well to keep the individual word entire and to

---

[1] The mediæval scribes often made the first line of a chapter
or book in uniform capitals (excepting the initial letter). The
succeeding line generally was smaller, and of a different colour
and type—even when a divided word was carried over into it.

let the heading or page contain the complete *initial phrase* or *sentence* (see fig. 91).

Generally the greater the number of capitals the *plainer* their forms are kept, and the closer their spacing. It is best to keep to the regular method of *spacing the lines of Versals one of the writing-line spaces (or more) apart*—though in special cases the Versals may be independent of the writing-lines.

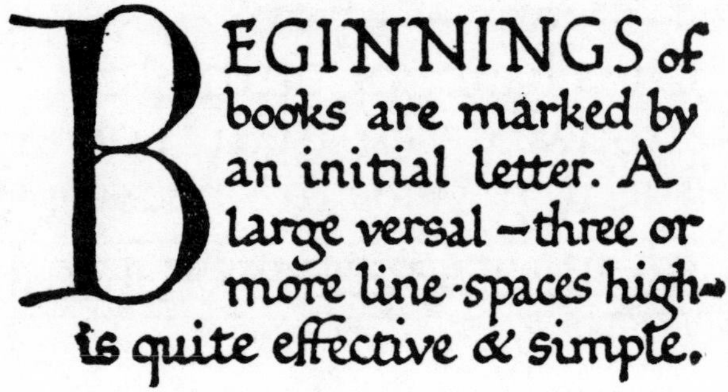

BEGINNINGS of books are marked by an initial letter. A large versal –three or more line ·spaces high– is quite effective & simple.

FIG. 88.

Spacing Out.—Coloured letters and ornaments are usually put in after the plain MS. has been written. A very little practice enables the scribe accurately to guess the amount of space which he should leave for the Versals, &c., whether it is designed to have several lines of them, or a single letter only on the page. A few pencil marks may be used to settle a doubtful point, but an elaborate sketching or setting out in pencil spoils the freedom of the work.

92

CHAPTER VIII

BLACK & RED

Rubricating—Initial Pages or Title Pages—Prefaces & Notes in Colour—Pages with Coloured Headings— Page or Column Heading & Initial—Versals in Column or Marginal Bands—Stanzas or Verses marked by Versals—Music with Red Staves— Tail-Pieces, Colophons, &c.—Rubricating: General Remarks.

RUBRICATING

"Red, either in the form of a pigment or fluid ink, is of very ancient and common use. It is seen on the early Egyptian papyri; and it appears in the earliest extant vellum MSS., either in titles or the first lines of columns or chapters. The Greek term was μελάνιον κόκκινον*; Latin* minium,[1] rubrica*."*—(Thompson's "G. & L. Palæography," p. 51.)

Rubricating, or the adding of Red, *or other coloured,* letters, line-finishings, or signs, to a MS. or Book, in which the main body of the text is already completed in black, constitutes in itself a very useful and effective form of decoration. It is, moreover, a connecting link between plain writing and illumination proper; and we may safely assume that the artists who made the beautiful illuminations of the Middle Ages were trained as *scribes* and *rubricators.*

INITIAL PAGES OR TITLE PAGES

Fig. 89 represents an *Initial Page* in Red Capitals. (The same arrangement may of course be used with a variety of colours and with gold: see Note (4)

---

[1] *Minium* = red-lead, used in early times for "rubrics" and drawings, hence is derived the word *"Miniature."*

93

below). Such a page is, as it were, an "illumination" to *all* the pages, following it in black text.

Title Pages came into fashion after printing was introduced. Early MSS. commonly began with the *opening words* written in large, decorated capitals, the *title* sometimes being written quite small, near the top of the page: other details were commonly put in the *colophon* in early books (see p. 108).

When the title is more important, in a literary sense, than the opening sentence, it may be well to follow the modern fashion. But when there is a finely worded opening sentence—perhaps the keynote to the rest of the text—while the title is merely for reference, it seems reasonable to magnify and illuminate the actual beginning of the book rather than the mere name of it (see p. 329).

NOTE (1). — In fig. 89 the title — (*JESU CHRISTI*) *Evangelium Secundum Joannem* — is written in as a decoration of the initial word; the old form "IHV XPI" is used for "Jesu Christi" (these letters, it will be noticed, are here employed to lighten the large capitals, see p. 174).

(2) Where IN is an initial word, to enforce narrow initial I, both letters may be magnified.

(3) The scale of the lettering corresponds with that of the ruled lines (these do not show in the figure): the letters and the interlinear spaces are each one line high; the initial word is four lines high. Such a mode of spacing is very simple and effective, and will save the rubricator much unnecessary trouble and fruitless planning (see *footnote*, p. 187).

(4) *Other Colour Schemes.*—All *Burnished Gold* (or with Title in *red*); or IN gold, with smaller capitals *Red* (or in *Blue* and *Red* lines alternately—or *Blue, Red, Green, Red:* see p. 147).

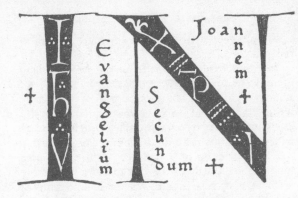

PRIN-
CIPIO
ERAT
VERBUM

FIG. 89

Fig. 90 represents a preface, or note, written in red.

It was a frequent practice in old MSS., where there were prefaces, or prologues, or notes—not actually part of the text—to keep these distinct by writing them in red. A somewhat similar usage still exists in modern typography, where such parts are sometimes distinguished by Italic type (see p. 279).

The distinction of a preface, "rubric," or note from the main body of the text makes a book more readable, and, as a page of red (or blue) writing is very pleasant and effective, we may certainly take advantage of such a reasonable excuse for introducing it. Entire books have been written in red, but this is a questionable mode, as too much red text would tire the eye.

NOTE (1).—The writing is founded on the tenth-century English hand given in Plate VIII.

(2) The flourishes on s and e fill gaps at the ends of the lines, and the spread out *A M E N* fills the last line.

(3) The Headline is in simple written capitals.

(4) The effect of colour contrast of the built-up Ps with the simple writing: the solid Ps (though really the same colour) appear to be a much deeper red than the writing, which is lightened by the intermingled white of the paper.

(5) *Other Colour Schemes.*—The *Versals* (Pp) in burnished gold; the rest in red or blue.

PATER NOSTER
qui es in coelis?
sanctificetur nomen
tuum. Adveniat reg-
num tuum. Fiat vo-
luntas tua, sicut in
coelo et in terra + + +
Panem nostrum quo
tidianum da nobis
hodie. Et dimitte
nobis debita nostra,
sicut et nos dimit-
timus debitoribus
nostris. Et ne nos in
ducas in tentation-
em. Sed libera nos a
malo. A M E N

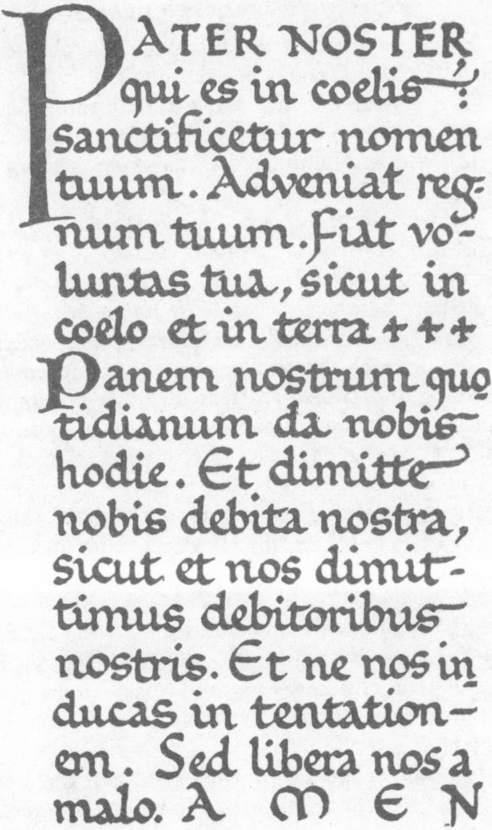

FIG. 90.

Red
& Black

Fig. 91 represents the first page of a chapter (or a book) with a *Heading* in red capitals.

It is convenient in practice clearly to distinguish between the two modes of beginning—

(*a*) with an illuminated Initial-*Page* (see fig. 89), or,

(*b*) with an illuminated *Heading* (see fig. 91). The former may be treated as though it were a decoration to the *whole* book. The latter is intended more particularly to decorate *its own page*.

The *Heading* should therefore be proportionate to the body of the text below it. About *one-third* Heading and two-thirds text make a good proportion. A "Heading" occupying half, or more than half, of the page is apt to look disproportionate, and it would be preferable to this to have a complete, or nearly complete,[1] *Page* of coloured capitals.

NOTE (1).—The full effect of black and red is obtained by an arrangement of the two colours in marked contrast.

(2) The lines are used as a scale for the Heading, the red capitals and interspaces each being one line high. If a Heading so spaced appear too close to the first line of black writing, another line space may be left.

(3) The round Es are used to fill out the second line, and the square, narrow E to relieve the crowded third line.

(4) *Other Colour Schemes.*—The entire *heading*, or the letters W, H, B, O, R, in burnished gold; or the whole variegated (see p. 146).

---

[1] An illuminated *Page* will allow of a few lines of black text at the foot (an arrangement very common in the elaborate Initial Pages of the fifteenth century), but these should be quite subordinate to the "Illuminatio."

WHO HATH BELIEVED OUR REPORT

and to whom hath the arm of the Lord been revealed ? For he grew up before him as a tender plant, & as a root out of a dry ground : he hath no form nor comeliness; & when we see him, there is no beauty that we should desire him. He was despised, & rejected of men; a man of sorrows, & acquainted with grief. & as one from whom men hide their face he was despised, & we esteemed him not.

FIG. 91.

99

Fig. 92 represents the first page of a book or chapter in two columns, beginning with a rather ornate Heading, in which the Initial is made the principal feature, and having coloured Versals and *line-finishings* throughout the text.

It is more difficult to get a good effect in this way than by means of a marked colour contrast (see p. 110), *or variegated colour, and gold* (see Note 7).

NOTE (1).—The lines bounding the text would naturally be indented, or pale (not black as in the block), and ruled from head to foot of the page (see Note (2) on the next figure).

(2) The red ornamental line-finishings (see p. 171) would be more effective if variegated.

(3) The Versals in the text are made about a line high, but are dropped below the line (p. 88).

(4) The Versals in the Heading are made one line high, with one-line spacing—between O and D increased to two lines (partly filled by a flourish from the D), in order to fit the U, O, and D in evenly beside the Initial.

(5) The Initial Q should project slightly up and out—beyond the bounding lines—to mark the top, left corner more strongly (see *footnote*, p. 177).

(6) *All* the rubricating on this page is done with the same pen (see pp. 171, 184).

(7) *Other Colour Schemes.* "QUOD FUIT AB INITIO," the *filigree ornament* and the V V in burnished gold (or the Q and VV in gold), the rest of the Versals and line-finishings in *Red and Blue*, or *Red and Green*, or *Red, Blue, and Green* (see pp. 147, 151).

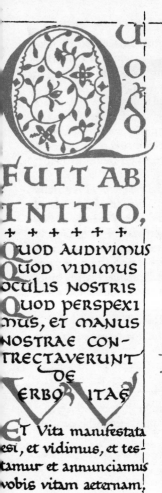

QUOD

FUIT AB INITIO,

✠ ✠ ✠ ✠ ✠ ✠

QUOD AUDIVIMUS
QUOD VIDIMUS
OCULIS NOSTRIS
QUOD PERSPEXI
MUS, ET MANUS
NOSTRAE CON-
TRECTAVERUNT
DE
VERBO VITAE

ET Vita manifestata
est, et vidimus, et tes-
tamur et annunciamus
vobis vitam aeternam,
quae erat apud Patrem

et apparuit nobis.
QUOD vidimus et
audivimus, annuncia
mus vobis, ut et vos
societatem habeatis no
biscum, et societas nos
tra sit cum Patre, et
cum Filio ejus JESU
CHRISTO
ET haec scribimus
vobis ut gaudeatis, et
gaudium vestrum sit
plenum
ET HAEC EST
ANNUNCIATIO
quam audivimus ab
eo, et annunciamus
vobis: Quoniam
Deus Lux est,
et tenebrae in eo non
sunt ullae
SI dixerimus quo-
niam societatem hab-
emus cum eo, et in
tenebris ambulamus,
mentimur, et veritat
em non facimus.

FIG. 92.

Fig. 93 represents two columns of black text, consisting of short verses, &c., which are marked by coloured capitals—forming bands of colour—in the margins.

NOTE (1).—The coloured capitals in the figure are made rather larger than usual, to enforce the effect of the two lines of red and mark their contrast with the columns of black text. In practice, however, they would be better and more distinct if rather smaller.

(2) The lines bounding the text would naturally be faint, or *grooved* (p. 307); but, ruled from head to foot of the page, they would be sufficiently apparent to add materially to the general effect of orderly arrangement. (Lines are printed here to show clearly the way the two columns are ruled and to *suggest* this effect, though the process block necessarily gives a false impression in making them appear too short and too heavy.)

(3) Extra width between the columns (and also in the margin) may be allowed for the coloured capitals (compare fig. 92).

(4) Words in simple written capitals are used to mark slight divisions, or changes of sense, in the text.

(5) A stiff Versal of a rather "Roman" type is used, partly because of the number of the capitals (see p. 92).

(6) *Other Colour Schemes.*—The larger capitals might be in burnished gold, the rest in red (or in *red*, *blue*, and *green*); or all might be in *red*, *blue*, and *green*.

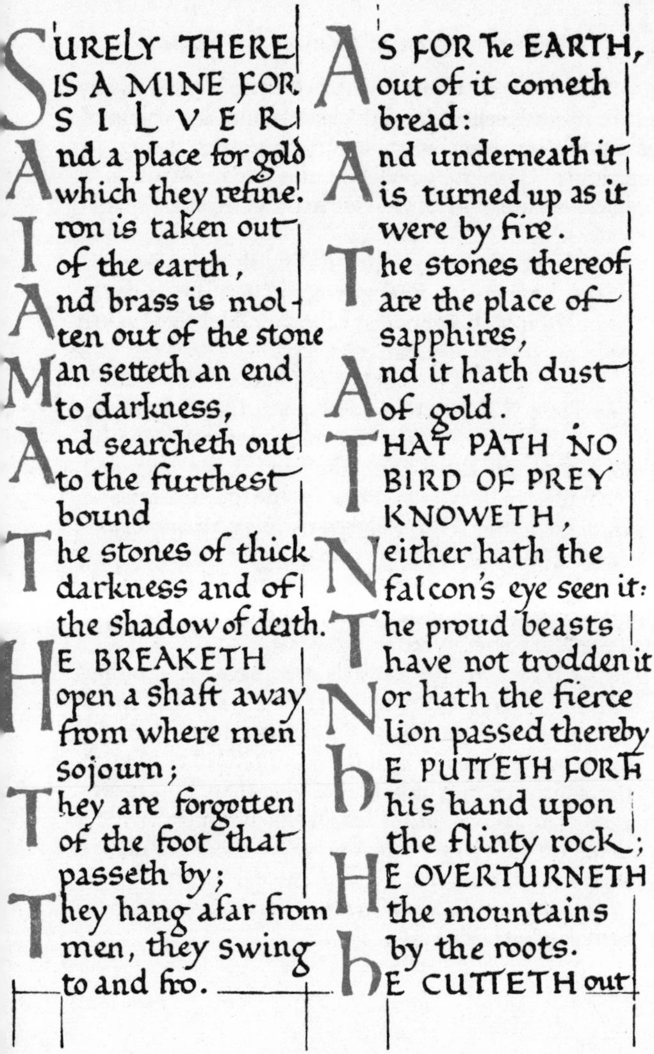

SURELY THERE
IS A MINE FOR
SILVER
And a place for gold
which they refine.
Iron is taken out
of the earth,
And brass is mol-
ten out of the stone
Man setteth an end
to darkness,
And searcheth out
to the furthest
bound
The stones of thick
darkness and of
the shadow of death.
HE BREAKETH
open a shaft away
from where men
sojourn;
They are forgotten
of the foot that
passeth by;
They hang afar from
men, they swing
to and fro.

AS FOR the EARTH,
out of it cometh
bread:
And underneath it
is turned up as it
were by fire.
The stones thereof
are the place of
sapphires,
And it hath dust
of gold.
THAT PATH NO
BIRD OF PREY
KNOWETH,
Neither hath the
falcon's eye seen it:
The proud beasts
have not trodden it
Nor hath the fierce
lion passed thereby
HE PUTTETH FORTH
his hand upon
the flinty rock;
HE OVERTURNETH
the mountains
by the roots.
HE CUTTETH out

Black
& Red

FIG. 93.

103

Fig. 94 represents a poem in two verses which are distinguished by interspaces and by coloured capitals—a brief introductory line also being in colour. (It is supposed that the poem occurs in a book—mainly in prose—written in Roman small-letters.)

It is generally best to distinguish the verses of poems by one-line interspaces. When this is done, coloured initials are not so necessary, and their value becomes chiefly decorative (see p. 89).

NOTE (1).—The writing is founded on "Italic" (see Plate XXI.), and (it is supposed that) it would be used here wherever the songs occurred; firstly, to distinguish them from the rest of the text, and secondly, to keep the lines of the poem entire—*Italics occupying less room than ordinary, round Small-Letters* (see p. 279).

(2) The story opens with the first line, which may in this case be regarded either as a *Title* or as a prefatory note in red.

(3) The two red capitals are made of a rather "Roman" type to match the Italic (and the small Roman text of the book). The difference in height made between the W and the S is intended to balance the difference in width, and to give them an appearance of equal weight. This may be permitted where there are only a few capitals; where there are many, their heights are generally kept more uniform.

(4) *Another Colour Scheme.*—W and S would look better in burnished gold.

WHO would list to the good lay
Gladness of the captive grey?
Tis how two young lovers met,
Aucassin and Nicolete,
Of the pains the Lover bore
And the sorrows he outwore,
For the goodness and the grace,
Of his Love, so fair of face.

SWEET the song, the story sweet,
There is no man hearkens it,
No man living 'neath the sun,
So outwearied, so foredone,
Sick and woful, worn and sad,
But is healèd, but is glad
Tis so sweet.

So say they, speak they, tell they the Tale:

FIG. 94.

Fig. 95 is a reproduction, in facsimile, showing
quarter of a page of a folio Service Book (probably
French, early sixteenth century). The page consists
of two columns of ten staves each, and is headed
❡ *In vigi* (lia), *natiuitatis dnī*. The book is printed
on vellum in red and black; the columns of music
have faint red bounding lines ruled by hand (not
shown in the figure).

The red stave is very effective, and it was commonly used in early MSS. and printed books. There
appears to be some doubt, however, as to its practical
value, and I have been advised that it is not so legible
as the black line stave, and also that, in *Church Service Books* (see p. 309), in order to make an absolutely
clear distinction, red should be reserved entirely for
the *rubrics*.

The "plain-song" chant, with its four-line stave,
has a simpler and finer appearance than the more
modern and elaborate five-lined stave and tailed
notes. The latter, however, may yet be treated
very effectively.

NOTE I.—The mark ❡ and the capitals 𝕊, 𝕓,
and 𝕔 were blotted—it can scarcely be called
"painted"—with yellow. Yellow or red were often
used in this way to mark the small black capitals in
printed books (& in MSS.—especially in the small
Bibles of the 13th century—p. 414, & *comp.* p. 266).
It is a questionable method. (These blots have been
removed from the figure—except, by an oversight,
in the case of 𝕊.)

(2) *Other Colour Schemes.*—(*a*) The title, or (*b*)
the text and the notes, might be in burnished gold
(the other parts in either case remaining in *red* and
black).

FIG. 95.

Fig. 96 represents a coloured Tail-piece or decorative finish at the end of a book (or chapter).

The Colophon (see p. 94 & figs. 13, 191), generally distinguished from the text by a smaller or different hand, and—especially in early printed books—by *colour* or other decorative treatment, occurs at the end of a book, where it is the traditional right of the penman and the printer to add a statement or a symbolical device. The *Name* (of craftsman and assistants), *Time*, and *Place* are commonly stated— preferably quite simply—*e.g. "This book, written out by me, A.B., in LONDON, was finished on the 31st day of DECEMBER* 1900." Any reasonable matter of interest concerning the *text*, the *materials*, *methods*, *lettering*, or *ornament*, and an account of the *number of leaves and their size, &c.*, may be added. But the craftsman, properly and modestly keeping his name off the title-page, is at liberty to exercise his right, marking the end of, and *signing* his work in any way he chooses—even in a speech or a sentiment—provided the form of the colophon be unobtrusive and its language natural. *Printer's devices* or *book-marks*, consisting of symbols, monograms, &c. (p. 326), were likewise used.

The opportunity generally provided by the final margin, and the natural wish to close the book with a fitting ornament, also led to the use of colour or capitals in the concluding lines; and sometimes the "tail" of the text was given a triangular form,
the lines becoming shorter and shorter
till they ended in a single
word, or even one
letter.

But I have not finished the five acts, but only three of them"— Thou sayest well, but in life the three acts are the whole drama; for what shall be a complete drama is determined by him who was once the cause of its composition, and now of its dissolution: but thou art the cause of neither—

Depart then satisfied, for he also who re-leases thee is satisfied.

FIG. 96

109

Contrast of Red and Black.—The most effective
arrangement of red lettering with black text involves
a sharp contrast, and, as a rule, the concentration of
the red in a line or mass (see figs. 91, 93, and 96,
where the red lettering is massed at the head, side,
and foot of the black). Too many red capitals scattered through a page lose their effect, and appear
as though they were *brown*-red rather than bright
red (see pp. 100, 151). Printed title-pages, &c., may
be seen with promiscuous lines of black and red, in
which the fine effect obtainable by the use of bright
colour is dispersed and lost; while the same, or even
a less, amount of red, massed in one or two places
in the page, would show to great advantage.

Notes in Red in Margins.—Red lettering, and
particularly small red writing, may be used freely
in the margins; being much lighter than black, it
appears there as a *marginal decoration*, not interfering with the regular look of the page. Indeed,
red may be used more freely, and I think its decorative effect is greater, in the form of rubrics, than in
any other simple form of ornament (see *Red in
Church Service Books* (pp. 106, 309) and *Red substituted for Italics* (p. 279)).

Paragraph and other Marks.—Various symbols,
numerals, and marks (such as ☞ ¶ ❡ * † ‡ §
✠ ℣ ℞—*Addenda*, p. xxiii) may be made in red.

Red Lines.—Lines made to divide, or outline,
pages ("rules" or "rule borders") should be sparingly used, and then rather in black than in red
(see p. 328). If in red, particularly between lines
of writing, these should be "ruled feint" with
diluted colour.

Red for Ornaments.—Red may be used pretty freely *with* other colours (blue, green, and gold), but by itself more sparingly.

OTHER COLOURS.—The foregoing remarks refer mainly to contrasts of black and red, but apply, to a certain extent, to black with any bright colour (or gold) (see "*Other Colour Schemes*" given above, and p. 146).

CHAPTER IX

LAYING & BURNISHING GOLD

Tools & Materials—Laying the Ground—Laying the Gold-Leaf — Burnishing the Gold — Remedying Faults in Gilding—Gold Writing—Other Methods & Recipes for Gilding—Appendix on Gilding (by *Graily Hewitt*).

TOOLS & MATERIALS

THESE should be kept together in a convenient box, as it is important that the process should not be interrupted by a search for a missing tool.

Tools and Materials.	Summary of Process.
HARD LEAD PENCIL.	For drawing forms if necessary.
POUNCE.	For preparing surface: "pouncing."
"SIZE" OR RAISING PREPARATION.	For raising and backing leaf.
SMALL SAUCER.	For mixing size in.
NEEDLE SET IN HANDLE.	For bursting bubbles, &c.
QUILL PEN.	For "laying" the size.
KNIFE.	For trimming size, &c.
GOLD-LEAF.	For gilding.

Tools and Materials.	Summary of Process.
SCISSORS.	For cutting gold-leaf.
BURNISHING-SLAB.	For backing the parchment or paper while under pressure
BREATHING-TUBE.	For damping size.
RUBBING-PAPER.	For pressing leaf on to size.
CHALK OR SOFT LEAD PENCIL.	For marking form on rubbing-paper.
BURNISHER, TOOTH SHAPE.	For (1) pressing down, and (2) burnishing gold-leaf.
FEATHER (Brush, &c.).	For dusting off the pounce.
BRUSH.	For brushing off waste leaf.
(HARD INDIARUBBER.)	(For removing gold from parchment.)
(POWDER GOLD & FINE BRUSH.)	(For "mending" in certain cases.)

LAYING THE GROUND

Drawing the Form.—Elaborate letters or ornaments may be drawn with a hard pencil, which will leave slight indentations in the surface of the page when the marks of the lead have been removed with indiarubber. In the case of free lettering or gold writing, however, the forms should be made directly with the pen (see pp. 114, 130).

Preparing the Surface: Pouncing.—The surface is thoroughly cleaned and prepared with powdered pumice stone, or other suitable "pounce" (see pp. 133, 140). This being rubbed well into the actual part which is to take the size absorbs grease and slightly roughens[1] the surface. The surrounding parts are also pounced to prevent the gold-leaf from sticking to them later.

Composition of the Ground or Size. The chief

---

[1] The surface of horny or greasy parchment may be slightly roughened with a pen-knife till little hairs are raised which will hold the size, care being taken that this roughening does not extend beyond the actual parts which are to be covered with size. (Oxgall: see *footnote*, p. 141.)

substance in a "size" or raising preparation is
generally some kind of earthy matter, to give it
body—such as *chalk, Armenian bole, slaked plaster of
Paris* (this is very good: see p. 132).[1] Other sub-
stances, having toughness and stickiness (such as *glue*
and *gelatin*, and *sugar*, *treacle* and *honey*) are used to
bind the earthy matter and prevent its breaking when
the page is turned over or bent, and also to make the
size adhere to the page and the gold-leaf stick to the
size. Yellow or red colouring matter is often added.
A preservative, such as oil of cloves—in a minute
quantity—may be present: this will permit of the
size being kept in a semi-liquid condition, in a
closed jar.

Mixing the Size with Water.—The size, if kept
semi-liquid, must be stirred very carefully and well,
and a little taken out of the jar is rubbed down in
a saucer—great care being taken to avoid making
bubbles. The right consistency is judged by experience—it should be thick rather than thin, but it
should be thin enough to flow easily.

It is essential that all the ingredients be present
in their right proportions, and the mixture should
be stirred every now and then. Otherwise the earthy

---

[1] Good results have been obtained from a mixture consisting
approximately of *Slaked Plaster of Paris* 10+*Whitelead* 3+*Fish-
glue* 3+*Treacle* 1 :—by weight.

Another recipe (given to me by Mr. G. Loumyer) is:—

> "*Chalk (Whiting).*
> *Oxide of Iron*—½ *grain.*
> *Glue (Carpenter's)*—4 *grains.*
> *Gum Arabic*—2 *grains.*
> *Water*—50 *grains.*
>
> *Melt the gum and the glue together in the water, then add the oxide
> of iron, and lastly put in enough chalk to make the whole a rather
> liquid paste. Apply to the parchment, which you have previously
> well rubbed with whiting, and, when dry, apply the gold-leaf with
> alcohol.*"

matter settles down, and the sticky parts, remaining in solution above, are liable to be used up. What is left in the saucer after use is apt to be deficient in its sticky parts, and it is best thrown away. Take out of the jar only what is required at the time, and mix a fresh lot the next time.

Bubbles, formed in the mixture, may be burst by a needle, or by adding a minute drop of oil of cloves.

Methods of Laying the Size.—The parchment or paper is laid *flat* on a table; if on a slope, the size would run down and lie unevenly. A quill pen with a finely cut nib and an extra long slit (about ⅝ inch) is used for laying the size. It is filled pretty full by means of a quill or a brush; if by the latter, special care must be taken to avoid bubbles.

Experiments should be made in various methods.

I. Perhaps the best way of sizing small forms, so that the size may set properly and the burnish retain its brilliance, is to put on a thin coat with a pen—in the direct manner in which coloured Versals are made (*q.v.*)—and afterwards add two or three thin coats, allowing each coat to dry thoroughly. This requires considerable patience and skill, as it takes a long time, and there is a danger, in adding several coats, of spoiling the form by going over the edges (*For extra coats, or for large forms, a brush may be used*).

II. The simplest method for ordinary gold letters is to make them with *one extra thick coat*[1] of size, exactly like coloured Versals—first a natural pen outline, and then the filling in (see fig. 81). This requires some practice to do well, as the thicker size

---

[1] If this, as is not unlikely, will require twenty-four hours to dry, make sure, before laying the size, that you will be able to lay the gold-leaf on it *at or near the same time on the next day* (see p. 117).

is more difficult to manage than the colour.[1] Very narrow parts—such as the thin strokes—are apt to be deficient in size, and therefore, while they are still wet, the pen—held nearly vertical with the nib in contact with the surface of the size—is moved slowly along it until the stroke has received sufficient size and is properly filled out.

III. A method that may be found more convenient for heavy forms, is to hold the pen across the form to be gilded (which has previously been marked on the parchment) with its nib resting on the further outline (*a*, fig. 97). The nib being

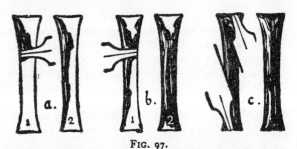

FIG. 97.

moved along that line, by contact with the parchment restrains the size from passing beyond it, while allowing it to flow out freely behind and below (*a*, 2). The opposite side is similarly treated, and, if the form be narrow, the size as it flows out blends with that already laid (*b*). The ends of the form are finished in like manner (*c*).

---

[1] Should a drop fall on the page it can be removed quickly with the knife, but it is safer to allow it to dry and then to pick it off carefully. Size which has flowed beyond the bounds of the form may be trimmed away when it has set.

The angle of the pen with the parchment is less for a wider form (*b*, fig. 98).

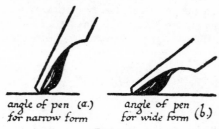

angle of pen (*a.*)
for narrow form   angle of pen (*b.*)
for wide form

FIG. 98.

As a general rule the size should stand pretty high when wet; it shrinks in drying, and, if it forms too thin a coat, it will neither hold the gold-leaf fast nor burnish well. While the size is still wet it is easy to raise it to any height desired by running more size into the form in the manner described above. It is well, however, not to raise the size too high, as burnished gold too much raised looks out of place on a page and has a heavy and vulgar appearance (p. 150). Very high raising also does not dry so well, and when dry it is more liable to chip.

The work of laying the size should be carried out as quickly as possible. If one part of the form is left any appreciable time before the remaining parts are sized, the first part will begin to settle and dry, and the different layings will not blend or lie evenly. Though the size is thick and awkward to use at first, a little skill will coax it quickly and evenly out of the pen, and it will all blend and dry with an even surface.

When it is sized, put the work away to dry in a

drawer or safe place where it cannot be smudged or
get dusty.

Drying the Size.—The time that the size is
allowed to dry varies very much with the weather
and the temperature; damp weather may make a
longer time necessary, and dry[1] weather or heat will
shorten the time. The thickness of the raising affects
the time very much; a very thin coat will dry in an
hour or two, while an extra thick coat may take
several days. Size not dry enough is too sticky to
burnish; if too dry, it is so absorbent that it sucks up
all the moisture which is breathed on it. To ensure
the gold-leaf's sticking thoroughly, it is safer on the
whole to gild the size while it is still slightly damp,
and delay the burnishing till it is drier.

The time to allow and the right condition of the
size for gilding can only be accurately judged by
experience.[1]

LAYING THE GOLD-LEAF

NOTE.—*In illuminated MSS., the simplest and best
method to follow is to lay and finish the gold before applying the colours (the gold may be laid last of all if there
should be a special risk of injury—pp.* 136–7).

The process of gold-laying must be carried out
steadily and quickly; all the necessary tools, &c.,
should be ready to hand (see p. 111).

The Gold-Leaf.—This is sold in books of twenty-
five leaves. The ordinary leaf, about $3\frac{1}{4}$ inches
square, consisting of gold and alloy, is said to be
beaten out to less than $\frac{1}{200000}$ inch in thickness. As
gold sticks readily to gold, especially when very thin
and liable to wrinkle and fold over, or to paper, red

---

[1] The dryness of east wind or frost makes gold-laying and
burnishing very difficult (see p. 129).

117

bole or ochre is scattered between the leaves of the ordinary book. This powder will come off on the work and give it an ugly colour, when burnishing, unless it is dusted off very carefully.

It is better to get gold specially prepared for fine work such as illuminating quite pure, and put up in white books (without bole). "Double" gold-leaf may be used for a final coat.

Cutting the Leaf.—With the scissors, which must be quite clean and sharp—*and not breathed upon*—(or else the gold will stick to them and tear), cut a whole or half leaf of gold, together with the paper leaf on which it lies, out of the book.

The gold is cut on one paper (fig. 99) (not

Fig. 99.

between papers, for then it would stick to both), and the cut edges of the paper and the gold stick together slightly. If the edge of the gold is anywhere loose and apt to flap about, it and the corresponding paper edge can be nicked together with the scissors (fig. 100). The gold-leaf being lightly held to the paper in this way is easily handled.

A piece of gold, about $\frac{1}{8}$ inch larger all round than the form to be gilded, is cut from the leaf in the manner described above (*a*, *b*, fig. 100). Except in the case of a very large form, it is not worth trying to save gold by cutting it out in the same shape. Square, oblong, and triangular shaped pieces are suitable for ordinary use; these are laid in a convenient place—the edge of a book cover will do very well (fig. 101) — ready to be picked up at the right moment.

The burnishing slab (a flat piece of vulcanite, celluloid, or metal) is placed under the page to give it a hard, firm back, which will make the pushing and rubbing of the burnisher effective.

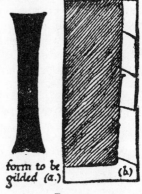

form to be gilded (a.)

(b)

FIG. 100.

Preparing the Size.—If the size has dried rough, it may be lightly scraped with the pen-knife—

FIG. 101.

removing as little as possible of the surface in which the essential *stickiness* frequently seems to be concentrated.

Ordinarily a form should not require trimming, though if its edges have accidental roughnesses, these may be trimmed a *little* with the pen-knife.

Damping the Size.—The breathing tube is about $\frac{1}{2}$ inch (or less) in diameter, and 6 inches or more in length; it may be made of paper or cane. One end of the tube being lightly held between the lips, the other is moved about over the size, which is gently breathed upon (fig. 102). The breath con-

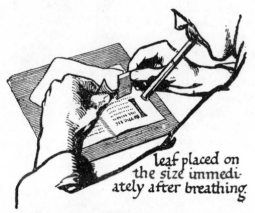

leaf placed on
the size immedi-
ately after breathing

FIG. 102.

densing on the surface of the size, moistens it and renders it sticky. The amount of moistening required depends on the condition of the size.

Care has to be taken that the breath does not condense in the tube and drop on to the work.

Laying the Gold-Leaf.—Immediately that the size has been sufficiently breathed upon, the piece of paper with gold-leaf adhering (held ready in the right hand) is placed upon it, gold-leaf downwards, care being taken to place it steadily down, and not drag it across the size (fig. 103).

FIG. 103.

The Rubbing Paper—a convenient piece of thin but tough paper (held ready in the left hand)—is immediately laid above the gold-leaf paper, and is then rubbed over firmly with the finger-tip, in order at once to attach the leaf to the size (fig. 104). It is then quickly rubbed with the soft pencil or chalk

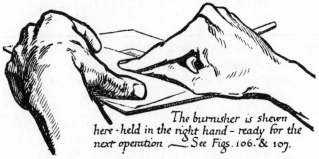

The burnisher is shewn here - held in the right hand - ready for the next operation —— See Figs. 106. & 107.

FIG. 104.

121

till the raised form underneath is indicated on the surface of the paper (fig. 105).

These two operations may be combined by having a little blue chalk either on the finger-tip or on the upper surface of the rubbing paper.

Round the outline of this form the point of the burnisher[1] is worked, pressing the gold-leaf firmly —through both the papers—against the size, in the angle formed by the size and the surface of the parchment (fig. 106).

The fore part of the burnisher is then passed rapidly all over the rubbing paper with a firm pressure (fig. 107).

The rubbing paper and the other paper are picked off, and an experienced eye can usually tell if the gold is sticking properly by a peculiar, smooth appearance which it then has.

Fig. 105.

Several Letters or Forms which are close together may be gilded simultaneously—with one piece of gold-leaf—as if they were one complex form. This saves time, but if too many forms are gilded together, some of them are liable to be less thoroughly and effectually treated.

Small Scattered Forms (dots, &c.).—For these the gold-leaf may be cut into a sufficient number of little pieces, which are allowed to fall (*gold side downwards*) on a sheet placed to receive them. They

---

[1] A finer metal or ivory point may also be used.

are picked up separately by means of a needle stuck into their backing-paper.

Additional Coats of Gold-Leaf.—A second leaf of gold may be laid on immediately on the top of the first; this will ensure richness and facilitate burnishing. Additional leaves may be laid *after* burnishing, but, unless the first gilding is absolutely clean, there is a risk of the second leaf peeling off when re-burnished.

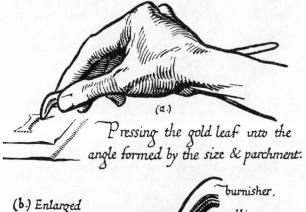

(a.)

Pressing the gold leaf into the angle formed by the size & parchment.

(b.) Enlarged diagram of above

burnisher.
rubbing-paper.
g.l. book paper.
gold leaf.
parchment &c.}
bearing-size. }
burnishing-slab.

FIG. 106.

NOTE.—*Heavy pressure with a cotton wool pad* on the back of the gold-leaf book paper (when that is sufficiently thin) may with advantage be used instead of the "rubbing-paper" and burnisher-point method here shown.

Note: The rubbing-paper
is held steadily by the
left hand and not al-
lowed to shift during
the time   that the
gold-leaf
is being pressed on
to the size. See figs.
106. & 10..

FIG. 107.

BURNISHING THE GOLD

The Burnisher.—A tooth-shaped agate burnisher
(fig. 108) is commonly used.

The *point* is used for pushing the leaf into angles
and for burnishing angles (*a*).

The *fore-part* for general burnishing (*b*).

The *bend* for cross-burnishing and for angles (*c*).

The *side* for very gentle and light burnishing (*d*).

The burnisher is kept scrupulously clean, and to
ensure this it is frequently rubbed on a cloth.

Dusting off the Pounce.—The edge of the parchment may be tapped smartly on the desk to shake
off the pounce, and a feather or a soft handkerchief
may be used, care being taken not to brush the
pounce over the gold.

124

Brushing off Waste Leaf.—The superfluous gold round the edge of the gilded form may be lightly brushed off with the brush, either after or before the burnishing—preferably *after* (see p. 136).

Any gold which may have stuck to the surrounding parchment, in spite of the pouncing, may be removed with the knife or with the hard indiarubber point, *care being taken not to touch the gilded size.*

For removing gold, ordinary baker's bread is very useful, and safe.

Burnishing the Gold. —The gold-leaf may be burnished immediately after laying when the size is *very dry*, but it is safer to wait for a quarter of an hour—or longer, if the size is at all damp (see *Drying*, p. 117).

The slab is again put under the work, and the burnishing is begun very gently and

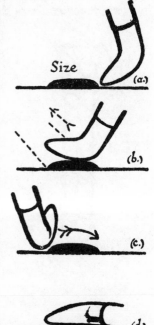

FIG. 108.

cautiously: should the burnisher stick in the very least, it is instantly stopped (or else the gold will be scratched off), examined, and cleaned.

The first strokes of the burnisher are generally carried all over the work, very lightly and with a

125

circular movement (fig. 109), till the gold begins to *feel smooth*, and the matt surface gives place to a dull polish.

As the gold gets smoother a little more pressure is used, and the burnisher is moved in straight lines in every direction across the gold (fig. 110). At

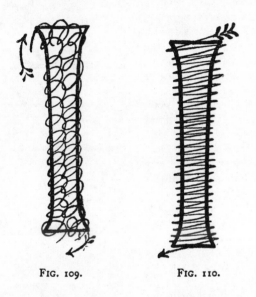

FIG. 109. FIG. 110.

this point the gold should have a peculiar and agreeable feeling of smoothness under the burnisher, an unmistakable sign that all is going well.

A rapid light polish with the bend of the burnisher across a gold stem will give a very good finish (*c*, fig. 108).

Properly burnished gold in a right light is at first as bright as a mirror, and in some lights may look quite dark by reason of its smoothness. A piece of white paper may be held at such an angle that the white light from it is reflected by the gold; this will show the quality of the burnish, and also show up any brown spots which the leaf may have failed to cover. It is helpful, moreover, during the actual process of burnishing to have a reflecting paper folded and standing beside the work (fig. 111).

Fig. 111

At first the size under the burnished gold is not thoroughly hardened, and great care should be taken of it (not to breathe on nor finger the gold in any way, nor allow it to lie about and get dusty). It is best to put it away safely in a drawer for a week or two.

After a week or fortnight, when the size has set a little more, it may be very gently re-burnished, and this may be done again at the end of another fortnight. This final burnishing, when the size is nearly hard, will give it a very lasting polish. It is well, however, to take every care of burnished gold, and to secure it from risk of damage as soon as may be. Illuminated miniatures were often protected by a piece of silk between the leaves—and this should be done now, in the case of fine work. That a bound volume protects the burnished gold within it is proved by the large number of MSS. in which the gold, laid and burnished 500 years ago, is in perfect and brilliant preservation.

REMEDYING FAULTS IN GILDING

To lay and burnish gold satisfactorily requires considerable experience. Careful practice with a good "size" (a "home-made" size for preference —try recipes on pp. 132 and 113) will overcome the chief difficulties: these, and their probable causes, are here summarised:—

To make the Size stick to the Surface.	*Probable Causes of Size not sticking to Parchment or Paper.*
Clean and pounce thoroughly: roughen if necessary (pp. 112, 133).	Dirty ⎫ Greasy ⎬ Surface. Horny or ⎪ Non-porous ⎭

Procure or make a proper composition, mix thoroughly always, and stir frequently when in use. If composition is at fault, add—
 	
  a. Sticky matter.
 	
  b. Toughening matter.
 	
(pp. 113, 132, and Appendix.)
	Size not sticky ⎫
	  enough. ⎪ due to faulty
	Size not tough ⎬ composition,
	  enough (and ⎪ or mixing.
	  c r u m b l i n g ⎪
	  off) ⎭

To make the Gold-leaf stick to the Size.	*Probable Causes of Gold-leaf not sticking to Size.*
Breathe on thoroughly and avoid delay in laying the gold (p. 120).	Size too dry, { due to being insufficiently breathed on, or the too absorbent nature or condition of, size. The dryness of frost or east wind makes the size dry, hard, and "*difficult.*"
Do not dry too long (p. 117).	
A fire with a steaming kettle having a long tube or spout will make gilding possible.	
More careful pressure (p. 122): use *thin* gold leaf.	Not sufficient rubbing and pressing on of gold.
See above (p. 128).	Size not sticky enough.
Raise the size sufficiently (p. 116). If not enough when dry, roughen surface and add another coat.	Not enough size, particularly in thin lines and edges.
Try re-gilding (p. 123), or, if spots persist, scrape them gently and try again: failing that, gently scrape off all the gold and try white of egg (dilute), or a slight re-sizing.	The gold may refuse to stick in *spots* with no apparent reason, but probably from one or other of the above causes. Or the size may have been touched accidentally and have become greasy or dirty
If the spots are very small and there is not time to spare for re-gilding, they may be touched with powder gold and dilute white of egg, and burnished when dry (p. 149).	

To make the Gold-leaf smooth and bright.	*Probable Causes of Gold-leaf's not burnishing properly.*
a. *b.* } Allow longer time (p. 117).	Size too sticky. { Due to— *a.* Damp weather. *b.* Insufficient time allowed for drying. *c.* Too much sticky matter in size.
c. Remove size and re-size with proper composition.	
Sometimes this difficulty may be overcome by using several coats of gold-leaf (p. 123).	
Scrape smooth with sharp knife. (Sometimes the size itself is burnished before the gold-leaf is laid.)	Size rough surfaced.
Clean burnisher frequently.	Burnisher becoming dirty.

129

Both paper and parchment when much wet with size are apt to cockle. Generally it is not possible, or desirable (see p. 140), to guard against this by first stretching the material, but the size may be used with less water, so that it will dry sooner. In cases where there is a gold background it may often be divided into small parts (to be sized at different times) by the pattern (see p. 157). For large unbroken patches of gold several thin coats may be put on, one after the other, with a brush.

Some sizes have a tendency to crack: this is difficult to guard against. But, if the cracks are very minute—such as may be seen in many instances in the best early MSS.—they do not constitute a serious blemish.

Burnished gold is often damaged by careless handling or insufficient protection.

GOLD WRITING

The page (having been ruled as for ordinary writing) is thoroughly pounced all over.

The pen has an extra long slit, and the size is made a little more fluid than usual to allow of its flowing freely and making true pen-strokes (p. 29).

The desk is lowered (fig. 46, *b*), or flat, so that the size may flow freely.

The nib sometimes makes only a wet downstroke on the parchment, but, by lightly pushing the pen up again, the stroke will be filled by the size which flows out from under the nib Simple pen-stroke in sallm writing hold but littl.e, and so ought to be filled as full of size as possible (pp. 116, 150). They will be found to dry much more quickly than larger forms, and may be gilded within a few hours of writing. Half-a-dozen or more letters are gilded together (see p. 122).

Laying & Burnishing Gold

OTHER METHODS & RECIPES FOR GILDING

Gold-leaf may be cut with a "*gilder's knife*" on a "*gilder's cushion*," and picked up with a "*gilder's tip*."

Water, white of egg, or alcohol may be used to make the gold-leaf adhere to the size.

"*Transfer gold-leaf*" is convenient, but the *greasiness* of the transfer paper is apt to dim the gilding.

Gold-leaf is made in many shades, from "red" (gold + copper) to "green" (gold + silver); though these may be used very effectively, they are liable to tarnish, and it is best to begin with pure gold (see pp. 118, 135).

Silver-leaf oxidises and turns black; platinum (a good substitute) costs about 5s., and *aluminium* (not so good) about 6d. per book.

"*Gold Ink*" has been made with powdered gold: its effect is inferior to *raised and burnished* writing.

The following is from "The Book of the Art of Cennino Cennini" (written about the beginning of the fifteenth century): Translated by Christiana J. Herringham, 1899:—

"Chap. 157.—*How you must do miniature-painting and put gold on parchment.*

"First, if you would paint miniatures you must draw with a leaden style figures, foliage, letters, or whatever you please, on parchment, that is to say, in books: then with a pen you must make the delicate permanent outline of what you have designed. Then you must have a paint that is a sort of gesso, called asiso, and it is made in this manner; namely, a little gesso sottile [see chap. 116, below], and a little biacca [whitelead], never more of this than equals a third part of the gesso; then take a little candy, less than the biacca; grind these ingredients very finely with clear water, collect them together, and let them dry without sun. When you wish to use some to put on gold, cut off a piece as large as you have need of, and temper it with the white of an egg, well beaten, as I have taught you. [*The froth is allowed to stand for one night to clear itself.*] Temper this mixture with it; let it dry; then take your gold, and either breathing on it or not, as you please, you can put it on; and the gold being laid on, take the tooth or burnishing-stone and burnish it, but hold under the parchment a firm tablet of good wood, very smooth. And you must know that you may write letters with a pen and this asiso, or lay a ground of it, or whatever you please—it is most excellent. But before you lay the gold on it, see whether it is needful to scrape or level it with the point of a knife, or clean it in any way, for your brush sometimes puts more on in one place than in another. Always beware of this."

"Chap. 116.—*How to prepare gesso sottile (slaked plaster of Paris) for grounding panels.*

"You must now prepare a plaster for fine grounds, called gesso sottile. This is made from the same plaster [plaster of Paris] as the last, but it must be well purified (purgata), and kept moist in a large tub for at least a month; renew the water every day until it almost rots, and is completely slaked, and all fiery heat goes out of it, and it becomes as soft as silk. Throw away the water, make it into cakes, and let it dry; and this gesso is sold by the druggists to our painters. It is used for grounding, for gilding, for working in relief, and other fine works."

APPENDIX: ON GILDING

(*By Graily Hewitt*)

Success with raised gilding can only be expected when practice has rendered attention to the details of the process automatic and there is no need to pause and think. Even then the results must be somewhat uncertain and experimental. For our own preparations of size are usually unsatisfactory, and the ingredients of the best we can buy are unknown to us. And our vellum is certainly not of the quality we find in the old books. Some one is badly wanted to investigate the chemistry of the one and an appropriate preparation of the other. But we can take as much care as our time allows, passing nothing as "good enough" which we have not well examined, and bringing to the business all the patience and deftness available.

Vellum is too stiff, or too dry, or too greasy. When stiff, it is too thick for books; when dry, too apt to crack or cockle; when too greasy, exasperating. And yet the soft and rather greasy sort can be rendered more agreeable than the rest with labour. It should be rubbed by the flat of the hand with powdered pumice (or even fine sandpaper on the rough side) and French chalk, especially on its split (or rougher) side, until it is serviceable. A few trials will teach how long to give to this. Five minutes for one side of a lamb's skin would not be too much. It can then be beaten with a silk handkerchief, but not rubbed with this until the size has been laid. It may be rubbed cleaner between the laying of the size and the gilding. Especially must those parts of pages be thoroughly rubbed clean which in the book, when made up, will lie upon and be pressed against gold letters on the page opposite; or the pumice left behind will scratch them. On the other hand, if the vellum has not been thoroughly pumiced on both pages, the greasiness in

133

it will dim the gold in time, both from above and below, or even make the size flake off altogether. The size is often blamed for faults of the vellum and its want of preparation.

Again size, or "raising preparation," is too sticky or too dry. If the former, the gold will not burnish well; if the latter, it will burnish, but will not stick at the edges, and will crack sooner or later. And though the essential quality of gilding is brightness, one may be content to fail of this rather than have letters ragged in outline or broken on the surface.

The size in use should be just liquid enough to flow evenly from the pen. More water makes it dry too brittle, and tends to cockle the vellum also; less tends to blobbiness and unevenness. Even when it is put on fairly an uncomfortable groove is apt to form as it dries down the centre of letters; but this can be either filled up as soon as the first layer is dryish, or the sides of the groove can be scraped (when the letter is quite dry) down to the level of the groove itself with a sharp knife. The knife must be sharp. As this scraping does not affect the extreme edges the power of the size there to hold the leaf is not impaired by it; and certainly a well-scraped surface is extremely even and pleasant to gild. If the surface, however, be burnished and not scraped before laying the leaf, it will not hold the leaf well, and remains lumpy also where lumps were there originally; while scraping gets rid of these. During use the size should be kept thoroughly mixed; and a small sable brush serves well for this purpose, as soon as it can be used so carefully as not to cause bubbles.

To know the exact time to allow between laying and gilding one had need to be a meteorologist, so much "depends on the weather." Very dry and very wet weather are equally unkind. Generally an interval of about twenty-four hours is right; but it is better to gild too soon than too late, provided one can be content, on testing the naked surface of the gilded letter with a burnisher, and noting that the glitter is reluctant to come, to leave the burnishing for a while, and only lay the leaf, pressing it well home to the outline of the letters. The burnishing can then be done in a few more hours. But if the size be too dry, the difficulty will be to make the leaf stick to it at all. In this case the leaf adhering can be scraped off, the size scraped down further, and another thin coat added and gilded after a shorter interval. If the letter be so fouled that such repairs are difficult, it should be entirely scraped away and the size relaid altogether. In doing this care is needed that the vellum be not injured round the letter.

The best gold-leaf for ordinary work costs about 3s. for twenty-five pages. More expensive leaf, being thicker, does not stick so well to the edges; cheaper is too thin to burnish well. Two kinds may be used together with good results, the finer leaf being put on next the size, and the thicker at once on to the top of that. The letter is then pressed and outlined as usual through paper, and the thin leaf will be found of considerable assistance towards the making of a clean cut edge. Generally, however, the piling on of several leaves is inadvisable, as bits are liable to flake away as the letter goes on drying, leaving dim specks where they have been. Yet if, after the outlining through the paper, the leaf is seen to be very dull or speckled with the colour of the size, this means that the size has been partly pressed through the leaf; and another laid immediately will have enough to stick to, and will burnish well. The best result comes of one moderately thick leaf laid and burnished at the right time as quickly as possible. Thicker leaves need only be used for large surfaces, where the edge can be scraped even and clean, or where a black outline is to be added.

As soon as the leaf is laid, and from that point onward, the breath must be kept from the letter with a shield (of cardboard or tin) held in the left hand or otherwise. Inattention to this is responsible for many failures. Not

only should the actual letters under operation be so protected, but where a quantity are sized ready for gilding
on the page these should be protected also, as well as
any parts already finished; for breath not only moistens
but warms, and on warm size moisture condenses less
easily. If the work to be done presently is so warmed,
it will be found more difficult to deal with when its time
comes. The first work done in the day is often the best,
and for this reason, that the size for it is cool; but in
gilding this portion one almost necessarily warms that to
be done later. Two pages, where possible, should therefore be gilded alternately, one cooling while a portion of
the other is gilded. Or thin plates of metal, or even
cardboard, may be placed about as shields to protect all
surfaces not under actual operation.

Superfluous gold is best removed by dusting lightly
with an old and very clean and dry silk handkerchief.
Indiarubber will certainly remove gold from the vellum,
but it will as certainly dim any part of the gilding it
touches. If the vellum was properly pounced to start
with the silk will easily remove all the leaf unstuck,
except little odds and ends, and these are safeliest taken
away with the point of a knife.

As the pressure of burnishing helps the leaf to stick, it
is best to wait till the letter has been burnished before
this dusting. Such spots as are visible ungilded may be
afterwards treated with a slight breath and transfer gold-
leaf, or gold dust, may be painted on them. In the latter
case the spots must be most carefully burnished, if burnished at all, or their surroundings will be scratched.

When a gold letter is to be set on a coloured background, or in the neighbourhood of colour, it is best put
on after the colour; as may be observed was the method
occasionally with the old books. If the gold is put on first,
it will certainly be dimmed by warmth and breath during
the colouring. On the other hand, if it is put on last,
great care must be taken that the gold-leaf shall not stick
to the coloured portions. Where possible, a stencil

pattern of the parts to be gilded should be cut out of paper. This is easily made from a pencil rubbing taken after the size is laid, the raised pattern being of course cut out carefully a trifle larger than the outline so obtained. The paper is then laid over all the work, and the sized portions showing through the cuttings can be gilded without injury to the colour.

All gilded work should be retained, if possible, for a week or more, and then re-burnished. And in burnishing generally the burnisher should not be used, even when the size is hard, with any great force or pressure at first. For the size in drying sets as if moulded, and this mould cannot be squeezed about or actually crushed without being loosened or cracked. Throughout the whole process a gentle and vigilant alacrity is required. Success will come easily if it means to come. It cannot be forced to come.

The binder of a book with gilding in it should be warned to press the sheets as little as possible, and to use all his care in handling it, so as to keep moisture, warmth, and fingering from the gold. The folding of the sheets, when left to him, should also be done rather differently from usual, for all gilded pages need to be kept as flat as possible. None of the sizes in use seem capable of resisting bending of their surfaces without crimping or cracking. Where there is much gilding, the book will be the better for being sewn with a zigzag[1] through the sections, as this helps to "guard" the gilded work.

---

[1] *Vide* D. Cockerell, "Bookbinding and the Care of Books," p. 81.

CHAPTER X

THE USE OF GOLD & COLOURS IN INITIAL LETTERS & SIMPLE ILLUMINATION

Tools & Materials for Simple Illumination—Parchment, "Vellum," & Pounce — Colours — Simple Colour Effects—Matt Gold—Burnished Gold—Burnished Gold Forms, & Outlines—Background Capitals—Applying the Background — Ornament of Backgrounds.

TOOLS & MATERIALS FOR SIMPLE ILLUMINATION

TOOLS, &c., FOR GILDING.—See Chapter IX (pp. 111-12).

IVORY TRACING POINT.—This is useful for various purposes, and for indenting patterns in burnished gold (see p. 157).

BRUSHES.—Red Sables are very good. A separate brush should be kept for each colour—or at least one brush each for *Reds, Blues, Greens, White,* and *gold "paint"*—and it is convenient to have a medium and a fine brush for each.

PENS FOR COLOUR.—Quill pens are used: "Turkey" or "Goose." The latter is softer, and is sometimes preferred for colour work. For very fine work (real) Crow Quills may be tried. A separate pen should be used for each colour.

COLOURED INKS.—Brown ink (tempered with black if desired) may be used for fine outlines: if the outlined forms are to be coloured afterwards, it is convenient if the ink be *waterproof.* Coloured inks seldom have as good a colour as the best paint colours (see *Colours for Penwork*, p. 142).

COLOURS.—(p. 141). *MATT GOLD* (see p. 149).

PAINT-BOX.—The little chests of drawers, sold by stationers for 2s. 6d., make very convenient "paint-boxes": pens, &c., may be kept in one drawer; gilding, tools, &c., in another; and colours and brushes in another.

PAPER (see pp. 17, 64, 69.—*PARCHMENT, VELLUM, & POUNCE* (see below).

PARCHMENT, "VELLUM," & POUNCE

(*See also Appendix on Gilding*, p. 133 *and pp.* 64, 320)

The name "Vellum" (strictly applicable only to calf-skin) is generally given to any moderately good skin prepared for writing or printing on. All the modern skins are apt to be too stiff and *horny*: chemical action (substituted for patient handling), followed by liberal sizing and "dressing," is perhaps responsible. The old skins have much more life and character, and are commonly much softer. Their surface is generally very smooth—not necessarily *glazed*—often with a delicate velvety *nap*, which forms a perfect writing surface.

Parchment (sheep - skin), as supplied by law-stationers, though rather hard, still retains the character of a skin, and is in every way preferable to the Vellum[1] which is specially prepared for illuminators. A piece of parchment about 26 inches by 22 inches costs about 2s. 6d. Lambskin is still better.

"*Roman Vellum*" is a fine quality of sheep or

---

[1] The very costly, specially prepared calf-skin is too highly "finished," and has much the appearance of superior cardboard. It is stiff and shiny, and its surface is objectionable to work on.

The Use of
Gold &
Colours in
Initial
Letters &
Simple
Illumination *"lamb"* *skin*, made in imitation of the Vellum used
in the Vatican.

The surface of a modern skin may be greatly
improved by *"pouncing*," but there seems to be a
danger of its becoming rough or porous.

Pounce.—Fine *powdered pumice* (as supplied by
drysalters) is very good. It is rubbed on with the
hand (p. 133), or with a pad or a piece of rag.
Law-stationers use a pounce in which the main
constituents are chalk (or "whiting") and powdered
resin. *Chalk*, *Whiting*, *French Chalk*, and *Powdered
Cuttlefish Bone* might be used as substitutes for
pumice, or as ingredients in preparing a pounce.
Sandarach (a resin) rubbed on an erasure appears to
prevent ink spreading when the surface is written
over: it also makes an excellent pounce. I have
not found any objection to its use before gilding,
though resin is said to make the parchment sticky.
(*Before Writing*, see Note 7, p. 323.)

A skin of parchment has a smooth (whiter) side
—the original flesh side—and a rougher, yellower
side—the original hair side. The penman will find
the *smooth* side preferable for writing on (though,
of course, both sides must be used in a book: see
p. 76). This side is more easily damaged, and
erasures have to be very carefully made with a *sharp*
knife, or by gentle rubbing with indiarubber. On
the rough side, erasures cause little or no damage
to the surface. A piece of rubber—or a paper
stump—dipped in pounce may be used. It is better
—as it is more straightforward—to avoid erasures
if possible, and to correct mistakes frankly, as in
ordinary writing (see p. 308).

For ordinary purposes parchment should be cut
to the size desired, and be held on the desk by the

tape, guard, &c. (see p. 16). It is generally a mistake to pin it down, or to damp and stretch it on the drawing-board (see p. 320).

The Use of
Gold &
Colours in
Initial
Letters &
Simple
Illumination

Parchment is stained a fine purple with "Brazil-wood": this may be obtained from a "store chemist." Three teacups full of Brazil-wood are stewed in about two pints of water, with two teaspoonfuls of alum (which acts as a mordant). The colour of this liquid is brownish-red, and, to make it purple, carbonate of potash is added (*very carefully*, or it will become too blue). The liquid is poured into a tray, and the parchment skin is placed in it for half a day or a couple of days. The colour dries lighter, so it should be prepared rather dark, and diluted if necessary: strips of parchment should be used to test it; they are taken out and dried at the fire.

The parchment skin is stretched on a frame, the edges being caught up over little buttons or pegs, and tied at these points with string. It is allowed to dry slowly.

COLOURS

POWDER COLOURS are the purest: they may be mixed with gum arabic and water. Yolk of egg and water is also used as a medium, and so is white of egg (pp. 145, 132). It is, however, more convenient for the beginner to use prepared colours.

CAKE COLOURS rank next to powder colours for purity: they seem to need tempering with a little gum or honey (or egg—see above) for use on ordinary parchment[1]: used on it with water alone, they are apt to flake off when dry.

---

[1] *OXGALL* may be used for a greasy surface; painted on it, or mixed with the colour. (*Experiment, and use in moderation.*)

141

The Use of
Gold &
Colours in
Initial
Letters &
Simple
Illumination

PAN COLOURS are safe for ordinary use.

TUBE COLOURS sometimes seem to have too much glycerine[1]; they are, however, very convenient for preparing mixed colours in any quantity, because of their semi-fluid condition, and because the amount of each colour in the mixture may be judged with considerable accuracy by the *length* which is squeezed out of the tube (p. 144).

COLOURS FOR PENWORK, *&c.*—For simple letters or decoration it is well to use a pure

RED—*neither crimson nor orange tinged:*
BLUE—*neither greenish nor violet:*
GREEN—*neither bluish nor "mossy."*

A little "body colour" is generally used with *blues* and *greens* to keep them "flat" (p. 84). These colours should be mixed as required, and be diluted to the right consistency with water (see p. 84). Colour which has been mixed and in use for some time — especially if it has been allowed to dry — is best thrown away (see *mixing size*, p. 114).

The paint pot, or saucer, may conveniently stand inside a larger vessel. A small tin, with the seam opened and the bottom melted off in a gas flame, will do.

FIG. 112.

If there is much rubricating to be done, a quantity of each colour sufficient to last several days may be mixed, and kept in a *covered* pot. A little pomatum pot is convenient —the smaller the better, as it keeps the colour together, and does not allow it to dry so quickly.

The filling-brush (a rough brush kept for filling the pen) may rest in the pot (see fig. 112), being given a stir round every time it is

---

[1] Glycerine is a doubtful medium, and, in letters, &c., heavily loaded with colour, is apt to remain moist and sticky.

used, to prevent the settling of the heavy parts of the colour. A drop of water is added occasionally as the liquid evaporates and becomes too thick.[1]

TINTS FEW AND CONSTANT.—*Red*, *Blue*, and *Green* (and perhaps *purple*) with *Gold*, *White*, and *Black*, are sufficient for everything but the most advanced type of Illumination. And it is in every way desirable that, until he has become a *Master* Limner, the Writer and Illuminator should strictly limit the number of his colours (see p. 181).

It is one of the "secrets" of good "design" to use a limited number of *elements*—forms or colours or materials—and to produce *variety* by skilful and charming manipulation of these.

It is well to follow the early Illuminators in this also: that these few colours be kept constant. When you have chosen a *Red*, a *Blue*, and a *Green*—as pure and bright as you can make them—keep those particular tints as *fixed* colours to be used for ordinary purposes. For *special purposes* (pp. 148, 168) paler tints may be made by adding white, and varied tints may be mixed, but even when your work has advanced so that you require a more complex "palette," you should stick to the principle of *constant tints and modes of treatment for regular occasions:* this is the secret of method.

RED.—Vermilion is prepared in three forms: *Vermilion*, *Scarlet Vermilion*, and *Orange Vermilion*. "*Orange Vermilion*," in spite of its name, properly mixed, is a pure *Red*, very like that of the medieval MSS., and, as the brightest red and most brilliant contrast to Black Writing (enhanceable by *gum*), it is the best for ordinary *Rubrications, etc.* (ch. VIII).

---

[1] And the nib is cleaned out now and then (with the filling brush), or wiped, to prevent the colour clogging it (see p. 36).

The Use of
Gold &
Colours in
Initial
Letters &
Simple
Illumination

Used with *Background Capitals, etc.* (pp. 154-163), vermilion is apt to be less happy. Large, adjacent areas in *Blue*, and patterning of surfaces, will help; but many such experiments, and also the old use of *Pink* or *Lake* reds for backgrounds must be tried.

Chinese Vermilion is a fine colour, but difficult to obtain; it was said that the genuine pigment was reserved exclusively for the Chinese Emperor (whose edicts were written with "The Vermilion Pencil").

GREEN.—Verdigris is a very fine colour, closely resembling, and possibly the same pigment as, the green in early MSS., but I believe that it has not been rendered permanent in modern use.

Green Oxide of Chromium (transparent) (or "Viridian") is a very good permanent green. It is rather a thin colour, and requires body, which may be given by a little *Chinese White;* being a rather bluish green, it is the better for some yellow—*Aureolin* is the safest. This (mixed) green is most conveniently prepared from tube colours.

BLUE.—*Ultramarine Ash Blue* is a very beautiful colour. (Powder *Ultramarine Ash*—$\frac{1}{4}$ oz. about 4s.—with a little gum, is best. The preparations are made unpleasantly *slimy.*) It is rather pale when used alone. A mixture consisting of *Ultramarine Ash Blue and Chinese White and (a very little) Prussian Blue* makes an extremely fine, pure blue. A similar mixture with *cobalt* as a base makes a good blue.

Ultramarine or Powdered Lapis Lazuli (unfortunately known as "Genuine Ultramarine"[1]) is a fine colour; it may have a slightly purplish tint and need

---

[1] *"French Ultramarine"* is an artificial compound, and a poor colour.

tempering with green to make a pure blue (whole cake about 18s.).

The Blue in common use in early MSS. (before Ultramarine came into use) has a fine, pure colour, and considerable *body:* it is more raised than any other colour; it is often seen to be full of little sparkles, as though there were powdered glass in it. It is supposed to have been prepared from a copper ore.

The following note on this blue has been given to me by Mr. C. M. Firth:—

" The blue is Native Carbonate of Copper finely powdered and tempered with white of egg (Vermilion is tempered with the Yolk)."

" The ore is of two kinds, a crystalline of a medium hardness found in France at Chessy, and hence called Chessylite, and a soft earthy kind which is obtained in Hungary, and largely now from Australia. The latter is from its ease of manipulation the best for paint making. It should be ground dry till it is no longer gritty and is of a sky blue (pale) colour."

" The Blue in MSS. was liable to wash off, but the oil in the Yolk prevented a similar result with the Vermilion. The Blue is identical with the Azzuro della magna (for d'allemaigne) of the Middle Ages. The frequently advanced hypothesis that the blue was due to a glass is based on the accounts of (I.) The Vestorian blue copper 'frit' for enamels probably; (II.) on the accounts in sixteenth century of the Manufacture of Smalt, which owes its colour to a glass tinted with Cobalt. This Azzuro is the oldest known Western blue, and was probably employed on Egyptian walls, where it has gone green, as also in Italian Frescoes."

" The Green tint of the chemical change in the Copper is seen in initials in books too much exposed to the damp. These exhibit a bright green tint in places where the colour was thinly applied."

145

The Use of
Gold &
Colours in
Initial
Letters &
Simple
Illumination

It appears that Yolk, besides being unsuited in colour for tempering this blue, changes it to a greenish colour (the effect of the oil, which forms about 22 per cent. of Yolk of Egg).

WHITE.—The tube *Chinese White*[1] is the most convenient to use when tempering colours.

"White Line or Hair Finishing" (see p. 183). Various tools have been recommended for this. A sable pencil with the outer hairs cut away, "the smallest brush" made, and even a fine steel pen. I am inclined to believe that some of the early Illuminators used a fine quill—such as a crow quill, or a goose quill scraped thin and sharply pointed.

PURPLE is seldom used in simple pen-work, lettering, &c., but largely and with very fine effect in complex illumination. A *reddish-purple* is to be preferred. A good colour can be made from the purple *stain* described on p. 141, or from Ruby madder and a little Rose madder, with a very little Ultramarine.

SIMPLE COLOUR EFFECTS

Simple "Rubrication" (see p. 93).—Red letters were most commonly contrasted with *blue* (the "warmest" and "coldest" colours),[2] in some MSS. with *green* alone, but more commonly the three

---

[1] For white lining, &c.—if in constant use—the Chinese White in bottle is said to be the best; a little Spirits of Wine should be poured into it, to keep it moist and make it work better. It should be stirred well, and a sufficient quantity for immediate use is taken out and mixed in a small saucer. The bottle is kept tightly corked.

[2] And single forms were often parti-coloured, as I I, IV, *Blue*, with *red* serifs, or *vice versâ* (see also pp. 174, 182).

colours were used together, the alternations being generally—

The Use of
Gold &
Colours in
Initial
Letters &
Simple
Illumination

Red cap.		**RED**	
Blue cap.	in columns of Versal letters (see fig. 93).	**BLUE**	in lines of Caps. (see fig. 89).
Red cap.		**RED**	
Green cap.		**GREEN**	
&c.		&c.	

Repetition and Limitation of Simple Colours (and Forms).—The uniform treatment of a MS. necessitates that no colour (or form) in it should be quite singular, or even isolated if it can possibly be repeated. If, for example, there be a Red capital on the "Verso" page, the *"opening"* is improved by some Red—a capital, a rubric, or even a line-finishing—on the "Recto" page. Very often the one piece of colour is very small, and, as it were, an *echo* of the other (compare Line-finishings and Initials, pp. 171, 159). While it is not always possible or desirable so to treat both pages of an *opening*, yet, in the book taken as a whole, *every colour used should be repeated as often as there is a reasonable opportunity*. And, therefore, where the opportunities for colour in a book are few and far between, it is well to limit the "colours" used to two, or even one.

This necessity for repetition applies to *simple* rather than to complex "Illuminated" Forms—*e.g.* a book need not have more than one Illuminated Initial—but within such complex forms themselves

147

The Use of
Gold &
Colours in
Initial
Letters &
Simple
Illumination *repetition* is recognised as one of the first principles
of "decorative design" (see p. 181).

Proportions of Colours.—In Harmonious Illumination, Blue very commonly is the predominating
colour; but no exact proportions can be laid down,
for the combined colour effect depends so much on
the arrangement of the colours.

Effects of Neighbouring Colours. [1]—When blue and
red are in juxtaposition, the blue appears bluĕr and
greener; the red appears brighter and more scarlet.
With Red and Green, the Red appears more crimson, and the green, greener and bluĕr. A greenish
blue will appear *plain blue* beside a pure green; a
blue with a purplish tinge will appear more purple.
Experiments might profitably be made with simple
arrangements of Red, Blue, Green, Black, White,
and Gold in combinations of two or more.

Tempering Colours with White.—Forms such as
flower petals, &c., may be painted in Blue or Red,
paled with White, and then be shaded with the
pure colour; this gives considerable richness, and
the effect may be heightened by very careful white
line work (*q.v.*). Green leaves, &c., may be made
very pale and then touched with *Yellow*—this gives
a brilliant effect.

Black Outlines.—The effect of these is to make a
bright colour appear brighter and richer, to define,
and, to a certain extent, *harmonise*, neighbouring
colours and shapes, and to keep the design flat (see

---

[1] In "white light" three rays (known as the "*Primary
Colour-Sensations*") have been distinguished—Red, Green, and
Blue; any two of these are complementary to the remaining
colour, and appear to be induced optically in its neighbourhood
(Yellow light is combined of Red and Green rays, and this
may partly explain the particular fitness of Blue and Gold
Illumination.)

p. 152). For one or more of these reasons, all coloured forms—patterns, charges, &c.—in a compound colour scheme have an outline—strong or delicate, according to the strength or delicacy of the work (see pp. 154, 187, 168, 153, 131).

White Lining.—A black outline is often separated from the colour by a fine white line (see fig. 129). White lines also are used to harmonise colours, one or more commonly being painted (or "penned") upon the colours. This tends to make the colours appear paler and lighter—brightening them if they are dark. Care must be taken not to overdo the white lining, or it will make the colours chalky and cold. White is also used in groups of dots, and in fine patterns on backgrounds (see pp. 179, 416).

Gold is even more effective than white or black for harmonising colours. It is commonly *Burnished* in bars or frames (p. 417), in spots (pp. 417, 153), or in large masses (p. 157). *Matt Gold* (see below).

MATT GOLD

Matt gold, or "shell gold"—the pure gold powder (as supplied by a gold-beater) with a very little gum, or white of egg, is best—is generally *painted upon colour*. It was much used in old miniatures for "hatching" and lighting landscapes, houses, costumes, &c.; and stars, rays of light, and outlines of clouds were painted in delicate gold lines upon the blue of the skies. Such gold lining has a very mellowing and pleasant effect upon colour, but it can easily be *overdone*. Matt gold may be used besides, for letters, ornament, and patterns *painted upon colour*. Such forms have either no outline, or a very faint one: their effect depends upon their lightness, and they are not made to appear *solid*.

149

The Use of
Gold &
Colours in
Initial
Letters &
Simple
Illumination

A very pretty effect may be obtained in a small
and not very formal manuscript by painting into
the spaces left for the capitals little squares of red
and blue, and painting upon these the letters and
ornament—all in gold powder—very freely and
quickly. The kind of treatment
is rather crudely suggested by
fig. 113. The pleasant appearance of the pages—as though
they were scattered over with
tiny squares of cloth of gold and
red and blue—is produced with
comparative ease, while the use
of leaf gold might entail an expenditure of more time and pains than the book
was worth. In the finest class of manuscripts,
however, these matt gold letters would be somewhat
informal and out of place.

FIG. 113.

BURNISHED GOLD

Gold is always raised, and burnished as bright as
possible, unless there is a special reason for using
matt gold.

The height to which it is raised varies, according
to the effect desired, from a considerable thickness
to the thinnest possible coat of "size." Extremely
thin and extremely thick raising are both objectionable (see p. 116): roughly speaking, a suitable height
for any ordinary purpose is between $\frac{1}{100}$ and $\frac{1}{32}$ of
an inch.

The surface, in the case of large forms, is generally made as smooth and perfect as possible, so that,
as Cennino Cennini says, the burnished gold "*will*

appear almost dark from its own brightness"; and its brightness is only seen when the light falls on it at a particular angle. The gilding of a manuscript, however, is slightly flexible, and a large gilded surface is likely to be bent, so that some part of it is sure to catch the light.

Small surfaces highly burnished very often do not show the effect of, or "tell" as, gold, unless they catch the light by accident. It is well, therefore, where the forms are small to have several on the page, so that one or another will always shine out and explain the rest. And while the proper craftsman tries always to get the best finish which he reasonably can, the natural, slight unevennesses or varying planes of small gilded forms may be of advantage to the whole effect. The pleasant effect of such natural variations may be seen in thirteenth-century Initials, where numbers of little gold pieces are fitted into the backgrounds, and their changing surfaces cause the whole to be lit up with little sparkles of light. A parallel to this may be found in the hand-tooling of a book-cover, which sparkles with gold, because the binder could not press in each piece of gold-leaf absolutely level. On the other hand, the "deadness" of a machine-stamped cover is largely due to the *dead level* of its gilding.

Black and Gold.—One of the finest effects in calligraphy can be obtained by the simple contrast of gold capitals with black writing (see p. 263).

While, as in the case of *black and red*, the strongest effects are obtained by a marked contrast, gold may yet be very effectively used for small capitals throughout the black text. It does not lose or blend its brilliance with the black of the writing as colour is apt to do, but lights up and illuminates the page.

151

The Use of
Gold &
Colours in
Initial
Letters &
Simple
Illumination

For this reason gold will "help out" and make agreeable a black and colour effect which, by itself, would have been a failure (see p. 100).

BURNISHED GOLD FORMS & OUTLINES

Plain gold letters, symbols, and other detached forms, not having backgrounds, are usually not outlined. An outline cheapens their effect, making them darker and heavier, and, if the line be at all thick, concealing the true form of the letter, and giving it a clumsy appearance.

It is an instructive experiment to make a gold (or plain white) letter with a thick outline (*a*, fig. 114), and then paint a background round it. The effect is quite altered, and greatly improved (*b*, fig. 114).

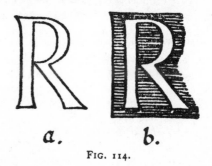

a.   *b.*

FIG. 114.

The outline no longer tells as the outer line of the form, but partakes more of the nature of the background, in which it cuts out, as one might say, a little *niche* for the letter to rest in.

Gold-leaf forms on coloured backgrounds are out-

The Use of
Gold &
Colours in
Initial
Letters &
Simple
Illumination

lined—generally in black—in order that letter and
background may together form a flat design, stable
and at rest in the page.

The distinction between the use of gold "*paint*"
and the treatment of a leaf gold form should be
carefully observed: the *matt gold powder* lies upon
colour, and may appear to blend with it (p. 149);
the *bright gold-leaf* constitutes a distinct form, which
either lies upon the surface of *a page*, or is, as it were,
set in a background.

Gold (leaf) Floral Ornament, &c.—If the stalk
and leaves are both gold: they are commonly not
outlined, unless on a background.

If there be a thin stalk in black or colour with
gold leaves: the leaves are outlined with the stalk-
colour (they were commonly *furred: c*, fig. 115).

If there be a *thick* coloured stalk with gold leaves:
both stalk and leaves commonly have a black outline,
the "leaves" often being treated as spots of gold
(below).

Gold Spots or Dots are usually outlined and *furred*
with black (fig. 115). The
effect produced is of a bright
gold form on a *grey* background.

A simple "leaf" or de-
tached spot of gold has a
formless look, much as a
small *blot* of colour or ink
would have. The black outline and the grey background-
effect seem in this case to give
form and interest to the spot;

FIG. 115.

at least they give it a place to *rest* in—a nest to hold
the small golden egg.

The Use of
Gold &
Colours in
Initial
Letters &
Simple
Illumination

Even a stalk and tendril (*d*, fig. 115) has the same effect of giving intention and meaning to what might otherwise be a mere blot.

When several spots of gold (or colour) are arranged in a simple design, together they constitute a simple form which does not require a background. Thus the *line-finishing* ∴ (*a*, fig. 126) has a formal and intentional arrangement in itself, and therefore need not be outlined.

BACKGROUND CAPITALS

Background Capitals or Initials frequently employ burnished gold, either for the letters or the ground. All the parts (including "solid" patterns) are generally outlined in black, or dark colour.

The commonest colours for grounds are Reds and Blues. The grounds are frequently countercharged, or made one colour *inside* and another *outside* the initial (p. 156). Sometimes little or no gold is used, and many fine white lines are employed to separate and harmonise the colours of the Initial and the ground. It is well, however, for the beginner to keep the letter and the ground distinct, by observing the Herald's maxim, and using "Metal on colour, *or* colour on metal."

The forms of the letters vary from those of ordinary capitals in being thicker in proportion to their height, and frequently in having no serifs. A very thin line or serif is apt to be lost in the background.

A very good form of background initial may be

made out of the ROMAN CAPITAL (*a*, fig. 116)

The Use of
Gold &
Colours in
Initial
Letters &
Simple
Illumination

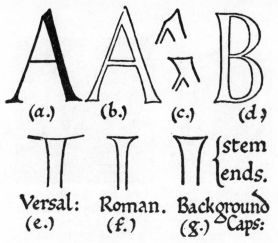

FIG. 116.

by thickening all its parts; in place of the serifs, curving out and shaping the ends of the stems (*b, d*) to a sort of "*blunderbuss*" pattern (*g*).

APPLYING THE BACKGROUND

It is well first to make the letter,[1] and then to *apply* the background to it (as though it were a sort of *mosaic*). The background is packed tightly round the letter, and the letter occupies the background,

---

[1] In the case of a burnished gold background, the actual *painting* of the Letter may be deferred until the adjacent gilded parts are finished (see p. 117).

The Use of
Gold &
Colours in
Initial
Letters &
Simple
Illumination

so that they appear to be in the same plane (*a*, fig. 117).

Diagram of (*a.*) simple, natural method of fitting together Initial & background. Note also counterchange.

Less satisfactory: (*b.*) Background too large: Or heavy ornament passing behind letter.

FIG. 117.

Such "flatness" is secured even more certainly and effectively by using two colours (*e.g.* red and blue) in the background—one inside and one outside the letter (see Plate XII).

The curves of the gold letter may with advantage slightly project, and so break the hard, square outline of the background.

The letter should not have the appearance of being "stuck on," as it is apt to if the background is large and empty, or if the ornament passes behind the letter (*b*, fig. 117).

In the case of letters with projecting stems or tails: the tail may be outside the background (*a*, fig. 118), or the background may be prolonged on

The Use of
Gold &
Colours in
Initial
Letters &
Simple
Illumination

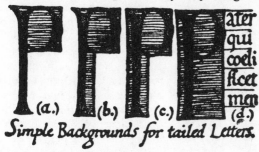

Simple Backgrounds for tailed Letters.

FIG. 118.

one or both sides of the tail (*b* and *c*), or the whole "field" may be enlarged to take in the complete letter (*d*).

There is no limit to the variety of shapes which backgrounds may take—symmetrical or asymmetrical, regular or irregular—provided they fit the initial or the ornament (which may *itself* partially, or entirely, bound them), are properly balanced (see Plate XII, and p. 381), and take their right place on the page.

ORNAMENT OF BACKGROUNDS

The ornament, as a rule, covers the background evenly, and is closely packed or fitted into its place.

Gold grounds are generally thin, sometimes bearing patterns in dots. These are indented in the surface by means of a point (p. 138) which is not too sharp. It presses the gold-leaf into tiny pits, but does not pierce it. Gold grounds may be broken up into small parts by coloured chequers (p. 181) or floral patterns.

157

The Use of
Gold &
Colours in
Initial
Letters &
Simple
Illumination.

Coloured grounds are, as a rule, more or less evenly covered with some form of decoration in thin white or matt gold lines, or in "solid" patterns in various colours (see pp. 168, 178). A simple and pretty diaper pattern may be made by diagonal lines of matt gold, cutting up the colour into small "lozenges," each alternate lozenge having a fleur-de-lis or little cross, or other simple ornament (fig. 119).

Simple Diaper
Background in
Shell Gold on
COLOUR.

FIG. 119.

A bolder design, in a broad white or coloured line, may be, as it were, woven through *counterfeited slits* in

FIG. 120.

the letter (fig. 120). This helps to preserve the

general flatness of the letter, background, and ornament, and gives additional interest.

The mimic slits are made by black lines drawn on the burnished gold of the letter. Where the stem of the ornament comes over the gold, the size is cut away with a pen-knife; the part hollowed out is painted with white to cover any blemishes, and then painted with the stem colour, and outlined.

A plain or pale stem may have a faint or brown outline, and be "shaded" at the sides (with *greys*, *browns*, or *yellows*) to give an effect of solidity; a stem that is painted in strong colour (*e.g.* red or blue) may have a central white line painted upon it.

Note that where the initials have backgrounds, the line-finishings are commonly made with backgrounds to match, though their treatment is naturally much simpler (see Plates XV, XVII).

The Use of
Gold &
Colours in
Initial
Letters &
Simple
Illumination

CHAPTER XI

A THEORY OF ILLUMINATION

Illumination—"Barbaric, or Colour-Work, Illumination"—"Filigree, or Pen-Work, Illumination"—"Natural, or Limner's, Illumination."

ILLUMINATION

IT is convenient to give a wide meaning to the word when we speak of an "*illuminated* manuscript," for the scribe works with a very free hand, and when he wishes to decorate his pages he can write the

words themselves in red, green, or blue, as easily as
he could have written them in black. He can take
a clean pen and a new colour and initial and "flourish" any part of the work to his heart's content. He
may acquire the art of laying and burnishing gold,
and no possible brilliance of effect is denied him—
within the limits of his skill as an illuminator (see
also pp. 262–263).

A limited number of specially prepared printed
books can likewise be illuminated. But the greater
the number of copies, the less labour may be spent
on each one, and the more their illumination tends to
be simple "rubrication"—adding coloured capitals,
flourishes, and the like (see p. 93). And, if a large
edition is to be decorated, the printer must be content to use black, or black and red, in woodcut or
"process" work (see pp. 329, 336).

Illumination proper may be defined as the decoration by hand, in bright gold or colours, of writing
or printing.

There are three broad types of illumination, which
for want of better terms I distinguish as "*Barbaric*"
(or colour-work), "*Filigree*" (or pen-work), and
"*Natural*" (or limner's). These types run naturally
one into another, and they may be blended or combined in every possible way, but it is convenient to
consider them and the distinctive treatments which
they involve separately.

"BARBARIC, OR COLOUR-WORK, ILLUMINATION"

(*See also pp.* 169, 174, 175, 181–4, 376, 407, 408)

This is mainly a colour treatment in which forms
seem to be regarded chiefly as vehicles for colour.

Its effect appeals to the senses, rather than to the
imagination; and such interest as the forms have lies
greatly in their skilful disposal or intricate arrangement. Sometimes in their fantasy—where organic
forms are introduced—as the "great fish" in the act
of swallowing Jonah (in order to make the *T* of
ET), Plate XII. This type of illumination appears
to have reached its climax of barbaric splendour in
the twelfth and thirteenth centuries.

Though its revival nowadays might seem a little
out of keeping with the more sedate and grown-up
point of view of modern life, we cannot doubt that
it is still *lawful* to decorate our work with the brilliance and splendour of gold and colours. Whether it
is *expedient* or not depends upon how it is done: to
justify our work, it must succeed; it must be bright
and splendid, and really gladden our eyes. And we
must really take pleasure in the making of it, for
if we do not, we can hardly expect that it will give
pleasure to others.

Simple and Complex Forms.—Between *simple forms*
—which are in a sense permanent—and *complex
forms*—which are always changing—it is necessary
to make a careful distinction.

An *equilateral triangle* drawn by "Euclid" and
one drawn by a modern Mathematician are, or
ought to be, practically the same thing. If the
ancients made an ornamental band of geometrical
forms, that is no bar to us; we also are at liberty
to make decorative bands of circles, lozenges, or
triangles.

The ancient Romans made a capital A—its *essential form* (see fig. 142) two strokes sloped together
and joined by a cross-bar (very like the "*Pons
Asinorum*"), it could hardly be simpler—they used

161

chisels and pens, which gave it its more characteristic
and finished form. If we use chisels and pens properly we shall get a similar result—not absolutely
the same—for no two chisels or two hands can
be quite the same—but closely resembling it and
belonging to our own time as much as to any
other.

The essential form of the "Roman" A is a purely
abstract form, the common property of every rational
age and country,[1] and its characterisation is mainly
the product of tools and materials not peculiar to the
ancient Romans.

But when there is any real *complexity* of form
and arrangement, or sentiment, we may reasonably
suppose that it is peculiar to its time, and that the
life and virtue of it cannot be restored.

It was common enough in the Middle Ages to
make an initial A of two *dragons* firmly locked
together by claws and teeth. Such forms fitted the
humour of the time, and were part of the then
natural "scheme of things." But *we* should beware
of using such antique fantasies and "organisms";
for medieval humour, together with its fauna and
flora, belong to the past. And our own work is only
honest when made in our own humour, time, and
place.

There are, however, an infinite variety of simple
abstract forms and symbols, such as circles, crosses,
squares, lozenges, triangles, and a number of Alphabets, such as Square and Round Capitals, Small
Letters—upright and sloping—which—weeded of

---

[1] It has even been supposed that we might make the inhabit-
ants of *Mars* aware of the existence of rational *Terrestrials*, by
exhibiting a vast illumination—in lamp-light—consisting of a
somewhat similar form—*the first Proposition in Euclid.*

archaisms—we may use freely. And all these forms
can be diversified by the tools with which they are
made, and the manner in which the tools are used,
and be glorified by the addition of bright colours and
silver and gold. Very effective "designs" can be
made with "chequers" and diaper patterns, and with
the very letters themselves. And I have little doubt
that an excellent *modern* style of illumination is quite
feasible, in which the greatest possible richness of
colour effect is achieved together with extreme
simplicity of form.

"FILIGREE, OR PEN-WORK, ILLUMINATION"

(*See also pp.* 171–4, 175, 184–6, 411, 414–15;
figs. 79, 92, 125–26, 150, 188–89; Plates XI,
XIII, XIV, XVII.)

This is a type of illumination which can safely be
attempted by one who, having learnt to write, is
desirous of illuminating his writing; for it is the
direct outcome of penmanship (see p. 170), and consists mainly of pen flourishes, or semi-formal lines
and shapes which can be made with a pen, suitably
applied to the part to be decorated. Its effect may
be very charming and restful: no colour standing
out as in a positive colour scheme, no individual
form catching the eye; but the whole having a richness of simple detail and smooth colouring more or
less intricate and agreeably *bewildering*.

It may be compared to the *tooling* of a book-
cover, both in the method of producing it, and in
its effect. A book-binder has a number of stamps
which bear the simplest forms and symbols, such as
little circles and "leaves" and stars and curved lines,

and with these simple *elements* he builds up a pleasant "design," which he tools, usually in gold-leaf, upon the cover.

The scribe can vary the forms which his pen produces, and the colours which he gives them, with a freedom that the set form and the method of using the binder's tools do not allow. But the skilled penman will find that his pen (or, at any rate, his *penmanship*) largely determines the forms of his freest flourishes and strokes, and that the semi-formal nature of such ornament demands a certain simplicity and repetition of form and colour, which do not unduly tax his skill as a craftsman.

Suppose, for example, that the scribe wishes to illuminate the border of a page of writing. He may choose a limited number of simple, pen-made forms for the elements of his design; say, a circle, a "leaf," and a "tendril," and a few curved flourishes and

FIG. 121.

strokes (fig. 121), and with these cover the allotted space evenly and agreeably.

The ornament being treated as though it were a sort of floral growth, requires a starting point or "root." The initial letter is the natural origin of the border ornament, the stalk of which generally springs from the side or from one of the extremities of the letter. The main stem and branches are first made with a very free pen, forming a *skeleton pattern* (fig. 122).

NOTE.—The numbers in the diagram indicate the order in which the strokes were made. The *main stem* (111) sweeps over and occupies most of the ground; the *secondary* stem (222) occupies the remainder; the main *branches* (333, &c.) make the occupation secure.

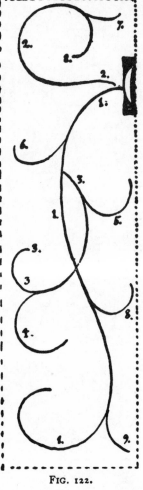

FIG. 122.

Fig. 123.

Next the minor branches are added to cover the space evenly, and then the *flowers, fruit,* and *buds* —made up of combinations of the "leaves," circles, &c. —are more or less evenly disposed in the spaces formed by the large, round curves at the ends of the branches (fig. 123).

The "leaves" are
placed all over, wher-
ever there is con-
venient room for them
(just as the leaves of a
real plant are). Then
the stalks of the leaves
are added, and, lastly,
the interspaces are
filled with "tendrils,"
which greatly con-
tribute to the pleasant
intricacy of the design
(fig. 124).

FIG. 124.

167

Colour Schemes.—The safest treatment of such a "design" is in black and gold (see p. 153). The leaves, which are kept rather flat, may be outlined *after* gilding. The flowers, &c., may be made up in red and blue (tempered with white: see p. 148). This is the colour treatment of the example, Plate XVII.

If the leaves are green, the stem and outline may be more delicately drawn in pale or grey-brown ink, and the green may be a delicate pale olive or grey-green. (A strong, black stem with bright green leaves is apt to look crude and hard.) In such a delicate green plant border, delicate blue and red flowers, and one or two rather flat gold "berries" (single, or in threes) may be placed.

A very effective colour decoration of a much simpler type may be made in red and green (or blue) pen-work—using the pen and the colours with which the Versal letters and line-finishings are made. A red flourished stem with red leaves or tendrils, and green berries (or leaves) or a green stem with green leaves and red berries.

A floral pattern may also be made in plain burnished gold—both stem and leaves—not outlined (p. 153 & Plate XXII).

A more complex decoration resembling the "floral filigree" has a "solid" stem in light or dark colour on a dark or light ground (or on a gold ground), as suggested in the rough diagram, fig. 120.

The examples of Italian fifteenth-century work in Plates XVIII and XIX show a related type of illumination, known as the "white vine pattern." Very carefully and beautifully drawn, it strongly suggests natural form.

"NATURAL, OR LIMNER'S,* ILLUMINATION"

(*See also pp.* 179, 185–7, 193, 409–10, 412–14, 422; figs. 131*a*–141; Plates XV, XVI, XXIII.)

This, the finest type of illumination, has very great possibilities; and it is to be hoped that some craftsmen, who have the necessary skill, will find an opening for their work in this direction.

---

* NOTE.—*Limning* strictly means *Illuminating*, but has come to imply drawing and painting, especially of portraits and miniatures. Here, *all* its senses are intended.

Plate XV is a thirteenth-century example of the transition from the "barbaric" to the "natural." The dragon-tailed initial with its wonderful scroll-work and "ivy-leaf" being the perfection of barbaric form, carrying brilliant colour and serving to support and frame the delicate and beautiful drawing which it contains.[1] But in the drawing itself the skill of a fine illuminator combines with the fancy of a cunning draughtsman to satisfy an æsthetic taste and appeal to the imagination.

Plate XVI shows a rare, and singularly interesting, treatment of an Italian fourteenth-century MS. decorated with plant and insect forms (p. 413).

Plate XXIII (*modern*) shows a border of wild roses and climbing plants: the colour treatment in the original is very brilliant (see p. 422).

The "natural" type depends very much on the beauty and interest of its form; and a draughtsman before he had become an illuminator, might be content to decorate MSS. and printed books with pen drawings only faintly coloured or tinted; but when he had mastered the limitations which the craft would impose on his drawing for pure and bright colour, there is no degree of brilliance, even unto "barbaric splendour," which he might not lay upon his trained and delicate forms.

---

[1] The modern illuminator, having no tradition for making such scroll-work, would find that natural or organic forms—as of trees or plants (see p. 187)—would serve the same end and have more "sweet reasonableness" in modern eyes. Excellent scroll-work, moreover, might be formed out of ornamental Capitals—if sufficient excuse could be found for introducing them: a large flourished L, for example, could be made exactly on the same lines as the pendant and scroll in Plate XV. Narrow gold rods also may be used in a border to support a floral growth, or as frames if necessary (compare *rules*, p. 328).

CHAPTER XII

The Development of Illumination—Line-Finishings—
Initial Letters—Borders & Backgrounds.

THE DEVELOPMENT OF ILLUMINATION

The Development of Illumination

An art or craft is so largely dependent on the tools and materials which are used by the craftsman, that we may reasonably say that it begins with the tools and materials, through which it has been produced. Now, "illumination" can be traced back step by step to simple penmanship. And its true development is most graphically sketched by Ruskin ("Lectures on Art," No. V) when he says—

"The pen . . . is not only the great instrument for the finest sketching, but its right use is the foundation of the art of illumination. . . . Perfect illumination is only writing made lovely; . . . But to make writing itself *beautiful—to make the sweep of the pen lovely—is the true art of illumination"; And also that those who have acquired "a habit of deliberate, legible and lovely penmanship in their daily use of the pen, . . . may next discipline their hands into the control of lines of any length, and, finally, add the beauty of colour and form to the flowing of these perfect lines."*

---

[1] The *steps in the development* sketched very briefly in this chapter, refer both to the past history of the art of illumination and to its practical revival (see p. xiv). Of something already done, of honour due, a friend reminds me: "William Morris was the first person in England to revive the art of writing and illumination, as he revived so many other arts, on the lines established by the ancient masters. Several books are in existence exquisitely written and decorated by him, notably a Horace, a Vergil, and two differently treated copies of Omar Khayyám."

Line-finishings are used to preserve the evenness of the text when lines of writing fall short. When the space left is small, or *occurs in the middle of a sentence*, a quick stroke of the pen—often a continuation of the last letter, or springing from it—is sufficient (fig. 125); but where there are many and long gaps (as, for example, in a psalter at the ends of the verses), they may be filled in with dots (see Plate VIII) or flourishes (*a, b, c*, fig. 126) either made in black with the script pen, or with another pen, in colour or gold.

Line-finishings commonly echo the treatment of the initials (see p. 147). In twelfth-century MSS. long delicate flourishes are commonly found, in red, blue, or green—matching the colours of the Versals, and probably *made with the same pen*. The latter being rather finer than the text pen keeps these flourishes from appearing too prominent (see *e, f*, fig. 126).

Such work should be simple and characteristic pen-work, showing the thicks and thins and crisp curves, the result of the position of the pen, which is usually "slanted" (see p. 9).

Bands of pen-made "geometrical" patterns—used with rather close writing—may be very simple and direct, though appearing pleasantly elaborate (see figs. 87 and (*g*) 126, Plate XIV, and pp. 181 & xxiii).

INITIAL LETTERS

(*See also pp.* xiv, 14, 78–80, 90, 100, 147, 154–159, 159–65, 177–81, *and the Plates*)

The main development of Illumination was—and still is—bound up with the growth and decoration of the Initial Letter (but see *footnote*, p. 179).

Line-finishings :
Pen-flourishing :
of Terminal strokes

e e f g e
e t s n
m v y
k r r r r r
E F L R
T z R
spread .... out ;
some-
times
IN
orna-
mental LETTERING,

FIG. 125.

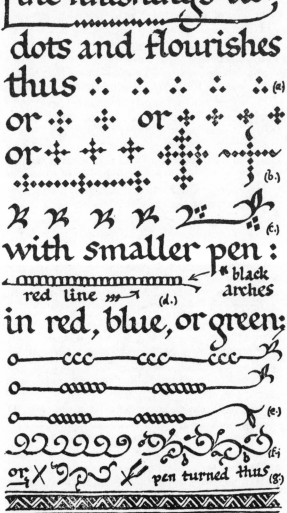

Line-finishings &c., dots and flourishes thus ∴ (a.)

or ⊹ or ⊹ (b.)

with smaller pen :

red line ⟶ (d.) black arches

in red, blue, or green:

ccc — ccc — ccc (e.)

(f.)

or ⫶ pen turned thus (g.)

FIG. 126.

The first step in this development is the mastery
of the pen-made Versal letter, and the right treatment of simple coloured capitals (see chapters VII,
VIII, and X).   The next step is their elaboration.
The simplest ornamental treatment is found in the
flourishing of a terminal of the initial letter (fig. 150),
or the arrangement of the *remaining letters of the
word* inside or beside it. Pen flourishes may consist
of the simplest curved and zigzag strokes (sometimes
springing from the actual letter: see p. 217), ending
with a "twirl" of the pen in a loop or a "bud"
(figs. 150, 79); or they may strike out a sort of
formal floral pattern, filling or surrounding the initial (fig. 92), and such a pattern in its turn may
spring from the letter into the margin, and grow into
a complete "illuminated border" (see p. 165).

Hollow Letters.—A large capital is often made
hollow, primarily with a view to lightening its appearance, which might be rather heavy if the letter
were made solid (p. 85). The hollow—which is
commonly left plain (*i.e.* the colour of the paper or
parchment)—may be a mere line, straight or curved
or zigzag (fig. 189), or a pattern, or lettering (fig.
89). Sometimes it is made large and filled in with a
contrasting colour, leaving a white line, however,
between the two colours. And sometimes half the
letter is made in one colour, and the other half (on
the opposite side of the hollow centre) is made in a
contrasting colour. A "hollow" letter (especially
if very large) may be strengthened and improved by
a filling of colour or ornament. (*Addenda*, p. xxiii.)

"Woven" Forms.—A simple form of ornament
(related to "Basket work") which effectually
strengthens the construction of a hollow letter—
without impairing its lightness—consists in a crossing

174

and "weaving" or knotting of its actual parts
(fig. 127). Plate XII gives a very fine example.

Woven=
hollow
Q

A "knot"

Elabor
ated
E, with
inwoven ornament: all
in burnished gold with red
outline and bands across the
three limbs of E. The interspaces
are filled with red, green & blue
& semee with white ∴ s

FIG. 127.

The elaborated E (in fig. 127) is from a 10th
or 11th century MS. (Brit. Museum, Egerton,
608). The Initial and its inwoven ornament cut
up the background into a number of distinct parts
(distinctly coloured). Note also that the entire
background is contained by the Initial.

The "knot" (fig. 127), or a basket-work ornament, is sometimes used as an arbitrary starting-
point for a filigree border (see p. 414) where an
initial is lacking.

Variety in Initials.—The *sizes* and *styles* of the
initials which are used *for the same purpose* throughout the book vary very slightly or not at all. Generally, the more important the division which the

initial marks, the larger the initial and the more ornate (p. 262). A slight complexity in the opening letter or word of a book does not seriously interfere with the readableness of the book as a whole. The general rule is followed that *the greater the number of (decorative) forms the plainer they are kept* (see p. 92), and if a book contained an "initial" on every page, it would be both an artistic and a working economy (if there were many pages) to make the majority of them rather plain.

But however simple the treatment of the initials may be, there is still room for considerable variety of *form* or *ornament* or *type*—as "round" or "square" letters (see fig. 80, and especially Plate XI). Such variety is found in the best work; it adds a liveliness and charm which are quite lacking where there is unnecessary or mechanical repetition.

"*Lombardic*" versus *Roman Capitals*.—The round, fat letters which are known as "Lombardic" (see fig. 1, and Plates XV, XVII) have been generally used for "illuminated initials" in Northern Europe since the thirteenth century. But—though they are capable of very beautiful treatment—they are rather doubtful models for us to follow. The fact that such letters will always pack neatly into a square niche or background—though an obvious convenience— is not an unmixed advantage. And the majority of examples show a debased type of Letters—often so unlike their originals, and so like one another, as to be scarcely readable. For the sake of readableness the stems should be made longer (fig. 128). The more slender "Roman" type of initial, commonly used in Italy (Plate XVIII), is in every way a more legible letter. The Roman Alphabet still remains the finest model, and it is better that fine lettering should be almost too slender and

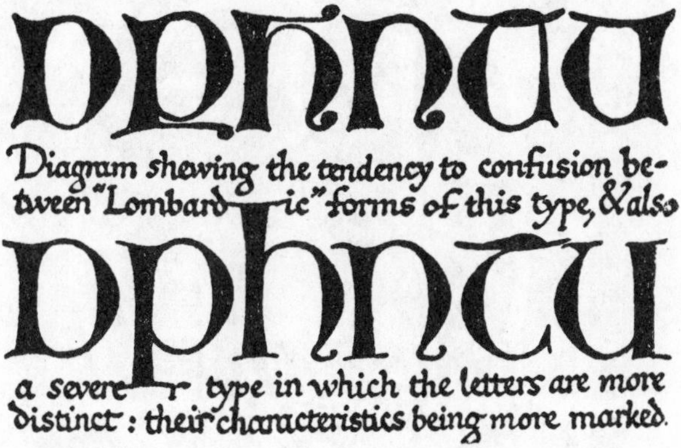

Diagram showing the tendency to confusion between "Lombard——ic" forms of this type, & also

a severe——r type in which the letters are more distinct: their characteristics being more marked.

FIG. 128

delicate, than that it should be at all heavy or clumsy.

BORDERS & BACKGROUNDS

The illuminated border was originally an extension or branching out of the initial decoration. It commonly occupied the greater part of the left-hand margin, and from thence it extended into the *head*[1] or *foot* margin (or into both), or completely surrounded the text, and even the eight margins of a

---

[1] Where it is possible it is desirable to mark the top left-hand corner of the "page" (and also the lower corner) by a branch, flourish, bud, or flower (see Plates XIX, XXII). A top left-hand corner appearing vacant or rounded off is apt to weaken the whole effect (see p. 100).

177

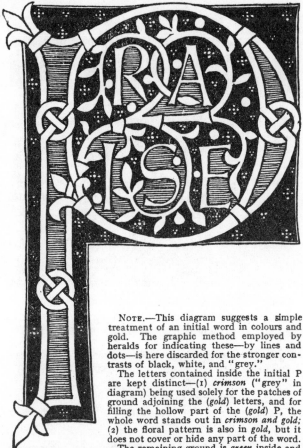

Fig. 129.

Note.—This diagram suggests a simple
treatment of an initial word in colours and
gold. The graphic method employed by
heralds for indicating these—by lines and
dots—is here discarded for the stronger contrasts of black, white, and "grey."

The letters contained inside the initial P
are kept distinct—(1) *crimson* ("grey" in
diagram) being used solely for the patches of
ground adjoining the (*gold*) letters, and for
filling the hollow part of the (*gold*) P, the
whole word stands out in *crimson and gold;*
(2) the floral pattern is also in *gold*, but it
does not cover or hide any part of the word.

The remaining ground is *green* inside and
blue outside the P. The doors •.• ••• are in
red on the green ground, in *cream* with a
red centre dot on the blue.

The gold throughout is outlined *black*, and the blue ground has a
black outline, separated from it by a *white* line.

complete *opening* are sometimes covered with illumination. In late and modern usage the border is frequently separated from the initial, constituting a "framing border."[1]

In some MSS. there are *two* side-borders on a page, one springing from the Initials on the left, the other sending branches into the gaps on the right (see Plates XVII, XVI). In some cases the two pages of an opening are balanced by a side-border in each of the wide side margins (p. 414).

Backgrounds of Initials (see pp. 154-9, 407-9) and borders are treated very similarly. It may be noted that, where a *solid-stem* pattern cuts up the ground into small pieces, these are often painted in different colours—commonly red, and green, and blue (see pp. 175, 416). And the *groups of dots* (fig. 129)—in white or other colours—may fill the interstices of a background, putting the finishing touch to the even covering and pleasant intricacy of the decoration (*comp.* p. 167). Or little flowers and leaves may be used instead—growing from a thin (white) stem which appears to twine throughout the main pattern—just as the smaller plants in a hedge creep and twine among the larger stems. There is no better model in nature for the illuminator than a country hedgerow.

---

[1] Narrow ornamental frames are to be found in early MSS. before the full development of the Initial Letter. These, like various other primitive *ornaments*, such as are suggested at pp. 161, 162 & 181-2, are not an outgrowth of the Initial.

Whether narrow or broad, *framing borders*, or borders which surround the text, should generally not encroach on the *writing-space* (which is kept uniform throughout the pages of the book), though broad framing borders may be allowed nearly to fill the entire marginal space.

CHAPTER XIII

"DESIGN" IN ILLUMINATION

"Design"—Elementary Patterns in Decoration—Scale
& Scope of Decoration—Of "Designing" Manuscripts Generally.

"DESIGN"

"Design" in
Illumination PERHAPS the nearest right definition of "design" is
"*contrivance*"—applied to the actual doing of the
work, rather than to the work when done: "*decoration*" (when that is the sense intended) is a safer
word,[1] because it implies "*of something.*" And
generally that "something" lies at the root of the
matter. For example: "illuminated initials" and
"illuminated borders," so called, are really illumi-
nat*ing*: they are properly *a decoration of manuscript
or print*.

To consider a "piece-of-decoration" as a thing
existing apart from that which it decorates, as
something drawn or copied, and, so to speak, *stuck
on* to the finished work, is as *un*natural as it would
be to contemplate the flame-of-a-candle as a thing
apart from the candle.

---

[1] "Design" has been associated so much with bad cleverness
in the artist, or clever badness in the natural man, that if we
use the word in a good sense it is apt to be misunderstood.

Decoration is derived from *decus, decor* = comeliness or grace.

180

The finest decoration is really part of the work itself, and may be described as *the finishing touches given directly to the work by the tools which are properly employed on it.*

The illuminator has, as a rule, to decorate a given manuscript with pen or brush work—it may be with the simplest pen flourishes, or with the most elaborate figure "design." *How* to make that illumination part of the work, he can learn only by patient practice and by careful handling of his tools.

ELEMENTARY PATTERNS IN DECORATION

Nearly all simple Decoration consists of a comparatively limited number of *elements*—simple form and pure colours—which are built up into more complex forms to occupy an allotted space. A primitive type of such built-up decoration is seen in the dotted patterns, which are found in every age—in the remains of the most ancient art, and in the shell decorations which children make on the sands at the present day. Examples of dotted "backgrounds" in the "Durham Book" are shown in fig. 130 (*a* and *b*). Chequers and Diapers—in which two or more elements are employed—are related patterns.[1] (*See also Addenda, p.* xxiii & *fig.* 191*a*.)

A simple way of filling a band (or long narrow

---

[1] Chequers in colours and gold were largely used in the fourteenth-century MSS. for backgrounds in miniatures. There is an example of very beautiful heraldic diapering (in enamel) on the shield of William de Valence, Earl of Pembroke, in Westminster Abbey (A.D. 1296). On p. 300 of this book there is a diagram of a very fine shield bearing a diapered chequer.

space) is to run a zigzag line along it (*c*). This may be treated either as a line or wavy stem, which may send out buds, leaves, or flowers into the spaces (*g*), or as two series of triangles which may be "*countercharged*" (*f*).[1] A second zigzag, cutting the first, would produce two series of triangles and a central row of lozenges (*d*). And it is not a very great step from this to the "twist" where the two lines pass over and under, the lines being made "solid" in white or gold on a coloured background (*e*, fig. 130). The main difference appears to be that while the one is of the nature of an abstract form, the other suggests a concrete form, such as might be made with twisted cords or rods.

These primitive patterns never become antiquated; they are still the root forms of "design," and the pleasant even covering of a given space by simple elements—which is their *mètier*—accounts for much of the unconscious pleasure which we take in good *bricklaying* or *sewing* or *writing*, and in a thousand things, where "*many littles make a mickle*."

For their decorative possibilities in Illumination we can experiment in the most delightful way— framing our writing with bands of countercharged triangles in burnished gold, and blue and white, or with golden zigzags on a blue ground, or chequering backgrounds with scarlet and blue, and trying a hundred and one other ways (p. 163). Such patterns have been made the most of in Heraldry, an art

---

[1] If the triangles were countercharged in colour and colour —*e.g.* red and blue—the zigzag would be made *white*, *black*, or *gold*, to separate and harmonise the colours (see pp. 148–9).

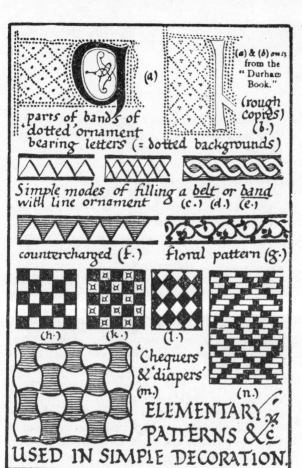

parts of bands of dotted ornament bearing letters (= dotted backgrounds)

(a) & (b) owts from the "Durham Book." (rough copies) (b.)

Simple modes of filling a belt or band with line ornament (c.) (d.) (e.)

counterchanged (f.)

floral pattern (g.)

(h.) (k.) (l.)

'Chequers' & 'diapers' (m.) (n.)

ELEMENTARY PATTERNS &c USED IN SIMPLE DECORATION.

FIG. 130.

183

"Design" in which in itself would form a foundation for a splendid
Illumination and complete scheme of Illumination.

SCALE & SCOPE OF DECORATION

Penmanship.—Many of the most beautiful MSS.
were made in pen-work throughout.[1] And it is well
that the penman should stick to his pen as much as
is possible. Not only does it train his hand to make
pen ornaments, the forms of which are in keeping
with the writing, but it helps to keep the decoration
proportionate in every way. It is an excellent plan
for the beginner to use the writing-pen for plain
black capitals or flourishes, and to make *all* other
decoration with similar or slightly finer pens than
the one used for the writing.

Again, the direct use of the pen will prevent much
mischievous "sketching." Sketching is right in its
proper place, and, *where you know exactly what you
wish to do*, it is useful to sketch in lightly the main
parts of a complex "design" so that each part may
receive a fair portion of the available space. But do
not spoil your MS. by experimental pencilling in
trying to find out what you want to do. Experiments
are best made roughly with a pen or brush on a piece
of paper laid on the available space in the MS., or
by colouring a piece of paper and cutting it out to
the pattern desired and laying it on. Such means are
also used to settle small doubts which may arise in
the actual illuminating—as to whether—and where

---

[1] A most beautiful twelfth-century MS., known as the
"Golden Psalter," has many gold (decorated) Initials, Red,
Blue, and Green (plain) Versals and Line-Finishings, every part
being pen-made throughout the book.

184

—some form or some colour should be placed on the page.

Filigree, Floral, & other Decoration.—The acquired skill of the penman leads very naturally to a pen flourishing and decoration of his work, and this again to many different types of filigree decoration more or less resembling floral growths (see figs. 125, 126; pp. 163–8; Plates XI, XVII).

Now all right decoration in a sense *arranges itself*, and we may compare the right action of the "designer's" mind to that necessary vibration or "directive" motion which permeates the universe and, being communicated to the elements, enables the various particles to fall into their right places: as when iron filings are shaken near a magnet they arrange themselves in the natural curves of the magnetic field, or as a cello bow, drawn over the edge of a sand-sprinkled plate, gathers the sand into beautiful "musical patterns."

And to most natural growths, whether of plants or ornament, this principle of self-arrangement seems common, that they *spread out evenly and occupy to the greatest extent possible their allotted space.* Branches and leaves most naturally *grow away from the stem and from each other,* and oppose elbows and points in every direction. In this way the growth fits its place, looking secure and at rest—while in disconnected parallels, or branches following their stem, there is often insecurity and unrest.[1] (*See also Addenda, p.* xxiii.)

For example: a circular space is filled more

---

[1] In a *spiral* the stem, following *itself,* may be tied by an interlacing spiral, or the turns of the spiral may be held at rest by the interlocking of the leaves (see G, Plate XXII).

decoratively by a cross (*a*, fig. 131) than by a contained circle; a square is better filled by a "lozenge" or a
circle (*b* and *c*) than by a smaller square set square

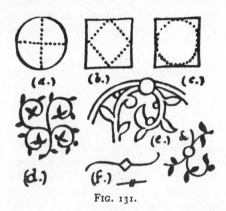

FIG. 131.

and parallel (compare the diapering of the chequers
in fig. 191 *a*). A circular or square space might be
filled on this principle with a filigree arrangement
such as is suggested by (*d*, fig. 131). *Note.*—In the
case of two curves in the ornament touching (either
internally or externally) they may be linked at this
point by a (gold) band or circle or lozenge (*e*, fig. 131,
see also Plate XVII).

Miniatures and Drawing.—In drawing and painting, the difficulty which is apt to beset the illuminator is how to strike a balance between "Natural-
ism" and "Conventionalism," so called. While the
only criterion is good taste, we may be guided by
certain general principles.

To limit the number of elements in a "design"
—whether of form or colour—is nearly always an

186

advantage (pp. 143, 147, 164). And the miniaturist,
while depicting the nature of a plant, usually *limits*
the number of its branches and leaves and shades of
colour. Every part of a "design" should be drawn
clearly and distinctly, and in proportion to the whole.
The miniaturist, therefore, usually *draws in careful*
outline every branch and leaf, making the whole propor-
tional with the MS. which it decorates.

In fact, the qualities of good illumination are the
same as the *qualities of good writing—Simplicity,*
Distinctiveness, Proportion, &c. (see p. 203). And
the "convention" (here literally a *coming together*)
required is only such as will make the drawing and
colouring of the illumination and the form and
colour of the writing *go well together*.

NOTE.—Figs. 135 to 141 (woodcuts—with part of the text—
from a Herbal printed at Venice in 1571 [p. 333]) and figs. 132,
133, and 134*a* (wood engravings by T. Bewick, printed 1791)
are suggested as examples of drawing—of plants and animals—
suitable for book-decoration (see also figs. 134*b*, *c*, *d*; Plates XV.,
XVI., XXIII., and notes on "limner's illumination," p. 169).

OF "DESIGNING" MANUSCRIPTS GENERALLY

Cultivate the simplest and most direct methods,
and make "rules of thumb"[1] for work-a-day use, to
carry you successfully through all routine or ordinary
difficulties, so that your hand will be trained and
your mind free and ready to deal with the harder
problems when they arise.

---

[1] As an example of a good "rule of thumb," *use the ruled lines*
of a manuscript as a scale for other measurements and proportions,
leaving one, two, three, or more of the line-spaces for capitals,
ornaments, &c.: you have this scale—as it were, a "ready
reckoner"—present on every page, and following it enables you
more easily to make the decoration agree and harmonise with
the written text and with the book as a whole (see p. 94 &
figs. 89, 91, 71).

Use a limited number of pure, bright colours, and keep your work clean, neat, and definite.

Go straight ahead, trusting to workman-like methods, and not calculating overmuch. Do the work in a regular order, settling, first, the general scheme, the size of the book, the writing, and the margins; then when you are ready—

1. Prepare the sheets (see pp. 65, 76, 133).
2. Write the text—leaving spaces for decoration.
3. Write (a) The coloured writing.
   in— (b) The coloured capitals.
        (c) The line-finishings.
4. Illum-(a) The Initials. ⎱ Following a regular
   inate— (b) Line-finishings. ⎰ order in the various
        (c) The Borders. ⎰ processes involved.
5. Bind the book (p. 310), or have it bound, in order to make a real and finished piece of work.

Practise an artistic economy of time and space: usually the quicker you write the MS. the better it is. Allow sufficient margins to make the book readable and handsome, but not so wide as to make it appear fanciful. Allow sufficient ornament, not overloading the book with it. Let the ornament be of a type suited to the book and to the subject—not *too painstaking* or elaborate in an ordinary MS.; not too hasty and slight in an important work.

Endeavour to strike a balance between what may be called "practical" and "ornamental" considerations: an illuminated MS. is not meant to be entirely "practical," but it is a greater failure if made entirely "ornamental." Let the text be *readable* in every sense, and let the ornament *beautify* it: there should be give and take, as it were, and that most desirable quality—"sweet reasonableness."

188

THE SPRINGER.

The *White-Antelope*, which is fuppofed to be the fame with the *Pygarg*, mentioned in the book of Numbers, is an inhabitant of the Cape of Good Hope, where it is called the *Spring-bok;* and is to be feen in herds of feveral thoufands, covering the plains as far as the eye can reach. Sparrman fays, that, having fhot at a large herd of them, they formed a line, and immediately made a circular movement, as if to furround him; but afterwards flew off in different directions.

The height of this beautiful creature is two feet and a

FIG. 132.

189

THE CHEVROTAIN AND MEMINNA.

The Chevrotain, or little Guinea Deer, is the smallest
of all the Antelope kind, the least of all cloven-footed
quadrupeds, and, we may add, the most beautiful. Its
fore legs, at the smallest part, are not much thicker than
a tobacco-pipe; it is not more than seven inches in
height, and about twelve from the point of the nose to
the insertion of the tail; its ears are broad; and its
horns, which are straight, and scarcely two inches long,
are black and shining as jet; the colour of the hair is a
reddish-brown; in some a beautiful yellow, very short
and glossy.

These elegant little creatures are natives of Senegal
and the hottest parts of Africa; they are likewise found
in India, and in many of the islands adjoining to that
vast continent.

FIG. 133.

190

FIG. 134.—Part of Fig. 133. Enlarged twice linear.

FIG. 134 *a*.

FIG. 134 *b*.

"The intricacies of a natural scene (fig. 134 *a*—after Bewick) may be simplified when rendered in such a simple medium as the pen drawings of a MS. (comp. fig. 134 *b*). Figs. 134 *c* & *d* are old examples of strong, simple drawing. Students should practise themselves by translating figs. 132, 133 into fine, Quill-pen drawings."—(N. R.)

FIG. 134 *c.*

(*This and fig.* 134 *d are copies from a fourteenth century MS. in the possession of Mr. Yates Thompson.*)

FIG. 134 *a.*

ARVNDO, Græcis, Κάλαμος.] Arabibus, Casab.]
manis, Roebr.] Hispanis, Canas:] Gallis, Cann
ARVNDO.

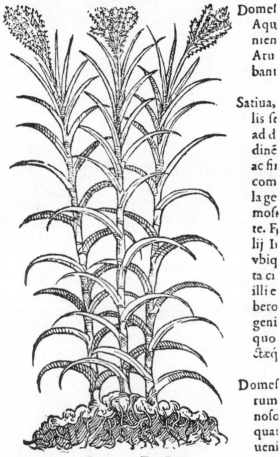

Domel
Aqu
nien
Aru
bant

Satiua,
lis se
ad d
diné
ac fii
com
la ge
mose
te. F,
lij I
vbiq
ta ci
illi e
bero
geni
quo
ctæq

Domes
rum
noso
quat
ueni

FIG. 135.—THE REED.

194

dixi-
)en-
ftre,
Pe-
voca

s, fa
iffe-
cau
oftq̄
, fo-
iris,
cau
ina-
:ibis
:eris
aina
vt ét
atur

ius,
ib⁹,
Cor-
, &
nit.
s,

inus
quæ

lliores, nec valétiores vires habent. Cęterùm Cor-

FIG. 136.—ASPARAGUS.

195

s.] Hiſpanis, *Lenteyas*.] Gallis, *Lentille*.

LENS.

.bum ,
, & in
colo-
aiore.

:, flore
iliqua
literq;
in qua
aterna
a preſ-
htecta.
irpura
nplici-

s, cum

s.

ate me
tamen
er quo
itaque
k ſiſtit
rò pro
gluti-
diſcu-

euora-
rò ius
tantur
a deli-
ietſio-
tea de-

FIG. 137.—THE LENTIL.

VITIS vinifera, Græcis, Αμπελος οινοφόρος.] Italis, bibus, *Harin Karin, seu Karm.*] Germanis, *Vuein*

VITIS VINIFERA.

"Design" in
Illumination

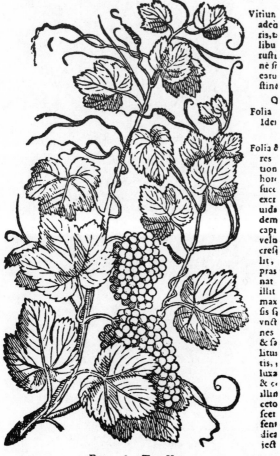

Vitiun
adeo
ris, t
libu
rusti
në si
earu
stine

Q

Folia
Ide

Folia δ
res
tion
hor
succ
exci
uida
dem
capi
velu
cresi
lit,
pras
nat
illit
max
sis si
vnct
nes
& si
litu
tis,
luxa
& c
illin
ceto
scet
sent
dica
iest

FIG. 138.—THE VINE.

197

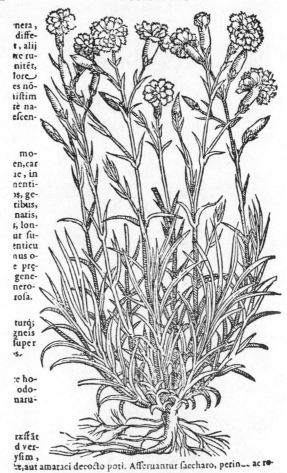

'nera,
diffe
t, alij
re ru-
nitêt,
flore,
es nō-
tiſſim
rè na-
eſcen-

mo-
en,car
ie, in
nenti-
s, ge-
ribus,
natis,
s, lon-
ur ſu-
enticu
nus o-
e prę-
gene-
nero-
roſa.

turq̃;
gneis
ſuper
s.

e ho-
odo-
naru-

rſſſt
d ver-
yſim,
ſ, aut amaraci decocto poti. Aſſeruantur ſaccharo, perin... ac re

FIG. 139.—THE CARNATION.

uidun-
mo cau
filiquæ
imiles,
:ütmul-
ra, aci-
a, inu-
be t ceu
m , au-
gia .

·us, fa-
cis .
:s.
.dſtrin-
m dul-
m den-
oniam
amar:
purga:
ruct.ò
x aci·
aute·
iccato
d tam.
aut a·
ò cali
attin.

, partu
et'mè-
tudine
ıs cum
:, valet

m, & renum, & veſicę dolores dęcocta in vino aluum ſiſtit .
s menſes ſiſtunt decem, aut duodecim pota ex vino a uſtero.

FIG. 140.—THE PEONY.

A .

n reperiuntur
enim rubent,
algent, aliæ vi-
nt, alia sangui-
, alia duracina
iriore sint pul-
n diducantur.
ja nuciperfica,
um faciem re-
ntur. Sunt etiã
hygdalam dul-
a amygdala ap

A .

st foliis Amyg
nilibus, quem-
bus, quamuis
urpurascentes
nateries fragi-
tilles, nec altè
b fit, quod hæc
cat , & cadat.

S .

h in Italia, sed
ma prouenit.

T E S .

rêtem habent
n. Alioqui fa-
medicamen-
o eius, nempe
sicum, humi-
r temperie.

S .

cohibent, sed
. Decoctum e
q; fluxiones si
unt, & quæ sa-
¶ Flores re-
n solum aluú
uones quoq;
orium aquam

sque ægrotantium incommodo. Lacnryma arboris datur ex plantaginis,
ad sanguinis reiectiones. tussientibus verò, & anhelosis ex Tussilagina
uento : facit quoq; ad raucedinem, & arteriæ impedimenta. Datur calcu-
haus, aut limonum duarum drachmarum pondere. Recentia folia illi

FIG. 141.—THE PEACH.

200

PART II

LETTERING

CHAPTER XIV

GOOD LETTERING——SOME METHODS OF CONSTRUCTION & ARRANGEMENT

Good Models—The Qualities of Good Lettering—Simplicity — Distinctiveness — Proportion — Beauty of Form—Beauty of Uniformity—Right Arrangement —Setting Out & Fitting In—"Massed Writing" & "Fine Writing"—Even Spacing—Theory & Practice.

GOOD MODELS

IF lettering is to be rightly constructed and arranged, the study of good models is essential. Some of the writing and lettering in the old MSS., and the letters used on various old tombstones and brasses, weeded of archaisms, will be found almost perfect models. Yet to select one of these from the many which are "more or less" good, requires much discrimination.

It is suggested below that the essential virtues of good lettering are *readableness*, *beauty*, and *character*. If, then, we can discover some of the underlying qualities which make for these, our choice will at least be better considered, and instead of forming our

201

Good
Lettering—
Some
Methods of
Construction
& Arrange-
ment

"style" on the first type of letter that pleases, we shall found our work on a good model, full of possibilities of development.

The Roman Capital (Chap. XV.).—The ancestor of all our letters is in undisputed possession of the first place: but it is open to comparatively few to make a practical study of its monumental forms by means of cutting inscriptions in stone with a chisel.

The Pen-formed letters are more easily practised, and the mastery of the pen acquired in the practice of a root form—such as the half-uncial—is the key to the majority of alphabets (which are pen developed) and to those principles underlying the right construction and arrangement of lettering, which it is our business to discover.

Doubtless a "school" of lettering might be founded on any fine type, and a beautiful alphabet or fine hand might be founded on any fine inscription: but the practical student of penmanship may be sure of acquiring a knowledge of lettering which would be useful to any craftsman concerned with letters, be he printer, book-illustrator, engraver, or even inscription carver.

THE QUALITIES OF GOOD LETTERING

The first general virtue of lettering is *readableness*, the second, *fitness* for a given Use. And the rational basis of the following summary is the assumption that such *fitness* is comprised in *beauty* and *character*, and that a given piece of lettering having *readableness*, *beauty*, *and character* has the essential virtues of good lettering.

The qualities on which these virtues seem chiefly to depend, and their special significations in the case of plain writing, may be set forth as follows:—

Good
Lettering—
Some
Methods of
Construction
& Arrange-
ment

READABLENESS

RIGHT FORM

1. *Simplicity:* As having no unnecessary parts (and as being *simply* arranged: see 6).

2. *Distinctiveness:* As having the distinguishing characteristics of each letter strongly marked (and the words *distinctly* arranged: see 6).

3. *Proportion:* As having no part of a letter wrongly exaggerated or dwarfed (and as the lettering being *proportionally* arranged: see 6).

BEAUTY

4. *Beauty of Form:* As having beautiful shapes and constructions, so that each letter is an individual and living whole (not a mere collection of parts) fitted for the position, office, and material of the object bearing the inscription.

5. *Beauty of Uniformity:* As the assimilation of the corresponding parts — "bodies," "limbs," "heads"—and as the "family likeness" of the different letters, so that they go well together.

RIGHT ARRANGEMENT

6. *Beauty of Arrangement:* As having a general fitness in the placing, connecting, and spacing of letters, words, and lines, in the disposal of the lettering in the given space, and in the proportioning of every part of the lettering and its margins.

CHARACTER

RIGHT EXPRESSION

7. *Essential qualities of (Hand and Pen) work:* As being genuine calligraphy, the direct outcome of a rightly made and rightly handled *pen*. (See p. 242.)

8. *Freedom:* As having skilled and unaffected boldness. (See pp. 88, 291, 287, 333.)

9. *Personality:* As having the characteristics which distinguish one person's hand from another's. (See also pp. 242, 287.)

203

Good
Lettering—
Some
Methods of
Construction
& Arrange-
ment

This summary, while not presuming to define the *Virtues*, or achieve *Beauty* by a formula, does indicate some guiding principles for the letter-maker, and does suggest a definite meaning which may be given to the terms "Right Form," "Right Arrangement," and "Right Expression" in a particular craft.

It is true that "Readableness" and "Character" are comprised in *Beauty*, in the widest sense; but it is useful here to distinguish them: *Readableness* as the only sound basis for a practical theory of lettering, and *Character* as the product of a particular hand & tool at work in a particular craft.

The above table, therefore, may be used as a test of the qualities of any piece of lettering—whether Manuscript, Printing, or Engraving—provided that the significations of those qualities on which "Character" depends be modified and adapted to each particular instance. It is however a test for general qualities only—such as may help us in choosing a model: for as to its particular virtue each work stands alone—judged *by* its merits—in spite of all rules.

SIMPLICITY

(As having no unnecessary parts)

Essential Forms and their Characterisation.—The "Essential Forms" may be defined briefly as *the necessary parts* (see p. 239). They constitute the skeleton or structural plan of an alphabet; and *One of the finest things the letter-craftsman can do, is to make the Essential Forms of letters beautiful in themselves, giving them the character and finish which come naturally from a rightly handled tool.*

204

If we take the "Roman" types—the letters with which we are most familiar—and draw them in single pencil strokes (as a child does when it "learns its letters"), we get a rough representation of their Essential Forms (see diagram, fig. 142).

Such letters might be scratched with a point in wax or clay, and if so used in practice would give rise to fresh and characteristic developments,[1] but if we take a "square cut" pen which will give a thin horizontal stroke and a thick vertical stroke (figs. 10 and 40), it will give us the "*straight-pen,*" or simple written, essential forms of these letters (fig. 143).

These essential forms of straight-pen letters when compared with the plain line forms show a remarkable degree of interest, brought about by the introduction of the thin and thick strokes and gradated curves, characteristic of pen work.

Certain letters (A, K, M, N, V, W, X, Y, and k, v, w, x, y) in fig. 143 being composed chiefly of oblique strokes, appear rather heavy. They are lightened by using a naturally "slanted" pen which produces thin as well as thick oblique strokes. And the verticals in M and N are made thin by further slanting the pen (fig. 144).

To our eyes, accustomed to a traditional finish, all these forms—in figs. 143 and 144, but particularly the slanted pen forms—look incomplete and unfinished; and it is obvious that the thin strokes, at least, require marked terminals or *serifs.*

---

[1] In fact, our "small-letters" are the formalised result of the rapidly scratched *Square Capitals* of the Roman era (p. 33 & fig. 3).

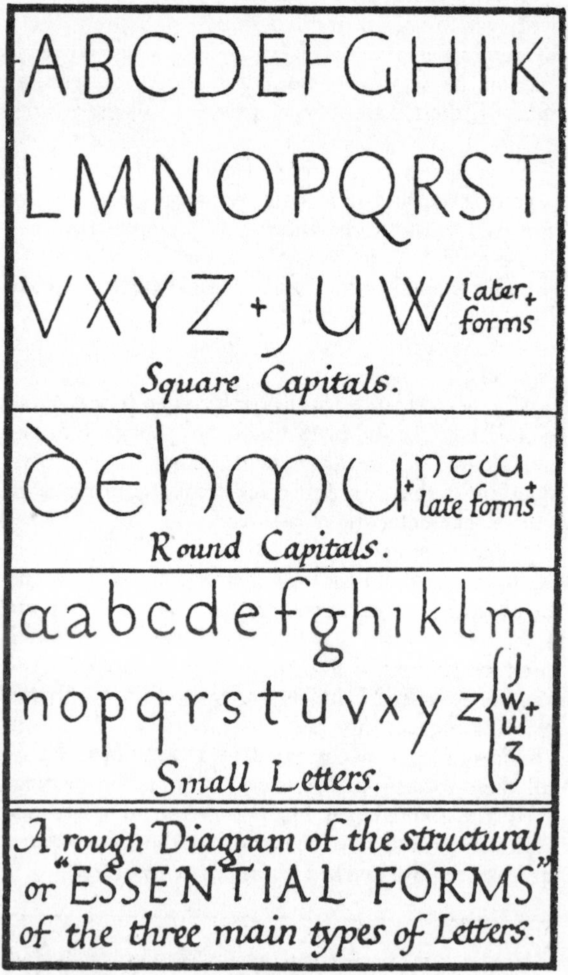

Good
Lettering—
Some
Methods of
Construction
& Arrange-
ment

ABCDEFGHIK

LMNOPQRST

VXYZ + JUW later + forms

Square Capitals.

ƆЄhmu + ntɯ + late forms

Round Capitals.

aabcdefghiklm

nopqrstuvxyz { J w + ɯ + 3

Small Letters.

A rough Diagram of the structural or "ESSENTIAL FORMS" of the three main types of Letters.

FIG. 142.

Good
Lettering—
Some
Methods of
Construction
& Arrange-
ment

ABCDEFGHI KLMNOPQRS TVXYZ&JUW

Square Capitals . (pen forms).

ⲆⲈⲎⲘⲨⲚⲦ

Round Capitals. (v. Uncials).

aabcdefghikl mnopqrst uvx yz&j w ա 3 *Small Letters.*

A Diagram of the "ESSENTIAL FORMS"
(of the three main types) AS
produced by a "straight Pen"

FIG. 143.

Good
Lettering—
Some
Methods of
Construction
& Arrange-
ment

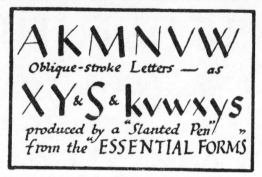

FIG. 144.

Finishing-Strokes.—The pen naturally produces a variety of finishing-strokes—"heads," "feet," serifs, &c.—each type of which strongly characterises the alphabet in which it is employed.

The main types (fig. 145) are—

(a) *Hooks or beaks.*

(b) *Straight (or curved) strokes,* thick or thin according to the direction of the pen.

(c) *Triangular "heads"* (and "feet"), straight or slanted, and more or less curved and sharpened.

(d) *Thin finishing-curves,* horizontal or oblique.

To give uniformity to the various letters of an alphabet it is necessary to treat similar parts as consistently as possible throughout (see No. 5, p. 203). And the remarkable way in which "heads" impart a "family likeness" to letters closely resembles the same phenomenon among human beings (see pp. 288, 218).

If we consider the four types of serif, *as applicable to straight-pen writing,* we find—

Good
Lettering—
Some
Methods of
Construction
& Arrangement

(a) *Hooks or Beaks*	Suitable only *for certain*
(d) *Thin Finishing-*	*parts of certain letters*
Curves	(and for *informal* writing).
(b) *Straight (or Curved)*	Informal (or Ornamental).
THIN Strokes	
(c) *Triangular*	Formal and capable of imparting great elegance and finish.
"Heads"	

For a formal, straight-pen writing, therefore, we may assume that a form of triangular head is, on

Fig. 145.

the whole, the most suitable, while some of the letters may be allowed to end naturally in finishing hooks and curves.

Good
Lettering—
Some
Methods of
Construction
& Arrange-
ment

Heads are easily built up at the ends of thick strokes, but some practice is required to enable a penman to make them on the thin strokes properly and skilfully. On the thin horizontals they are made with an almost continuous movement of the *point* of the nib from the thin stroke itself (see (*a*) to (*h*) fig. 146) closely resembling the termination

horizontal (a.)
& curve (b.)

pen turns here (c.)
on to left
half-nib point

(d.)
which
runs up

"head"
(or Serif)
filled in (e.)

Reverse head:
Above action
is reversed (f.)

Combined
head: Actions
combined (g.)

E. shewing
three heads
(h.)

Heads on obliques
(i) and on vertical
thins. (k.)

Heads on
vertical
thicks (l. m.)

FIG. 146.

of some of the thin strokes in the Irish half-uncial (Plate VI). On the thin oblique or vertical stems a thin crossing stroke is first made, and then shaped with the pen point to meet the stem (see *(i)* and *(k)* fig. 146).

We may write out the letters now with their suitable serifs, and we see that the Pen character and finish, given to the "Essential, or Skeleton, Forms" (fig. 142) result in a very formal and highly finished alphabet (fig. 147).

Slanted-pen characters and serifs (see fig. 145)—

(a) *Hooks or Beaks*
(d) *Thin Finishing-*
     Curves
} Suitable for most of the letters, but tending to be informal.

(b) *Straight (or Curved)*
     THICK Strokes
} Formal and strong.

(c) *Triangular Heads*
{ Formal and suitable for small-letters, and free capitals (see fig. 168).

The alphabets (fig. 148), produced from the skeleton forms (fig. 142) by the *slanted pen*, while not having such a conscious air of finish as the straight-pen letters, are much easier to write, and have in a greater degree the virtues of strong,[1] legible, natural penmanship.

They are eminently suitable for general MS. work (see p. 269) when the beginner has mastered an early form of round-hand (see pp. 36, 268).

DISTINCTIVENESS

(As having the distinguishing characteristics of each letter strongly marked)

The "*Characteristic Parts*" are those parts which most particularly serve to distinguish one letter from

---

[1] Their *greater strength* may not at first be apparent in fig. 148, as the nib used therefor is narrower, in proportion to the height of letter, than that used for fig. 147 (see also fig. 151).

Good
Lettering—
Some
Methods of
Construction
& Arrange-
ment

ABCDEFG
HIJKLMN
OPQRST&
UVWXYZ

abcdefghij
klmnopqrs
tuvwxyz;ȝ:

Formal types of Letters 1904
produced chiefly by "Straight"-PEN ✠

FIG. 147.

212

ABCDEFG
HIJKLMN
OPQRST&
UVWXYZ

abcdefghij
klmnopqrs
tuvwxyz:z:

Good
Lettering—
Some
Methods of
Construction
& Arrange-
ment

"Slanted-Pen" characterization of Letters.

FIG. 148.

Good
Lettering—
Some
Methods of
Construction
& Arrange-
ment

another (fig. 149). We should therefore, when constructing letters, give special attention to their

FIG. 149.

preservation, and sometimes they may even be accentuated with advantage—always with an eye to the life-history, or evolution, of the letter in question, and allowing for the influence of the special tool with which it is to be made (see *Proportion*, below, also *Roman characterisation*, p. 246).

214

PROPORTION

Good
Lettering—
Some
Methods of
Construction
& Arrange-
ment

(As having no part of a letter wrongly exaggerated or dwarfed—see pp. 238, 241-2)

The right proportioning of letters entails the

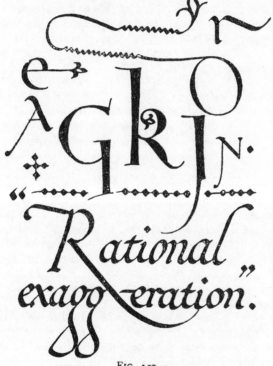

FIG. 150.

preservation of their Essential Forms and their Characteristic Parts, and, provided these are not

215

Good
Lettering—
Some
Methods of
Construction
& Arrange-
ment

seriously interfered with, a certain amount of exaggeration (and dwarfing)[1] is allowable in special
cases; particularly in ornamental writings, and Pen-
flourished capitals or terminal letters (see figs. 79
and 125).

Rational exaggeration usually amounts to the
drawing out or flourishing of tails or free stems, or
branches—very often to the magnifying of a *characteristic part* (see fig. 150, & pp. 214, 295). It is
a special form of decoration, and very effective if
used discriminately.

BEAUTY OF FORM

*(As having beautiful shapes and constructions, so that
each letter is an individual and living whole (not
a mere collection of parts) fitted for the position,
office, and material of the object bearing the inscription)*

To choose or construct beautiful forms requires
good taste, and that in its turn requires cultivation,
which comes from the observation of beautiful
forms. Those who are not accustomed to seeing
beautiful things are, in consequence, often uncertain whether they think a thing beautiful or not.
Some—perhaps all of us—have an intuition for
what is beautiful; but most of us have to achieve
beauty by taking pains.

At the least we are apt to be misled if we label
abstract forms as *essentially beautiful* or *essentially ugly*
—as by a mistaken *recipe* for beauty. For us as
craftsmen "achieving beauty by taking pains," means
acquiring skill in a special craft and adapting that

---

[1] The exaggeration of one part may be said *relatively* to dwarf
the other parts of a letter; but it is seldom advantageous, and
often not permissible, to dwarf part of a letter absolutely.

216

Good
Lettering—
Some
Methods of
Construction
& Arrange-
ment

skill to a special piece of work. And perhaps the surest way to learn, is to let our tools and materials teach us and, as it were, make beautiful shapes for us.

"*Inside Shapes.*"—The beauty of a letter depends very much on its inside shape—*i.e.* the shape of the space enclosed by the letter form. As this is often overlooked, it may be briefly referred to. Frequently when it seems difficult to say what is wrong with a piece of bad lettering, a glance at the inside shapes will reveal the fault. In *simple writing*, if the pen be properly cut and properly held, these shapes will generally take care of themselves, and internal angles

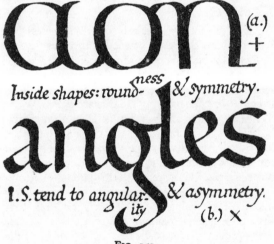

FIG. 151.

or asymmetrical lines which occur are characteristic of that particular form of penmanship, and not accidental (*b*, fig. 151).

217

Good
Lettering—
Some
Methods of
Construction
& Arrange-
ment

In making *Built-up* letters—which have both outer and inner strokes—the inner strokes should generally be made first (see p. 87).

Plain and Ornamental Forms.—Not only for the sake of readableness, but to promote a beautiful and dignified effect, the forms of letters are kept simple when the text is long. And, generally, the less frequent the type, the more ornamental may be its form (see pp. 92, 176, 262, 294).

BEAUTY OF UNIFORMITY

(As the assimilation of the corresponding parts— "bodies," "limbs," "heads"—and as the "family likeness," of the different letters, so that they go well together)

Right uniformity makes for readableness and beauty, and is the result of good craftsmanship.

Readableness.—Where the text letters are uniform, the reader is free to give his attention to the sense of the words, whereas the variations in an irregular or changing text are distracting.[1]

Beauty.—The abstract beauty-of-uniformity may be said to lie in this, that the different letters, or individual elements, *"go well together."* The beautiful effect of uniform lettering is thus caused by the united forces, as it were, of all the letters.

Good Craftsmanship.—A pen, or other letter-making tool, being handled freely and regularly, the uniform movements of the tool in similar cases will produce uniform strokes, &c. (On the other hand, the interruption and loss of freedom to the

---

[1] As when the construction of a part of some letter is peculiar (all the **y** or **g** *tails*, for example, catching the eye, and standing out on the page), or, as when promiscuous types are used, giving the impression of a confused crowd of letters.

writer who is irregular, or who forces an unnatural variety,[1] results in inferior work.)

RIGHT ARRANGEMENT

BEAUTY OF ARRANGE-MENT

(*As having a general fitness in the placing, connecting, and spacing of letters, words, and lines, in the disposal of the lettering in the given space, and in the proportioning of every part of the lettering and its margins*)

The particular fitness of a given inscription depends upon considerations of its particular *office, position, material,* &c. (see pp. 66, 315). For general use, however, the craftsman has certain regular modes of disposing and spacing the lettering, and proportioning the whole. And, as in constructing individual letters, so in treating lettering as a whole, he endeavours to give his work the qualities that make for readableness: viz. *simplicity, distinctiveness, and proportion.*

Simplicity in the Disposal of the Lettering.—For convenience of construction, reading, or handling, the simple, traditional arrangement of lettering is generally followed in dealing with flat surfaces (paper, vellum, &c.):[2]—

THE TEXT FORMING A RECTANGLE, CON-SISTING OF A NUM-BER OF EQUAL LINES

---

[1] *Variety.*—There is a variety both readable and beautiful (see pp. 176, 333), but it is founded on uniformity (and sincerity).

[2] "*Bands*" and symmetrical or asymmetrical *groups* of lettering adapted to the available space are used—usually as ornament—upon friezes, furniture, chests, book covers, flagons, dishes, and the like (see fig. 156 & p. 300). The special treatment of such things is a matter for the craftsman who makes them.

Good
Lettering—
Some
Methods of
Construction
& Arrange-
ment

Distinctiveness in the Spacing of the Lettering necessitates sufficient interspaces: the following common
spacing of Letters, Words, Lines, &c., may be
modified to suit special circumstances.

Letters, as a rule, are not equidistant, but their interspaces are
approximately equal (*a*, fig. 152).

Words, commonly *less than* one letter-space apart (*b* and *c*).

Lines of Capitals, frequently *half* (*d*) or *whole* (*e*) letter-height
apart. Lines of Small-Letters, commonly *ascenders* and
descenders just clearing (*f*).

Divisions of Text a clear line apart, or marked by a difference
in colour or size (see figs. 94, 96, 186, &c.).

*Proportion in the Treatment of the Whole Inscrip-
tion.*—The spacing-proportions referred to above
apply to lettering generally, but the proportions of
an *inscription as a whole* involve the consideration of
a special case. Example:—

The Proportions to be Considered in the Case of a
Manuscript Book (see pp. 66–74, 305, &c.).

(1) Size and shape of the Book and its page (proportion of width to height) (see p. 69).

(Set by custom, use of Book, size of material, &c.) (see figs. 69, 70, and pp. 67, &c.).

(2) Width of *Margins*—
Proportions—
  (*a*) to each other.
  (*b*) to size of page.
  (*c*) to the lettering.

(*a*) (Commonly about $1\frac{1}{2}:2:3:4$) (see fig. 70, and pp. 69–70).
(*b*) (Frequently about, or more than, *half the area of the page*).

(3) Size of *Writing*—
Proportion of height of letter to length of line.

(Set by page, and margin, and number of words in the line; usually more than *four* words to the line) (see pp. 73–4).

(4) Number of *lines*—
Proportion of text to page.

(Set by page, margin, and height-of-letter, and modified by treatment of *spacing*) (see pp. 74, 226).

(5) Size of *Large Capitals, Initials, &c.*

(Set by Small-Letter; commonly one, two, three, or more of the writing - line - spaces high) (see *footnote*, p. 187).

(6) Size of Decorative *Divisions* of the Text (marked by different treatment, colour, ornament, &c.).

(Set by page, &c.; usually such Division is relatively small or large—as a definite "heading," or a whole page) (see p. 98).

Good
Lettering—
Some
Methods of
Construction
& Arrange-
ment

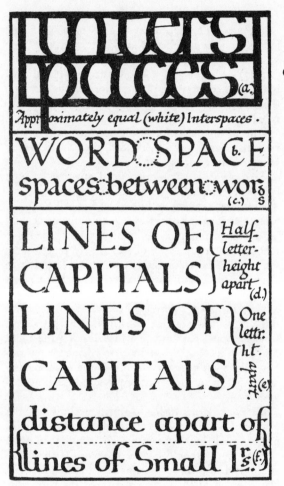

FIG. 152.

221

Good
Lettering—
Some
Methods of
Construction
& Arrange-
ment

Ruling.—The approximate sizes ommargins and letters, and the number of lines of text, having been estimated, guiding lines are ruled on the surface (see p. 307)—a right and a left vertical marginal line, with the necessary number of horizontals between them. (In the case of a manuscript, these lines are ruled faintly (or *grooved*), and are left to form a feature of the page; for inscriptions on other materials than paper, parchment, &c., they are generally removed after setting-out.)

Setting-out.—An inscription of any size, or one requiring complex or very nice arrangement, is set-out in faint, sketchy outline of lead pencil or chalk. *Simple writing* is not set-out, but such slight calculation or planning as is necessary is carried out mentally, or on a scrap of paper. By practice the scribe, like the compositor, can fit his lettering to the given space with ease and accuracy. For *writing* and (to a large extent) *printing*, both *combine setting-out and the act of "lettering" in one operation.* And this shoans how practice gives foreknowledge of the "mechanical" part of the work, leaving the mind free to take pleasure in its performance; and also how slight—if necessary at all—is the experimental *setting-out* of simple forms required by the practised workman.

Dividing Monosyllables.—In simple writing—the beauty of which depends on freedom rather than on precision—I think that even such an awkward word as "through" should not be broken. If the space at the end of a line is insufficient, it should be left blank, or be filled in with a dash of the pen. But in the case of words in LARGE CAPITALS, especially in title-pages and the like, where spacing is more difficult, and smooth reading less essential, any word may be divided at any point if the necessity is sufficiently obvious. But (even when the division is syllabic) breaking words, as interfering

Good Lettering—
Some
Methods of
Construction
& Arrange-
ment

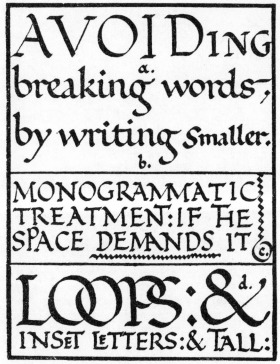

FIG. 153.

with the ease of reading, may often be avoided with advantage, and divisions which give accidental words, especially when they are objectionable, as

Good
Lettering—
Some
Methods of
Construction
& Arrange-
ment

"TH–ROUGH," or "NEIGH–BOUR," should not be
allowed. Among other ways of dealing with small
spaces, without breaking words, are the following:—

Ending with Smaller Letters.—The scribe is always at liberty to compress his writing *slightly*,
provided he does not spoil its readableness or beauty.
Occasionally, without harming either of these, a
marked difference in size of letter may be allowed;
one or more words, or a part of one, or a single letter,
being made smaller (*a*, *b*, fig. 153; see also Plate V).

Monogrammatic Forms, &c.—In any kind of lettering, but more particularly in the case of capitals,
where the given space is insufficient for the given
capitals, monogrammatic forms resembling the ordinary diphthong Æ may be used; or the stem of
one letter may be drawn out, above or below, and
formed into another (*c*, fig. 153).

Linking.—Letters which are large enough may
be linked or looped together, or one letter may be set
inside another, or free-stem letters may be drawn up
above the line (*d*, fig. 153, but see p. xxiv).

Tying up.—One or more words at the end of a
line of writing—particularly in poetry (see p. 61)—
may be "tied up," *i.e.* be written above or below the
line, with a pen stroke to connect them to it (fig. 67).

Care must be taken that none of these methods
lead to confusion in the reading. Their "Quaint-
ness"—as it is sometimes called—is only pleasing
when their contrivance is obviously made necessary.

"MASSED WRITING" & "FINE WRITING"

We may distinguish two characteristic modes of
treating an inscription, in which the treatment of
the letter is bound up with the treatment of the
spacing (fig. 154).

Good
Lettering—
Some
Methods of
Construction
& Arrange-
ment

And if I bestow all
my goods to feed
the poor, and if I
give my body that I
may glory, but have
not love, it profit=
eth me nothing ✠

Love suffereth long,
  and is kind ;
  love envieth not ;
love vaunteth not itself,
  is not puffed up,

FIG. 154

225

Good
Lettering—
Some
Methods of
Construction
& Arrange-
ment

"Massed Writing" (*Close Spacing*). The written or printed page is very commonly *set close*, or "massed," so that the letters support and enforce one another, their individual beauty being merged in and giving beauty to the whole. The closeness of the *letters* in each word keeps the *words* distinct, so that but little space is required between them,[1] and *the lines of writing are made close together* (ascending and descending stems being shortened, if necessary, for this purpose).

"Fine Writing" (*Wide Spacing*).—An inscription in "Fine Writing" may be spaced widely to display the finished beauty of the letters, or to give free play to the penman (or letter-craftsman). It consists generally of a number of *distinct lines of Writing* (or other lettering).

The two modes may be contrasted broadly, thus—

MASSED WRITING { Lines near together.	FINE WRITING { Lines spaced and separated.
Has an effect of richness, depending on tone of mass and close, even spacing.	Has an effect of elegance, depending on form of letter, and distinct arrangement of lines.
Simple method (for ordinary use); saving of time and space, ∴ suited for long inscriptions or small spaces.	Refined method (for special use); lavish of space and time, ∴ suited for large spaces or short inscriptions.
Lines generally of equal length, or if some fall short, end-fillings may be used—gaps are avoided if possible.	Lines may be of unequal length, giving irregular, right-hand edge, as in poetry (see p. 227)—gaps allowed on either side.

---

[1] By closing up the letters and the words one may generally avoid *"rivers"* or accidental spaces straggling through the text. The presence of "rivers" is at once made evident by slanting the page and looking along its surface, across the lines. Note, that whether the *lines* be close or wide, the inter-spacing of the *Small-Letters* does not vary very much.

Good
Lettering—
Some
Methods of
Construction
& Arrange-
ment

Ascending and descending stems — medium or short: serifs simple, and not strongly marked.	Stems—medium or long: long stems often a marked feature, ending in carefully made heads and feet, or flourishes.
Suited for slanted-pen forms of "gothic" tendency, and heavy, black writing (ex ample, "black letter").*	Suited for *straight and slanted* pen forms of "roman" tendency, and slender, light writing (ex., *light* "Italic").*
Requires generally contrasts of colour or weight (p. 294), and will bear more and heavier illumination (Line-fillings, Initials, Borders, &c.).	Allows variety in size of Letters (see pp. 262, 292): its typical treatment is as plain, *fine lettering* — better without heavy Borders, &c. (p. 263).

* NOTE.—Both modes are suited for *Roman Capitals and Small-Letters.*

These two modes may not have been recognised by the ancient letter-craftsmen: their comparison here is intended chiefly as a stimulus to definite thought, *not* as a hard-and-fast division of two "styles"; for there may be any number of possible compromises between them. In practice, however, it will be found convenient to distinguish them as *two modes of treating* LINES OF WRITING *which produce markedly different effects, the one, as it were, of* COLOUR, *the other of* FORM.

Plates XI, XIII, XIV, XV, XVII may be taken as examples of "Massed Writing," Plates IV., V, VI, VII, IX, (XXI) of "Fine Writing"; the other plates suggest compromises between the two.

Poetry (see p. 61), or any text consisting of, or which is conveniently broken up into, *unequal lines*, may be treated as "Fine Writing." There is no objection to a *straight left-hand edge* with an *irregular right-hand edge*,[1] where the cause of the irregularity

---

[1] The gaps on the right may be filled with line-finishings to preserve a "Massed" effect, but for many purposes this would be apt to look too ornamental (see pp. 171, 409).

Good
Lettering—
Some
Methods of
Construction
& Arrange-
ment

is natural and obvious, and no fault of the scribe's. Such an arrangement, or rather, *straightforward writing*, of poetry is often the best by virtue of its freedom and simplicity (see p. 335).

In many cases, however, a more formal and finished treatment of an irregular line text is to be preferred (especially in inscriptions on stone, metal, &c.), and the most natural arrangement is then an approximately symmetrical one, inclining to "Fine Writing" in treatment. This is easily obtained in inscriptions which are previously set-out, but a good plan—certainly the best for MSS.—is to sort the lines of the text into *longs* and *shorts* (and sometimes *medium* lines), and to set-in or indent the short lines two, three, or more letters. The indentations on the *left* balance the accidental irregularities on the *right* (fig. 154, and Plate IV), and given an appearance of symmetry to the page (see *Phrasing*, p. 348).

Either mode of spacing (*close* or *wide*) may be carried to an unwise or ridiculous extreme. "Leading" the lines of type was much in vogue a hundred years ago, in what was then regarded as "high-class" printing. Too often the wide-spaced line and "grand" manner of the eighteenth-century printer was pretentious rather than effective: this was partly due to the degraded type which he used, but form, arrangement, and expression all tended to be artificial. Of late years a rich, closely massed page has again become fashionable. Doubtless there has been a reaction in this from the eighteenth century to an earlier and better manner, but the effect is sometimes overdone, and the real ease and comfort of the reader has been sacrificed to his rather imaginary æstheticism.

By attaching supreme importance to readableness,

228

the letter-craftsman gains at least a rational basis for his work, and is saved from the snares which lurk in all, even in the best, modes and fashions.

EVEN SPACING

In the spacing of a given inscription on a limited surface, where a comparatively large size of letter is required, what little space there is to spare should generally be distributed evenly and consistently (*a*, fig. 155). Lavish expenditure of space on the margins would necessitate an undue crowding[1] of the lettering (*b*), and wide interspacing[2] would allow insufficient margins (*c*)—either arrangement suggesting inconsistency (but see p. 316).

NOTE.—*A given margin looks larger the heavier the mass of the text*,[3] and *smaller the lighter the mass of the text*. And, therefore, if lettering be spread out, as in "Fine Writing," the margins should be extra wide to have their true comparative value. The space available for a given inscription may in this way largely determine the arrangement of the lettering, comparatively *small* and *large* spaces suggesting respectively "*Massed Writing*" and "*Fine Writing*" (see p. 226).

In *certain decorative inscriptions*, where letters are merely treated as decorative forms—readableness

---

[1] In (*b*) fig. 155, the letters have been unintentionally narrowed. The natural tendency to do this forms another objection to such undue crowding.

[2] In (*c*) the letters have been unintentionally widened.

[3] *Experiment*.—Cut out a piece of dark brown paper the exact size of the body of the text in an entire page of this Handbook, viz. $5\frac{1}{16}$ inches by 3 inches, and lay it on the text: the tone of the brown paper being much darker than that of the print makes the margins appear wider.

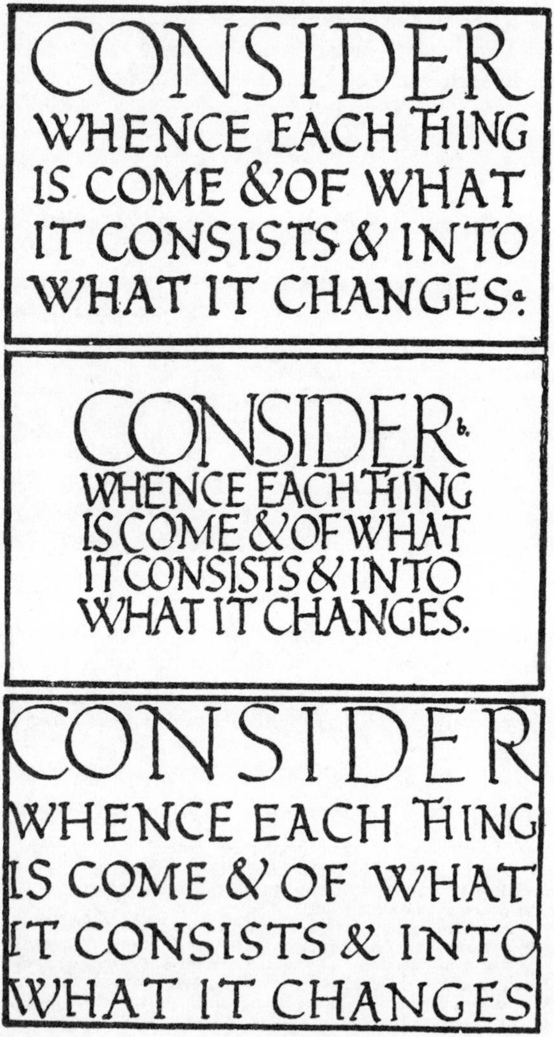

Good
Lettering—
Some
Methods of
Construction
& Arrange-
ment

CONSIDER
WHENCE EACH THING
IS COME & OF WHAT
IT CONSISTS & INTO
WHAT IT CHANGES:

CONSIDER.
WHENCE EACH THING
IS COME & OF WHAT
IT CONSISTS & INTO
WHAT IT CHANGES.

CONSIDER
WHENCE EACH THING
IS COME & OF WHAT
IT CONSISTS & INTO
WHAT IT CHANGES

FIG. 155.

being a matter of little or no moment—the treatment of the spacing is adapted to a particular surface; and, for example:—

THE LETTERS MAY BE KEPT VERY

CLOSE, FORMING ORNAMENTAL

BANDS, THO' THE LINES MAY BE

WIDELY SPACED AND LEGIBLE.

OR THE LETTERS
MAY BE FAR APART
& THE LINES CLOSE,
TO COVER SURFACES.

Fig. 156.

THEORY & PRACTICE

The above discussion of theories and "rules" for the construction and arrangement of good lettering is intended to suggest some useful methods—not to provoke excessive fitting or planning, but rather to avoid it. Straightforwardness is perhaps the greatest virtue in a craft, and whatever "rules" it may break through, it is refreshing and charming.

An excellent example for the scribe or inscription maker is the method of an early printer, who had only four or five sorts of type—say, "Small-Letters" and "Capitals" (Roman and Italic) and "Large Capitals," and who, without any elaborate "design," simply put his types into their proper places, and then

231

Good
Lettering—
Some
Methods of
Construction
& Arrange-
ment
pulled off his pleasant sheets of "commonplace" printing.

The scribe should choose the best and simplest forms and arrangements, and master them before going further; he should have a few definite types "at his finger tips," and, for everyday use, a matter-of-course way of putting them down on paper.

Ambiguity is one of the greatest faults in a craft. It comes often from vague ambitions. One may be inspired by good ambitions, but the immediate concern of the craftsman is to know what he is capable of doing at the present, and to do it.

Let the meaning of your work be obvious unless it is designed purely for your own amusement. A good craftsman seeks out the *commonplace* and tries to master it, knowing that "originality" comes of necessity, and not of searching.

CHAPTER XV

THE ROMAN ALPHABET & ITS DERIVATIVES

The Roman Alphabet—Proportions of Letters: Widths —Upper & Lower Parts—Essential or Structural Forms — Characterisation of Forms — Built-Up Forms — Simple - Written Capitals — Uncials — Capitals & Small-Letters—Early, Round, Upright, Formal Hands — Slanted - Pen Small - Letters — Roman Small - Letters — Italics — Semi - Formal Hands—Of Formal Writing Generally—Decorative Contracts—Ornamental Letters.

THE ROMAN ALPHABET

THE Roman Alphabet is the foundation of all our alphabets (see Chapter I). And since the full development of their monumental forms about 2000 years ago, the Roman Capitals have held the supreme place among letters for readableness and beauty. They are the best forms for the grandest and most important inscriptions, and, in regard to lettering generally, a very good rule to follow is: *When in doubt, use Roman Capitals.*

The penman may with advantage devote some study to a fine monumental type of Roman Capital (such as that of the Trajan Column Inscription: Plates I and II), and endeavour to embody its virtues in a *built-up pen form* for use in MSS. (p. 258).

PROPORTIONS OF LETTERS: WIDTHS

The marked distinction between the "Square" and the "Round" forms, and the varying widths of the letters—as seen in the early inscriptions,[1] are *characteristic* of the Roman Alphabet. We may broadly distinguish *Wide* and *Narrow* letters thus—

WIDE {
    O Q C G D   *"Round."*

    M W

    H (U) A N V T (Z) } *"Square."*
}

NARROW {
    B E F R S Y (X)

    I J

    K L P
}

---

[1] Such inscriptions contrast favourably with that nineteenth-century style in which it was customary to make every letter occupy the same space and look as much like its neighbour as possible.

The "Round" Wide Letters—O, Q, C, G, D.—
O may be regarded as the Key letter of an
alphabet. Given an O and an I of any
alphabet, we can make a very good guess at the
forms of the other letters.

In fine Inscriptions the external line of O is
commonly an almost perfect circle (see Plate II)
—*i.e.* its height and width are equal. This may be
regarded as the ideal shape, though a slight widening or narrowing of the letter (fig. 157) is quite
permissible.[1]

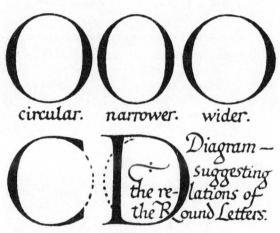

circular. narrower. wider.

Diagram—
suggesting
the re-lations of
the Round Letters.

Fig. 157.

Q, C, G, and D follow the proportions of O

---

[1] NOTE.—There is less danger of spoiling letters by narrowing
them than by widening, because the limits to the *possible* narrowing of a letter are more obvious than the limits to its *possible*
widening. Further, when letters are widened there is a tendency to thicken their parts and make them heavy and vulgar.

234

very nearly, and, though C, G, D are a little narrower, they have the same effect of roundness and
width.

The *"Square" Wide Letters*—*M*, *W*, *and H*,
(*U*), *A*, *N*, *V*, *T*, (*Z*)—

M & W   Their mean width is properly
about equal to their height.

H   Width equal to, or a little less than, height
(fig. 158), but if made too narrow it would
look heavy, being *double-stemmed*.

U   (see pp. 251, 248) resembles H.

A, N, & V   are *double-stemmed*, and have
internal angles, moreover,
which would become too sharp—and tend to close

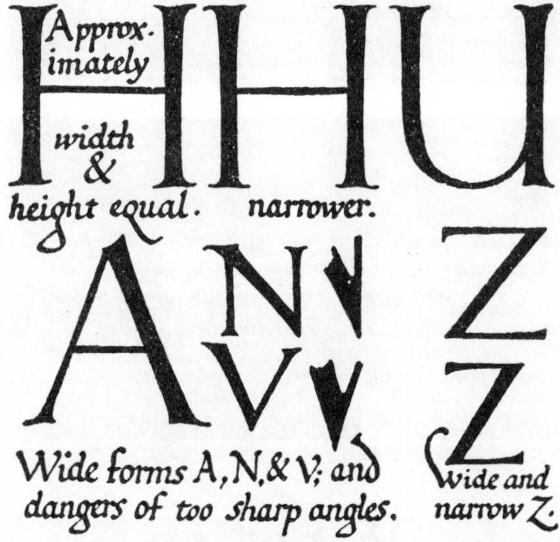

Wide forms A, N, & V; and
dangers of too sharp angles.   wide and
narrow Z.

FIG. 158.

235

up—if they were made too narrow (fig. 158).

T The cross-bar—the *characteristic part* of T —projects a fair way on either side of the stem.

Z Either *wide* or (moderately) *narrow* (fig. 158).

The Narrow Letters, B, E, F, R, S, Y (X) (see fig. 159).

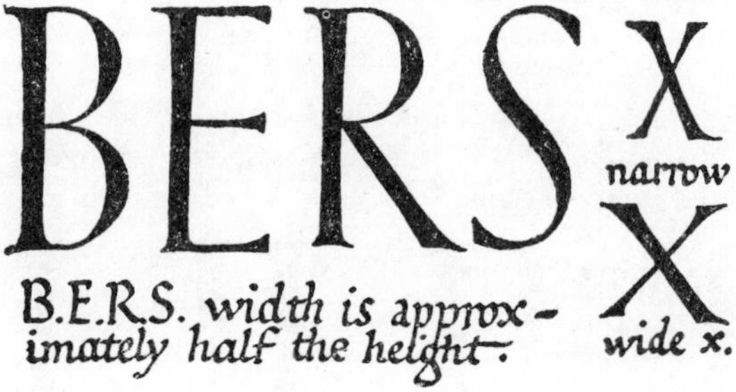

BERS X *narrow* X

B.E.R.S. width is approx-imately half the height.

wide x.

FIG. 159.

There is a point of division in these letters about the middle of the stem or a little above (see p. 237), and we may argue that each being composed, as it were, of two little letters—which are *half-height*, they are proportionate *half-width:* and this will be found approximately correct. B may be said to consist of one little D on the top of another, averaging respectively *half* the height and width of a full-sized D.

E, F, & R follow the proportions of B (see also E, 4, p. 246).

236

S may be made of one little *tilted* O on the top of another—joined together and having the superfluous parts removed.

Y is like a little V upon a little I.

X Either *narrow* or *wide* (fig. 159).

The Narrow letters, K, L, and P—

These forms are related to the B, E forms, but it is permissible to make them a little wide to give clearance to the angles of the K and force to the single *arm* and *loop*—the characteristic parts (see fig. 149)—of L and P.

UPPER & LOWER PARTS

In the letters B, E, H, K, X (A), F, R, P (S), Y there is generally a tendency to enlarge the lower part, the cross-bar—or division—being set above mid-height. This tendency may reasonably be accounted for as follows:—

The natural division of B, E, H, K, & X, regarded as abstract forms, would be symmetrical—*i.e.* at the centre of the stem.[1] In order that its *apparent position* may be central, however, it is necessary, for optical reasons, to make

---

[1] The primitive forms of these letters were vertically symmetrical, I believe.

its actual position above the centre.[1]   And further, by a reasonable enlargement of the lower part, these letters acquire a greater appearance of stability.

It would be well, I think, for the letter-craftsman to begin by making such divisions at the *apparent centre* (*i.e.* very slightly above mid-height; see E, F, X, Plate II), so keeping most nearly to the *essential forms* (see p. 239). Later he might consider the question of stability (see B, Plate II). The exaggerated raising (or lowering) of the division associated with "Art Lettering" is illegible and ridiculous.

A The lower part is essentially bigger, and the cross-bar is not raised, as that would make the top part disproportionately small.

F usually follows E, but being asymmetrical and open below it may, if desired, be made with the bar at—or even slightly below—the actual centre.

R In early forms the bow was frequently rather large (see Plate II), but it is safer to make the tail—the characteristic part—more pronounced (see Plates III, XXIV).

P The characteristic part of P is the bow, which may therefore be a little larger than the bow of R (see Plate III).

S In the best types of this letter the upper and lower parts are approximately equal; there is a tendency slightly to enlarge the lower

---

[1] It is interesting to note in this connection that the eye seems to prefer looking upon the *tops* of things, and in reading, is accustomed to run along the *tops* of the letters—not down one stroke and up the next. This may suggest a further reason for smaller upper parts, viz. the *concentration* of as much of the letter as possible in the upper half.

part. (In Uncial and early round-hands the *top* part
was larger: see Plates IV to VII.)

Y varies: the upper part may be less than that
of X, or somewhat larger.

ESSENTIAL OR STRUCTURAL FORMS

The *essential or structural forms* (see p. 204) *are
the simplest forms which preserve the characteristic
structure, distinctiveness, and proportions of each individual letter.*

The letter-craftsman must have a clear idea of
the *skeletons* of his letters. While in every case the
precise form which commends itself to him is matter
for his individual choice, it is suggested in the
following discussion of a typical form—the Roman
B—that the rationale of his selection (whether
conscious or unconscious) is in brief *to determine
what is* ABSOLUTELY *essential to a form, and then how
far this may be amplified in the direction of the* PRACTI-
CALLY *essential.*

The letter B reduced to its simplest (*curved-bow*) form—*i.e.*
to the bare necessity of its distinctive structure—comprises a
perpendicular stem spanned by two equal, circular bows (*a*, fig. 160).
In amplifying such a form for practical or æsthetic reasons,
it is well as a rule not to exceed one's object—in this case to
determine a reasonable (though arbitrary) standard essential
form of B, having a distinctive and proportionate (*f*) structure.
We may increase the arcs of the bows till their width is nearly
equal to their height (*b*), make their outer ends meet the ends
of the stem (*c*), and their inner ends coincide (*d*). Raising the
division till its *apparent position* is at or about the middle of the
stem entails a proportionate increase of width in the lower part,
and a corresponding decrease in the upper part (*e*).

The very idea of an essential form excludes the
*un*necessary, and its further amplification is apt to
take from its *distinctiveness* and legibility. Where

239

no limits are set, modification is apt to become
exaggeration. And, though special forms and

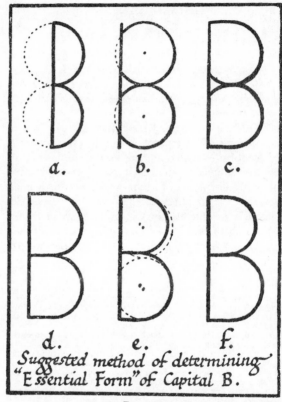

a.   b.   c.

d.   e.   f.

*Suggested method of determining
"Essential Form" of Capital B.*

FIG. 160.

ornamental letters may be produced by "reasonable
exaggeration" (*k*, *l*, *m*, fig. 161), if the tool be kept

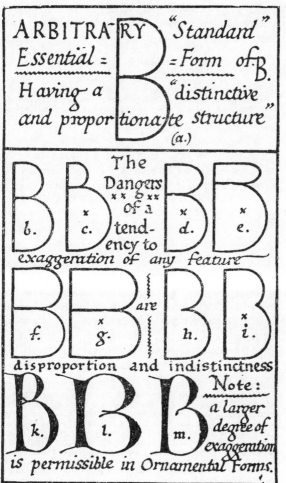

The

ARBITRARY "Standard"
Essential =
Having a = Form of B.
and proportionate structure"
(a.)

B.

Dangers
xx o xx
Of a
tend-
ency to
b. c. d. e.

exaggeration of any feature

are

f. g. h. i.

disproportion and indistinctness

Note:
a larger
degree of
exaggeration
k. l. m.

is permissible in Ornamental Forms.

FIG. 161.

241

under proper control, yet, generally, such *structural* changes do not improve the appearance of the plain letter forms.

We may test our "Standard" (*a*, fig. 161) by considering the effects of further amplification.

(1) *Raising the division* [1] slightly is permissible (*b*, fig. 161)—too much makes the top part disproportionately small (*c*).

(2) *Widening both bows*, or *separating their junction from the stem*, tends to dissociate the bows from the stem, making the letter less distinctive (*g* and *i*, fig. 161).

Widening and narrowing are both allowable and occasionally desirable, but assuming that a standard or ideal width can be approximately determined, it is well to keep to it for common and ordinary use.

CHARACTERISATION OF FORMS

(See also Built-Up Forms, pp. 255–60, & pp. 204, 217)

That the tool [2] gives character and finish to the Essential Forms of letters, can easily be proved by a little practical experience of the natural action of a properly cut pen (see figs. 142 to 148, and 162). And the penman—or indeed any other letter-maker—is advised to allow the pen to train his hand to

---

[1] The extremely beautiful and finished B in the "Trajan Alphabet" (Plate II) has the division a little higher, and a marked enlargement of the lower part; until the letter-craftsman can approach the perfection of its execution he will find a simpler form more suitable for his "standard." A curious form, in which the top lobe has nearly or quite disappeared (*comp. c*, fig. 161), is found in early Roman inscriptions. This form (which may have helped to give us the useful small **b**) is not suitable for a modern Capital, and would lack the *distinctiveness* of B.

[2] *Chisel-made* Roman Capitals (possibly influenced by *brush*, &c., pp. 256, 355), Plates I, II: (modern), XXIV. *Pen-made* Plates III, XVIII: (modern), figs. 147, 148, 167, 168, &c.

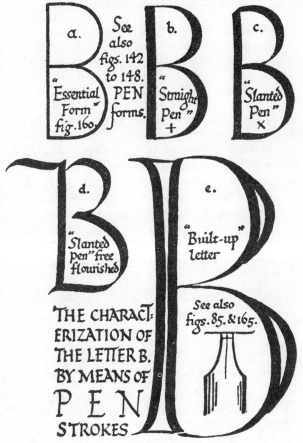

a. See also figs. 142 to 148. PEN forms.

"Essential Form" fig. 160.

b. "Straight Pen" +

c. "Slanted Pen" ×

d. "Slanted pen" free flourished

THE CHARACTERIZATION OF THE LETTER B. BY MEANS OF PEN STROKES

e. "Built-up" letter

See also figs. 85. & 165.

FIG. 162.

243

make the proper strokes automatically: then he may begin to master and control the pen, making it conform to his hand and so produce Letters which have every possible virtue of penmanship and are as much his own as his common handwriting.

Most of the letters in a good alphabet have specially interesting or *characteristic parts* (p. 214), or they exhibit some general principles in letter making, which are worth noting, with a view to making good letters, and in order to understand better the manner in which the tool—whether pen, chisel, or brush—should be used.

The characterisation of the Roman Capital Form.
NOTE.—*The large types below are* indices—*not models.*

A 1. A pointed form of A, M, and N (see Plate II) may be suitable for inscriptions in stone, &c., but in pen work the top is preferably *hooked* (fig. 167), *beaked* (fig. 147), or *broken* (fig. 158), or specially marked in some way, as this part (both in Capital A and small **a**) has generally been (fig. 189).

2. The oblique strokes in A, K, M, N, R, V, W, X, Y, whether thick or thin, are naturally finished with a short point *inside* the letter and a long, sharp point, or *beak, outside* (see serifs of oblique strokes, p. 253).

3. The thin stem may be drawn out below for an occasional form (see F, 3).

B 1. B, D, R, and P are generally best made *round-shouldered* (fig. 162 & *Addenda*, p. xxiv).

2. B, D, E, F, P, R (and T) have generally an *angle* between the stem and the top horizontal, while

3. *below* in B, D, E (and L) the stem curves or
blends with the horizontal.

4. See O, 2.

C 1. C, G, (and *round* ∈) may have the
top horizontals or 'arms' made straighter
than the lower arms (see fig. 187).

2. C, G, S, &c.; the *inside* curve is generally best continuous—from the 'bow' to
the ends of the 'arms'—not being broken by the
serifs (except in special forms and materials), and

3. it is best to preserve an unbroken inside curve
at the termination of all free arms and stems in
built-up Roman Capitals. In C, G, S, E, F, L,
T, and Z the upper and lower arms are curved on
the *inside*, and squared or slightly pointed outside
(the vertical stems curve on either side) (fig. 163).

4. 'Arms' are best shaped and curved rather
gradually out to the terminal or serif, which then is
an actual part of the letter, not an added lump
(p. 253).

5. See O, 2.

D 1. See B, 1.

2. See B, 2 and 3.

3. The curve may be considered as
springing from the foot of the stem, and
may therefore for an occasional form be
separated from the stem at the *top* (*D*, fig. 177).

4. See O, 2.

E 1. See B, 2 and 3.

2. See C, 3 and 4.

3. The lower limb in E, L (and Z) is
often drawn out: these, however, are properly to be regarded as *occasional* or *special*

245

forms: the lower serif of this type commonly points
out (see figs. 206, 188).

4. E's three *arms* (& F's two) are approximately
equal in length in the best early forms (Plate II, &c.).

F
1. See B, 2.
2. See C, 3 and 4 (and E, 4 *above*).
3. The development and traditions of each
letter being considered, nearly all of the
free stems of A, F, G, H, I, J, K, L, M,
N, P, R, T, V, W, X, Y may be drawn out for
occasional forms (see fig. 188).

4. The elongated stems of F, I, J, P, T, Y may
hang below the line, or they may (occasionally)
stand on the line and overtop the other letters.

G
1. See C, 1, 2, 3, and 4.
2. The stem may be drawn out below
the line (F, 3).
3. The stem sometimes forms an
angle with the lower 'arm' (this is
safest: see fig. 148), sometimes they blend (fig. 147).

4. The point of the lower 'arm' may project a
very little beyond the stem to mark the *outer* angle.

5. The round "gothic" G (as also the other
"*round*" letters: p. 85) may generally be used
freely together with the "*square*" Roman Capitals.
6. See O, 2.

H
1. The *left-hand* stem is occasionally
drawn out above (F, 3 & *comp*. fig. 3), and
2. this form is sometimes associated
with an ornamental cross-bar (fig. 189).
3. H and N may slightly widen out
above.

246

I 1. The stem may be drawn out above
(see Plate XXIV) or below (F, 3 and 4).
2. See J, 2.

J 1. The stem or tail may be drawn out (F,
3 and 4).
2. NOTE.—With regard to the use of I for
J (and V for U):[1] this—the classical Latin
usage—is correct (for the capital forms) in a
modern Latin inscription. But for modern English,
in which these letters are strongly differentiated, the
tailed J and the round U are to be preferred. Besides the suspicion of affectation attaching to the
other mode, its strangeness gives an appearance of
awkwardness—almost amounting to illegibility—
to common words, such as "A QVAINT IVG"
or "IAM IAR." And, at the least, very careful

---

[1] J. C. Egbert in an "Introduction to the Study of Latin
Inscriptions" says, "*J was not specialised as a letter until the 15th
Century.*" It would seem that in early inscriptions a tall I
was frequently used for J *between* vowels, and for I at the *beginnings* of words: later, while the medial I remained straight, the
initial form was curved to the left and used for both I and J; this
curved initial form, J, at length became identified with the
letter J.

Similarly, it appears that V was used for an initial, and U
for a medial; and later, the V form became identified with
the consonant.

In the words 𝕵𝖓 𝖇𝖎𝖌𝖎, 𝖓𝖆𝖙𝖎𝖚 in fig. 95, the
initial I is curved like a J, while the medial i's are straight;
the *initial* V has a v form, while the medial V in *nativ(itatis)* has
a u form.

247

discrimination is desirable: "IVBILATE" may pass, but "IVIVBE" is not really readable.

3. The tail of the J may be slight, provided it be distinct, and the second stem of the U may match the first (fig. 158); the ugly J and U in common use need not be copied.

4. See also *Tails*, pp. 253–5.

K 1. The stem is sometimes drawn out above (F, 3).

2. Both arms are occasionally lengthened, and the width of the letter increased, by joining the thin arm to the stem lower down; the thick arm, or tail, then springs from the side of the thin arm (*compare* R). This tends away from the essential, and is therefore a less safe form.

3. The tail may be curved or drawn out occasionally (see *Tails*, pp. 253–5).

4. Serifs on *arms*. See A, 2.

L 1. See B, 3.
2. See C, 3 and 4.
3. See E, 3.
4. See F, 3 (*compare* LL *Appendix* p. xxii).

M 1. The stems are commonly slightly spread out to give greater clearance for the inner angles. An occasional form is widely spread Λ. The v part being shortened M, or widened M, has a like effect.

2. NOTE.—There are inscriptional forms of M

248

and N without the top serif (Plate II). But the pen forms and others have top serifs, and these commonly extend *outward*—tending to *beaks* (see A, 1 and 2)—rather than *in*. (V, W, X, Y (and N) show a similar tendency—see p. 253.)

3. The thin stem of M is occasionally drawn out (F, 3).

N 1. See C, 3 and 4.
   2. See H, 3.
   3. See M, 2, and A, 1 and 2.
   4. The first stem is drawn out below the line for an occasional form (most suitable for an Initial Letter): the right-hand stem is very occasionally raised (when a final letter) (F, 3).

5. NOTE.—The stems of N (the only vertical *thins*—not counting M's—in the Roman Capitals) tend sometimes to be thicker: see Plate II.

O 1. O is the key letter of the curved forms and, in a sense, of the whole alphabet (p. 234). The upright form—

O — may be regarded as the ideal simple letter.

2. Very commonly, however, O is tilted— O —(see fig. 163), and when this is the case, all the curved letters—B, C, D, G, P, Q, R, S, U—*are correspondingly tilted* (see Plate II). The tilted form is more easily made, but both are good forms.

P 1. See B, 1 and 2.
   2. See O, 2.
   3. (P with stem below line (see Plate IV) must not be allowed to confuse with D) (see F, 3 and 4).

249

4. The bow of P appears to be attached (to the stem) *above*: in certain forms it is slightly separated from the stem *below*: see Plate II.

1. Q resembles O with a tail: see O.

2. There are many characteristic varieties of the tail: see *Tails* (pp. 253–5).

3. NOTE.—Q being always followed by U, it is convenient often to deal with the two letters together. (See Plate II.)

1. See B, 1 and 2.

2. See O, 2.

3. In the form nearest the essential, the junction of the Bow and the Tail touches the stem. If the tail springs from the curve of the bow (Plate II) greater care in construction is necessary (compare K). The treatment of the tail is very important. It may end in a serif (see A, 2), or it may be curved and pointed (see *Tails*, pp. 253–5). It may be drawn out (see fig. 150).

4. See F, 3 (& *conf.* fig. 169).

1. See C, 2, 3, and 4.

2. See O, 2 (and p. 237).

3. S very often leans slightly forward.

1. See B, 2.

2. See C, 3 and 4.

3. Drawing out of stem: see F, 3 and 4.

4. NOTE.—The *right arm* is occasionally extended—to fill a line—when T is a terminal letter (in this case it is generally made lighter, and the left arm heavier—somewhat as in the Uncial T, figs. 56 & 188).

U 1. NOTE.—The curve—if it be modelled on the common tilted O (see O, 2)—is thin where it meets the second stem.

2. (V for U). See J, 2, 3, and footnote.

3. The *foot* of the second stem projects on the right only, and gives clearance to the angle of the curve on the left. Sometimes the second stem ends in a *hook* or *beak*, which (very occasionally) is drawn out below.

V 1. See M, 2, and A, 2.

2. The *thick* stem may be drawn up (F, 3), in which case the *thin* commonly curves over for strength (see figs. 89, 95).

3. (See note on V for U, under J.)

W 1. See M, 2, and A, 2.

2. The best form is of two V's crossed, W.

3. The first or both the *thick* stems may be drawn up and the thins curved over (see V, 2).

X 1. See M, 2, and A, 2.

2. There is sometimes a slight curving in of the stems, especially the thin stem (see fig. 80).

3. The thin stem is sometimes drawn out below (F, 3), and commonly curved.

Y 1. See M, 2, and A, 2.

2. See F, 3 and 4. (Y with stem below line (see Plate V) must not be allowed to confuse with V.)

3. An occasional rather interesting form

251

of Y has the arms curving out and ending in points (see fig. 167).

Z 1. See C, 3 and 4.

2. The lower arm of Z is sometimes drawn out (see E, 3): it may be curved and pointed (or flourished).

General Remarks on the characterisation of Roman Capitals and related forms, illustrated in fig. 163.[1]

VERTICAL STEMS.—(*a*, fig. 163) *Thick* (excepting in the thin stemmed N and M).

(*b*) *Slightly curved* in on either side (see fig. 116), or appearing so because of the outward curve of the serifs (see figs. 204, 206).

(*c*) A fine effect is obtained when the stem is made *wider above* than below (see p. 85).

(*d*) Free stems occasionally are *drawn out* (see above, F, 3 and 4, and pp. 215, 224, 296).

OBLIQUE STROKES or STEMS.—In A, K, &c., from the left \ *thick*, to the right / *thin*—otherwise like VERTICAL STEMS (above), see also SERIFS (*e*) (below).

HORIZONTALS, ARMS, BRANCHES, or BARS.—*Thin:* free ends sometimes drawn out and flourished (see figs. 125, 188).

BOWS and CURVES.—Gradated, and following the O (see pp. 10, 87, 234, 249).

SERIFS or FINISHING STROKES. — (*a*) NOTE.—*Terminals* of some sort are practically essential to the proper characterisation of an alphabet (see figs. 147, 148, 162), and should generally have a certain uniformity (p. 288).

---

[1] The more *ornamental* treatment of *Stems, Bows, Serifs, Tails.* &c., is referred to in p. 295, and in figs. 188, 189.

(*b*) The serifs, &c., of simple-written forms are treated at p. 208 (see fig. 145).

(*c*) In *Versals* and certain other forms the mode of making requires the serif to be a distinct addition to the letter (see figs. 116, 166).

(*d*, fig. 163) In the finest *built-up* A B Cs serifs are treated as the actual finishing and shaping of the ends of the *stems and branches*, rather than as added parts (see C, 3 & 4, p. 245 and p. 204). This particularly affects the construction of the thin strokes (see figs. 165, 167).

(*e*) *The serifs of the oblique strokes* in A, K, M, N, R, V, W, X, Y are commonly not placed centrally, but projecting in the direction of the stroke (*i.e.* away from the letter, thus: ✕), branching out from the parent stem (see *tails*, below), and avoiding an acute angle (as ⟍). This has tended to produce *hooks* and *beaks* (see fig. 163), which are often used for the oblique strokes, particularly of A and N (see figs. 189, 158), and the tails of K and R (see below).

(*f*) There is a similar natural tendency to *hook* or *flourish* the terminals of *vertical stems* on the left, particularly of B, D, I, J, K, L, P, R; less often of E, F, H. A very interesting and beautiful effect may be obtained by delicately curving down the upper serifs on *the left* (like thin *beaks*). Such serifs are sometimes very slightly *turned up on the right*, and it may be noted that this tendency of the "horizontals" to *curve up and forward* ⌣ is natural and characteristic of freely made, vigorous lettering (see Uncial T, pen dashes, &c., figs. 169, 125, &c.).

TAILS.—(*a*) The tails of K, Q, R (and J)—

FIG. 163.

254

and the strokes in A, F, G, I, M, N, P, Y, &c., which may be drawn out tail-wise—play an important part in the right construction, and the occasional decoration, of plain lettering. They may end either in *serifs* or in *curves* (see *SERIFS* (*e*), above, and fig. 188).

(*b*) NOTE.—It is a characteristic of vigorous forms that *branches, &c., stand out well from their stems* (pp. 185, (*e*) 253, (N) 235), and a good tail should stand out well from the letter (K, Q, fig. 167).

(*c*) An excellent form of tail for ordinary use, combining strength and grace, consists of a (strong) *straight stroke* ending more or less abruptly in a (graceful) *finishing curve*.

(*d*) An extraordinarily long tail requires a slight double curve to take off its stiffness.

(*e*) A good tail may be made by the addition of a double curved stroke on the under side of a straight tail (or of a single curve above).

(*f*) In treating the tail of J, or the drawn-out stems of A, F, G, I, M, N, P, Y, it is important to preserve the essential straightness of the stems. Therefore, if a *finishing curve* be used, its size is related to the length of the straight stroke, and, unless this be extraordinarily long, the curve is usually made rather small and abrupt. A curve which is too large is apt to weaken the form and "pull it out of the straight" (*g*, fig. 163).

BUILT-UP FORMS

Built-up Letters are composed of compound strokes (*c*, *d*, fig. 164); *Simple-written Letters* of simple strokes (*a*, *b*).

The Pen being *an instrument which produces*

definite thick and thin strokes on a smooth surface, is perfectly adapted to the construction of either simple or compound forms; *other tools*, such as the stylus, needle, graver, &c., *produce various scratches, stitches, or cuts, generally of the nature of rather varying thin strokes*, and to produce thick strokes a *building-up* process is required.

In making built-up forms the control exerted by the tool is less obvious, and more depends upon the craftsman, who must therefore use greater care and judgment. Not only is it possible, but, occasionally, it may be desirable to depart from the more obvious tool-forms; though generally the more simply and naturally *tool-made* a form is, the better it is.

The fine early inscriptions are supposed to have been first *drawn* or *painted* (in outline) and then cut into the stone. The *chisel forms* were doubtless affected in this way by *brush* (and indirectly by *pen*) *forms*, but these were of the simplest—nothing was sketched in that was unfitted for the chisel to make into a natural and true *chisel-form*.

The action of the brush or "pencil" to a certain extent resembles that of the pen, but their effects are really distinct. In contrasting pen-made and brush-made letters, we may observe that *a pen form tends to abrupt changes from thin to thick: a brush form to gradation* (fig. 164). The pen particularly affects curved strokes (*comp. a & b*), generally making them more quick and abrupt (or even *broken*, see * * *c*), than brush curves. The brush will give more graceful and finished but less uniform letters (see p. 340).

The character of a pen-letter depends greatly on the *nib-width* (p. 288), and *narrow, medium,*

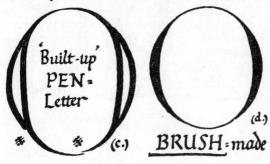

Simple-written PEN curves

'Built-up'
PEN=
Letter

(c.)

BRUSH=made

(d.)

FIG. 164.

or *broad* nibs are used according to the type of letter
required.

A narrow nib may be used for special (built-up)
Initials and Capitals, which are *drawn* rather than
written (*a*, fig. 165). The horizontal arms (made
by the pen held horizontally) are markedly affected,
and if a very fine nib were used, the necessity of
strengthening and thickening them would tend
further to reduce the pen character.

A broad nib gives strong, uniform pen-letters
(*b*).

For ordinary use letters are perhaps best made
with a "medium" nib (*c*). The width of the

257

ordinary writing-pen, or rather narrower, gives a
good proportion for initials, &c. (see pp. 84, 184).

(a.)   (b.)   (c.)

Proportion
of width of
nib to size
of letter.
Narrow:
Broad:
Medium:

FIG. 165.

In MS. books the early built-up Capitals were
commonly of a rather severe type—approaching
the Roman Capital, but having the sharp contrast
between the *thicks* and the *thins* characteristic of
pen-letters (fig. 166). They make very simple and
effective "Versals."

A more highly finished type of pen-made Roman
Capital may be made by blending the serifs and
stems (*d*, p. 253): it is nearer to the inscriptional

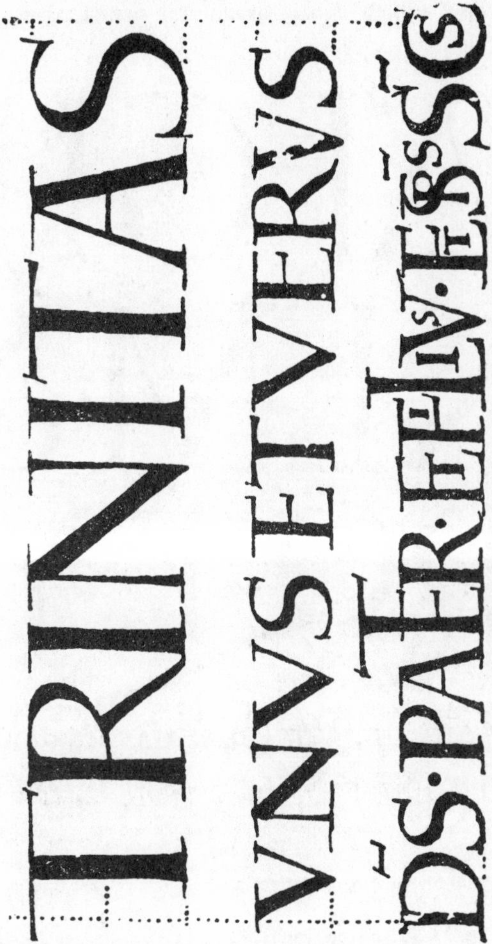

FIG. 166.— Pen-capitals from a tenth-century MS. (writing-lines dotted in fig. to show spacing method)

TRINITAS

VNVS ET VERVS

DS·PAER·ẽĒΙΙV·ES̃S̃Ē

259

form, but it exhibits a more curved and supple
outline, which comes of natural pen-strokes (fig.
167).

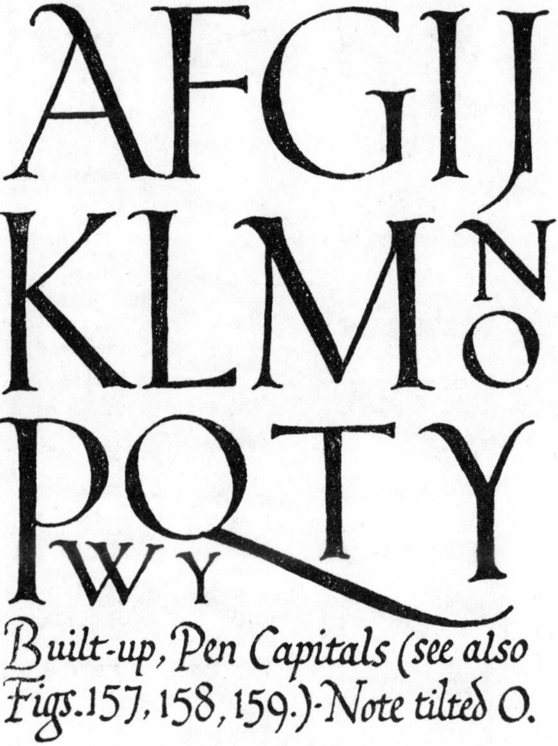

AFGIJ
KLM N O
PQTY
W Y

*Built-up, Pen Capitals (see also
Figs. 157, 158, 159.) - Note tilted O.*

FIG. 167.

The remarks in Chapter VII. on the treatment
of the more elastic "Gothic" Versal (a free variety

of the Roman) may be taken as applying generally
to (Coloured) Built-up Capitals — due allowance
being made for the characteristic differences of the
various types.

SIMPLE-WRITTEN CAPITALS

"*Rustic Capitals*" (fig. 4) may be referred to here
as typical, simple-written capitals. Though not a
very practical form,[1] they are full of suggestions for
a semi-ornamental lettering in which the pronounced
treatment of the *heads* and *feet* might be a feature
(*comp.* fig. 203). They were used as ornamental
letters for titles and the like (see Plates VIII, IX,
&c.) for centuries after they had gone out of ordinary
use.

Simple - written Roman Capitals. — (Examples:
Plates III, XVIII, XIX, XXI, figs. 147, 148,
168, 175, 179. See also pp. 211, 415.)

Uncials.—(Examples: see p. 264.)

Simple - written Capitals ordinarily conform to
the writing line—as set by the small text (p. 48).
This applies even where several *words* in capitals
have to be inserted in the small text, though in
special cases where these might look too crowded
such capitals might be written on alternate lines.

Used for *Initial Words, headings, whole pages,* or
books, in black or colour, they are written with
greater freedom and accorded more special treatment
(as indicated below).

Simple-written Capitals are best composed of
sharp, clean, pen-strokes: they may be quite plain

---

[1] Their thin *stems* and heavy *branches* may tend to weakness
and illegibility—*e.g.* such letters as E, F, I, L, and T (see
fig. 4) are not always easily distinguishable.

261

or more or less decorative (fig. 168), subject to the
general rule *that the fewer the number of letters or the
more ornamental their office, the more elaborate and
fanciful may be the forms employed* (see p. 294).

Simple-Written Capitals : roughly
copied from Plate XVIII.

FIG. 168.

A freely used pen naturally produces occasional
varieties for special or ornamental purposes: these
tend to elegance and drawn out flourished strokes
(p. 295); they vary chiefly in being extra large.[1]

---

[1] *Increasing the size of letter* affects the form as though the *nib
were narrowed* (see p. 288).

Several of these may be used with fine effect in a page of plain Capitals, their *"weight"* (and generally their colour) being the same as that of the text (see Plate V, and p. 292).

Whole Books or Pages written in Capitals.—A very grand effect may be produced by these at the expense of a little more time and material than a Small-letter MS. entails. The lines of writing are commonly made one-letter-height apart: this requires ordinary simple ruling—the capitals being written between every alternate pair of lines (see p. 374).

Such writing may conveniently be treated as *"Fine* Writing" (p. 226). It justifies the use of wider margins. It is generally more difficult (and less necessary) to keep the right-hand edge as straight as a small text permits. The irregularities of this edge may be balanced by setting out in the *left* margin the first letters of sentences, verses, and the like (see p. 228). Such initials may be written larger or more ornamentally as suggested above; or, if built-up Letters are required, plain, rather slender Roman Capitals are the most suitable: these look best in burnished gold.

Perhaps the finest and most beautiful work which the penman can produce, is a book written entirely in *gold*[1] *capitals*[2] *on purple vellum* (see pp. 130, 141). This is only possible in special cases, but a book rightly so made being illuminated from within, has an incomparable simplicity and grandeur, surpassing that of the finest post-decorated and illuminated manuscripts.

---

[1] Some may be in "silver" (p. 131).
[2] In a very short book these might even be *built-up* capitals.

UNCIALS

Examples: Plates IV, V; figs. 5, 169 (enlarged);
(modified, fig. 56).

Uncials are typical pen-capitals.[1] Though not
of such practical use as the simple-written Roman
Capitals, their great possibilities and their beauty
make them worth practising. (See *Round, Upright,
Formal Hands*, p. 268.)

Their use is limited by two considerations—

First: that while the round ᵭ.є.ɦ.ɱ.ʋ
are essentially legible (p. 203), people generally are
not accustomed to them, and may find them hard to
read; and

Secondly: that ᵭ.ꜰ.ɢ.ɦ.ɪ.ᴋ.ʟ.ᴘ.ǫ.ʏ
have ascending and descending strokes which are
apt to become too pronounced and give an unpleasant appearance of "*tailiness*" to a page of
Uncial Writing (in *English*, see *footnote*, p. 290).

The first difficulty may be met by keeping Uncials
for special MSS.—for private use—and introducing
them sparingly or not at all in Service Books,
Placards, &c., where ease and quickness of reading
are essential.

The appearance of "*tailiness*" (not so obvious in
Latin) may be avoided by making the tails shorter
and keeping the lines of writing well apart. Or
freely made Roman Capitals without *tails* (see D,
tail-less, fig. 57) may be substituted for one or more
of the chief offenders.

---

[1] Palæographers call them "majuscules" (= "large letters"),
but distinguish them from "Capitals." For the purposes of
the modern penman, however, they may be regarded as *Round
Capitals*. (For their treatment, see pp. 261–3, and 268.)

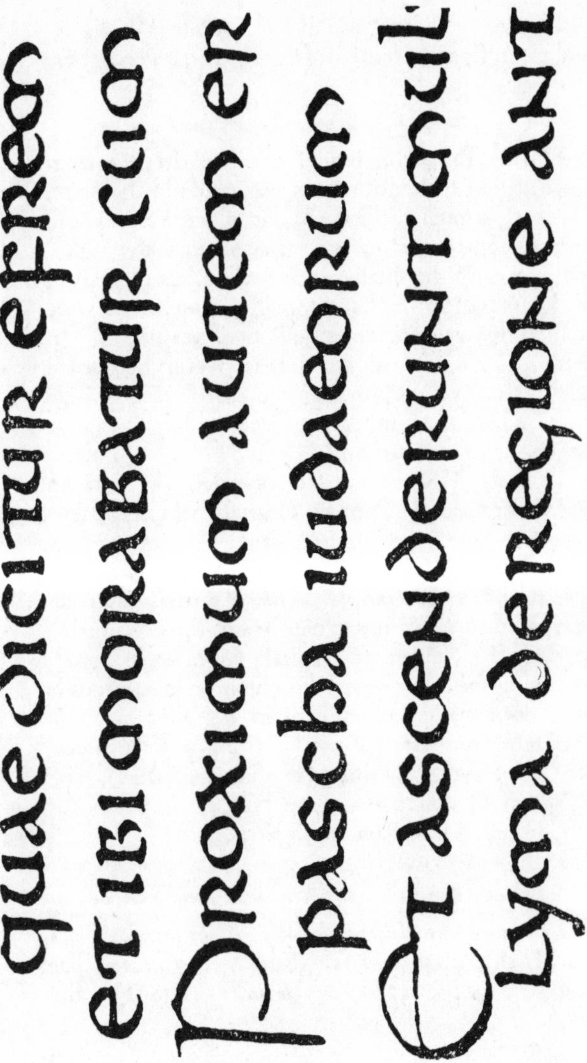

quae dicitur efream

et ibi morabatur cum

Proximum autem er

pascha iudaeorum

Et ascenderunt mul

Lyma deregione ant

FIG. 169.—*Part of Plate V. (q.v.), enlarged three times linear.*

Uncials may be "round" (see Plate IV, fig. 5,
and p. 268), or "pointed" (see fig. 169 and p. 375).

CAPITALS & SMALL-LETTERS

During the development of Small-Letters from
Capitals but little distinction was made in their use,
and such capital forms as N and R were freely and
promiscuously used in the *round minuscule* writings,
together with the small-letters n and r (see Plates VI,
VII). On the other hand, Small-Letter forms were
frequently written larger and used as initials. In
Irish and Anglo-Irish MSS. these were filled inside
with green, yellow, or red, and surrounded outside
with red dots, or otherwise decorated with colour
(see fig. 7, and Plate VI).

In early MSS., therefore, one does not find an
alphabet of Simple-Written Capitals, which is peculiar to a given small text. But we may employ
a kindred capital—such as the round *Uncial* for
the round *Half-Uncial*. And a fitting alphabet
may always be constructed, from the "Roman"
or "Uncial" types of Capitals (*footnote*, p. 264),
by taking the same pen with which the small-letters
have been made and using it in a similar manner:
"straight" for "straight-pen" writing, and "slanted"
for "slanted-pen" writing (see figs. 147, 148).

When in doubt as to the type of Capital—for
any purpose—use Roman Capitals.

EARLY, ROUND, UPRIGHT, FORMAL HANDS

Examples: *Half-Uncials*—fig. 6 (Roman); Plate
VI (Irish), Plate VII (English) fig. 170 *later;* see
also pp. 6, 10, 375–7. *Uncials* (Plate IV and
p. 4).

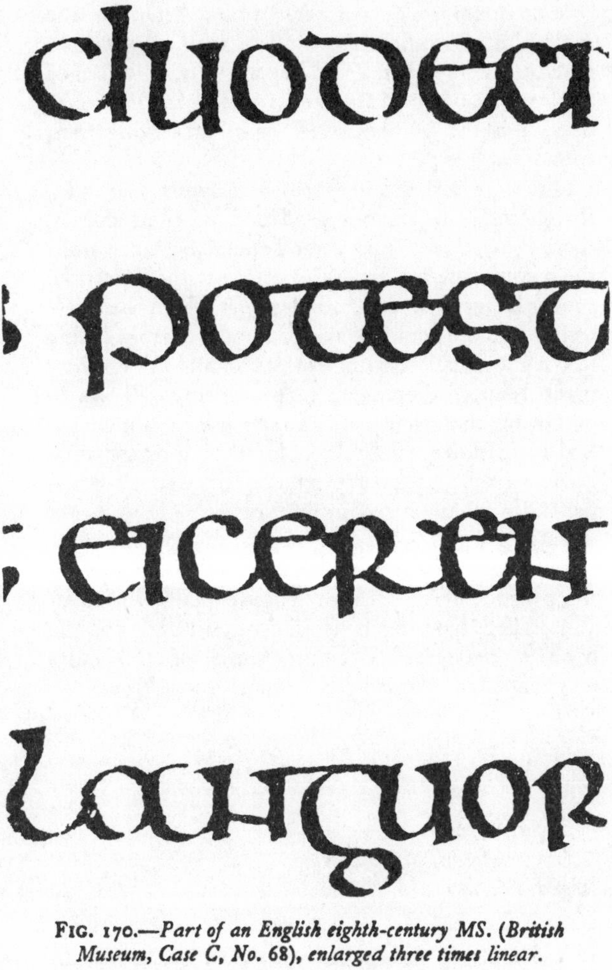

cluodea

potest

eiceret

lanquor

FIG. 170.—*Part of an English eighth-century MS. (British
Museum, Case C, No. 68), enlarged three times linear.*

267

The main types are the "round" Uncial and
Half-Uncial, commonly written with an approximately *"straight pen."*[1] They are generally treated
as *fine writing* (p. 226), and *written between ruled
lines:* this has a marked effect in preserving their
roundness (see p. 376).

They are very useful as *copy-book* hands (see p. 36),
for though the smooth gradation of their curves,
their thin strokes, and their general elegance unfit
them for many practical purposes, yet their essential
roundness, *uprightness*, and *formality* afford the finest
training to the penman, and prevent him from falling
into an angular, slanting, or lax hand. Their very
great beauty, moreover, makes them well worth
practising, and even justifies their use (in a modernised form) for special MSS., for the more romantic
books — such as poetry and "fairy tales"— and
generally where speed in writing *or reading* is not
essential.

With an eye trained and a hand disciplined by
the practice of an Irish or English Half-Uncial, or
a modified type, such as is given in fig. 50, the
penman may easily acquire some of the more
practical later "slanted-pen" types.

"SLANTED-PEN" SMALL-LETTERS

Typical Examples:—
Carlovingian ninth-century MS. — Fig. 8 *(enlarged, fig.* 171):

---

[1] The writing in fig. 170 shows a slightly *slanted pen*. To
make *quite* horizontal *thins* is difficult, and was probably never
done, but it is worth attempting them *nearly* horizontal for the
sake of training the hand.

English tenth-century MS. — *Plate VIII (en-arged, fig.* 172):

English eleventh-century MS. — *Plate IX (enlarged, fig.* 173):

Italian twelfth-century MS.—*Plate X (enlarged, fig.* 174).

The use of the "slanted pen" generally produced *stronger, narrower,* and *stiffer* letters. Its effects are detailed in pp. 9–13, and fig. 11, and may best be studied in the tenth-century example (fig. 172—the letter forms are described on p. 378).

In the Carlovingian MS.—which does not show these effects in any marked degree—we may note the wide letter forms, the wide spacing, the long stems (thickened above by additional strokes), the slight slope of the letters, and the general effect of gracefulness and freedom (see fig. 171). Carlovingian MSS. may be said to represent a sort of mediæval *copy-books,* and their far-reaching influence on writing makes them of great interest to the modern penman, who would, moreover, find one of these hands an excellent model for a free "formal hand."

For practical purposes the "slanted-pen" letter is generally superior to the "straight-pen" letter. The "slanted-pen" letters have greater strength and legibility, due mainly to the presence of the *thick horizontals*—often equal in width to the verticals. Their use saves both space and time, as they are narrower, and more easily and freely written[1] than the straight-pen forms.

The real importance to us of these early types

---

[1] NOTE.—*Single*-line ruling is commonly used—the writing being *on,* or a little *above* or *below,* the line: this allows of greater freedom than the double line (see p. 268).

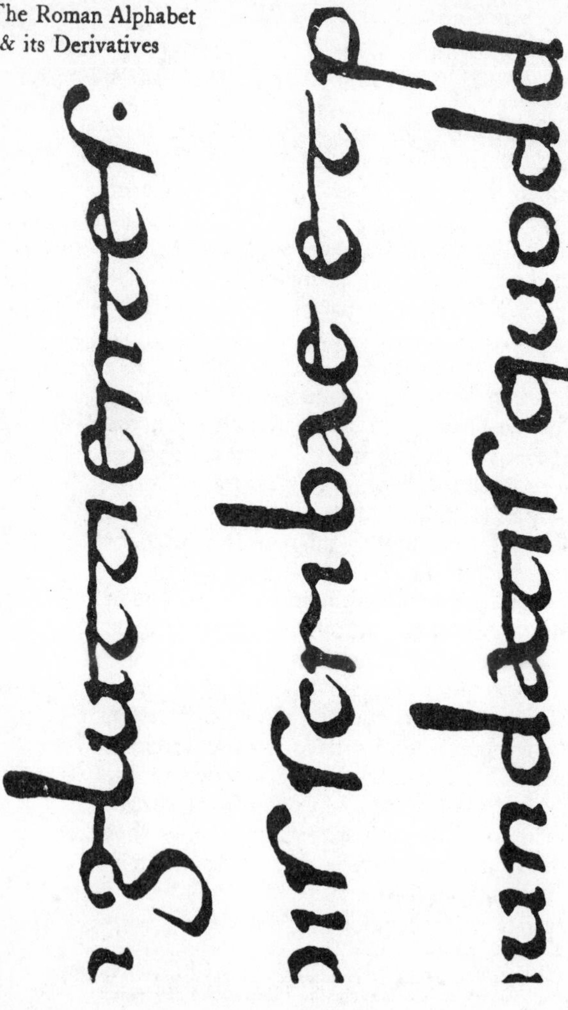

Fig. 171.—Part of fig. 8, enlarged three times linear (see p. 269).

angeli dmi dno.b

aquae omnſ quae

τ dno.b omnſuir

ſol & luna dmo .

FIG. 172.—Fig. 12, *enlarged twice linear* (see p. 269 & *Plate VIII*). *Note: top line is cut down.*

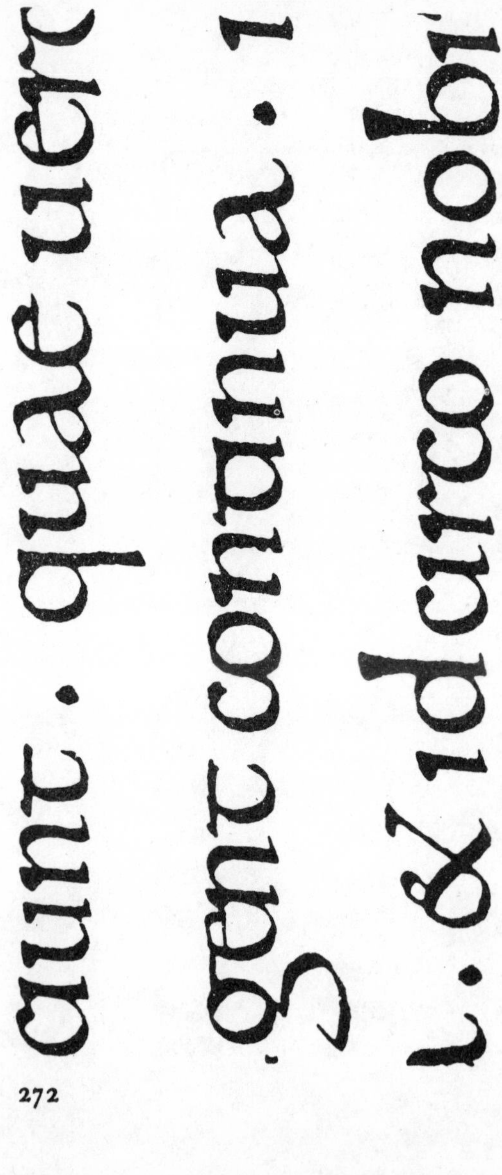

aunt . quae uer

gent contanua . 1

l . & id arco nobi'

FIG. 173.—Part of Plate IX (Charter of CNUT), enlarged three times linear (see p. 378).

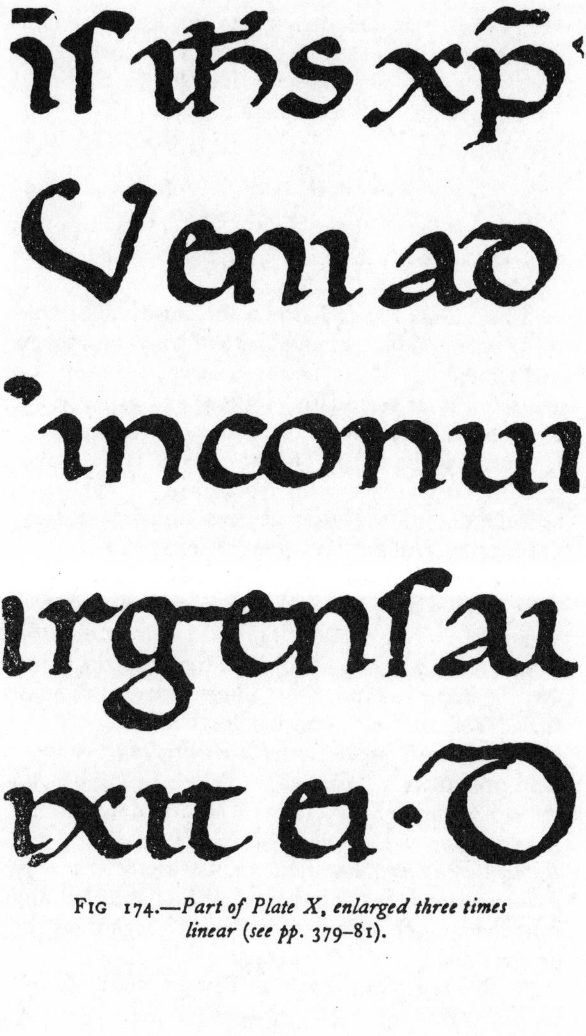

il ihs xp̄

Ueni ad

in conui

irgenſau

xtt ei · D

FIG 174.—*Part of Plate X, enlarged three times
linear (see pp.* 379–81).

lies, I think, in their relation to the Roman Small-
Letter (pp. 380–1 & 415–20), and their great
possibilities of development into modern formal
hands approaching the "Roman" type.

ROMAN SMALL-LETTERS

Ex.: (Italian) Plates XIX, XX (15th century);
figs. 175, 176 (16th century): figs. 147, 148 (*modern
MS.*).

The *Roman Small-Letter* is the universally recognised type in which the majority of books and papers
are printed. Its form has been in use for over 400
years (without essential alteration) and as far as we
are concerned it may be regarded as permanent.

And it is the object of the scribe or letter-maker
gradually to attain a fine, personal, formal hand,
assimilating to the Roman Small-Letter; a hand
against the familiar and present form of which no
allegations of unreadableness can be raised, and a
hand having a beauty and character now absent or
*un*familiar. The related *Italic* will be mastered for
formal MS. work (p. 279), and the ordinary handwriting improved (p. 287). These three hands point
the advance of the practical, modern scribe.

The Roman Small-Letter is essentially a pen form
(and preferably a "slanted-pen" form; p. 269), and
we would do well to follow its natural development
*from the Roman Capital—through Round Letters and
Slanted-Pen forms*—so that we may arrive at a truly
developed and characteristic type, suitable for any
formal manuscript work and full of suggestions for
printers and letter-craftsmen generally.

A finished form, such as that in Plate XX—
or even that of fig. 175—would present many

difficulties to the unpractised scribe, and one who so
began would be apt to remain a mere copyist, more
or less unconscious of the vitality and character of
the letter. An earlier type of letter—such as that
in Plate VIII—enables the scribe to combine speed
with accuracy, and fits him at length to deal with
the letters that represent the latest and most formal
development of penmanship.

And in this connection, beware of practising with
a fine nib, which tends to inaccuracy and the substitution of prettiness for character. Stick to definite
pen strokes, and preserve the definite shapes and the
uniformity of the serifs (p. 288): if these be made
clumsily, they become clumsy lumps. It may be
impossible always to ascertain the exact forms—
especially of terminals and finishing strokes—for the
practised scribe has attained a great uniformity and
some *sleight of hand* which cannot be deliberately
copied. But—whatever the exact forms—we may
be sure that in the best hands they are produced by
uniform and proper pen strokes.

ITALICS

Ex.: Plate XXI, and figs. 94, 177, 178 (enlarged).

Italics[1] closely resemble the Roman Small-Letters,
but are slightly narrowed, slightly sloped to the

---

[1] It is convenient to use the term "*Italics*" for both the
cursive formal writing and the printing resembling it. *Italic
type* was first used in a "Virgil" printed by Aldus Manutius
of Venice in 1500. The type was then called "Venetian" or
"Aldine." It was counterfeited almost immediately (in Germany and Holland it was called "cursive"); Wynkin de
Worde used it in 1524. Aldus printed *entire texts* of various
Classics in his italic *lower-case* type, but his Capitals are small
ordinary ROMAN (*in contrast* with the l.c.—p. 279).

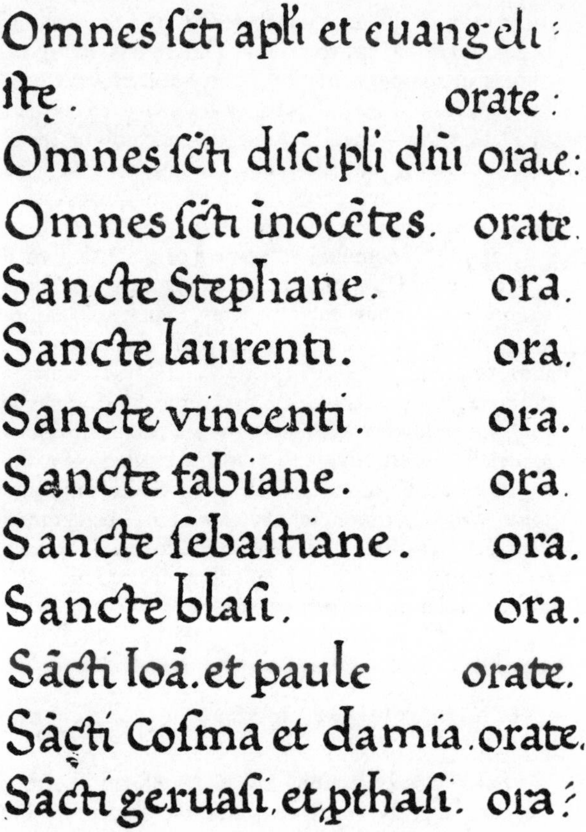

Omnes ſcti apli et euangeli
ſtę .   orate :

Omnes ſcti diſcipli dñi oraꞇe:

Omnes ſcti inocētes.   orate

Sancte Stephane.   ora.

Sancte laurenti.   ora.

Sancte vincenti.   ora.

Sancte fabiane.   ora.

Sancte ſebaſtiane.   ora.

Sancte blaſi.   ora.

Sācti Ioã.et paule   orate.

Sācti Coſma et damia.orate.

Sācti geruaſi.et pthaſi. ora ⸴

FIG. 175.—*Italian Prayer Book: 16th century* (*see opp. p. &
p. 309*).

276

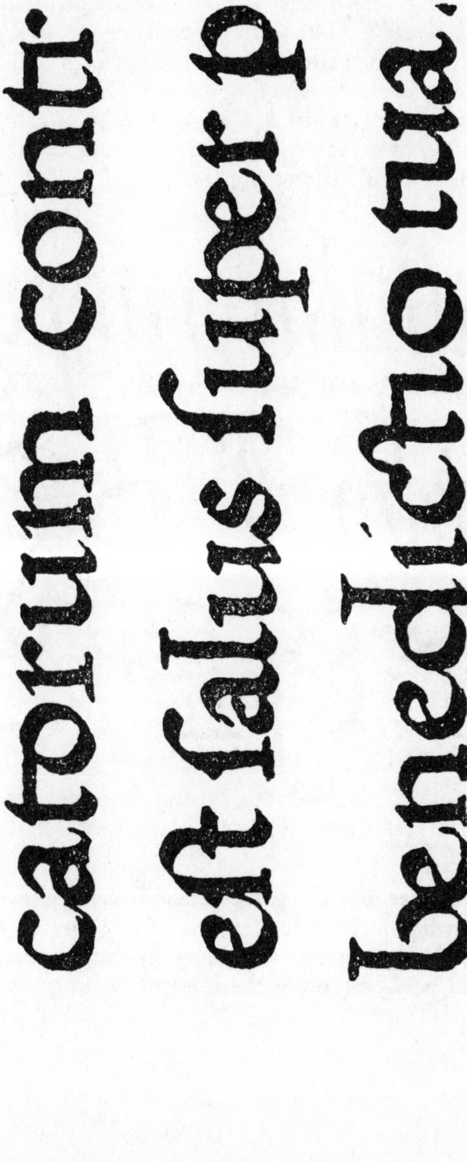

catorum contr

est salus super p

benedictio tua.

FIG. 176.—(From same MS. as fig. 175, enlarged three times linear.)

277

right, and very freely written (commonly with a "*slanted pen*"). The serifs generally consist of slight natural terminal hooks, &c.—though in *p* and *q* a finishing stroke is sometimes *added*. *Ascending* and *descending* strokes (in *b, d, f, h, k, l, g, j, p, q, y*) are commonly rather long, and often end in curves, sometimes in flourishes (fig. 177).

FIG. 177.

The lines of writing are generally widely spaced —allowing for the long stems: the *bodies* of the letters being narrow are generally rather closely packed, and frequently the lines of writing appear as almost continuous light but compact writing, while the *ascenders* and *descenders* and parts of the Capitals may be flourished freely in the spaces between the lines—sometimes filling them with ornamental pen work, which contrasts strongly with the extreme plainness and regularity of the *bodies*.

Italic Capitals are a variety of the Roman Capitals, slightly sloped (frequently less sloped than the accompanying small-letters), and sometimes much flourished (fig. 177). These still bear the seventeenth century name of "Swash Letters." We might try also the early *contrast of Caps & l.c.* (note p. 275).

Use of Italics.—In printing, after Aldus (pp. 275, 337), they served to mark such portions of the text as—

Introductions, *Prefaces,* *Indexes,* *Notes,*	and subsequently were used for	*Quotations,* *Emphasising,* *Words not part of the Text,* (*e.g.* Chapter headings in the Bible, &c.).

In MSS. when it is not desirable to alter the character, Red Writing (see p. 96) may be substituted for italics. Italics—either in black or red —go best with "Roman" characters.

Like the Roman Small-Letter, the Italic is a generally recognised and accepted form: this and other considerations, such as the peculiar elegance and charm of the letters, their formal relation to modern handwriting, their compactness and economy of space in the line, and the fact that they may be written easily and with extreme regularity —*being indeed the most rapid of formal hands*—are practical reasons for a careful study of the type, and justify the writing of certain MS. books entirely in Italics.

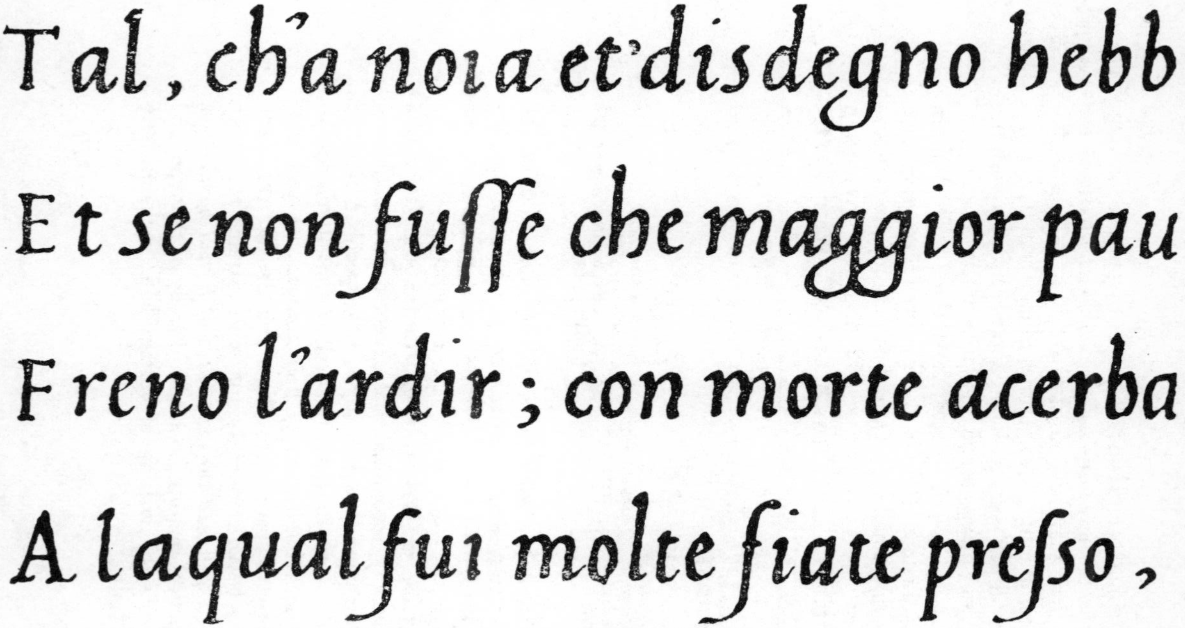

Tal, ch'a noia et disdegno hebb

Et se non fusse che maggior pau

Freno l'ardir; con morte acerba

A laqual fur molte fiate presso,

Fig. 178.—*Part of Plate XXI, enlarged (approx.) four times linear (see p. 419).*

Figs. 179, 180, and 181 are taken from a six-teenth-century Italian MS.[1] written in a semi-formal cursive hand in dark brown and red-brown inks (probably originally nearer *black* and *red*), on 150 leaves of fine paper.

The proportions of the Book,[2] together with the good writing, have a very agreeable effect, and are interesting as being used by a writer over 300 years ago. The extra width of the side margins may have been allowed for annotations—some notes were written in by the scribe himself.

Page — 11¼ inches high, 8 inches wide.

Margins
- *Inner* (⅞ inch + ⅜ inch allowed for Small Capitals) — 1¼ inch (approximate).
- *Top* — 1¾ inch (constant).
- *Side* — 2¼ inch (approximate).
- *Foot* — 3 inch (approximate).

Writing-Line Space nearly ⁵⁄₁₆ inch high: length (varies), average 4 inches.

Text Column nearly 6¾ inches high, consisting of 22 lines of MS.

Character of the Writing.—The good shapes of the letters, their great uniformity, and their easy yet formal arrangement, mark this MS. as the work of a skilful penman. But, while pen character of a sort is very evident, the writing approaches the *stylographic* (apparently a rather narrow blunt nib was used), and the absence of definite *thicks* and *thins* distinguishes it from all the formal hands hitherto discussed: it may conveniently be termed *Semi-formal*.

---

[1] The Book is a catalogue of early Roman inscriptions: apparently a written copy or a printed book.
[2] With a sheet of paper 11¼ inches by 16 inches the student might reconstruct these.

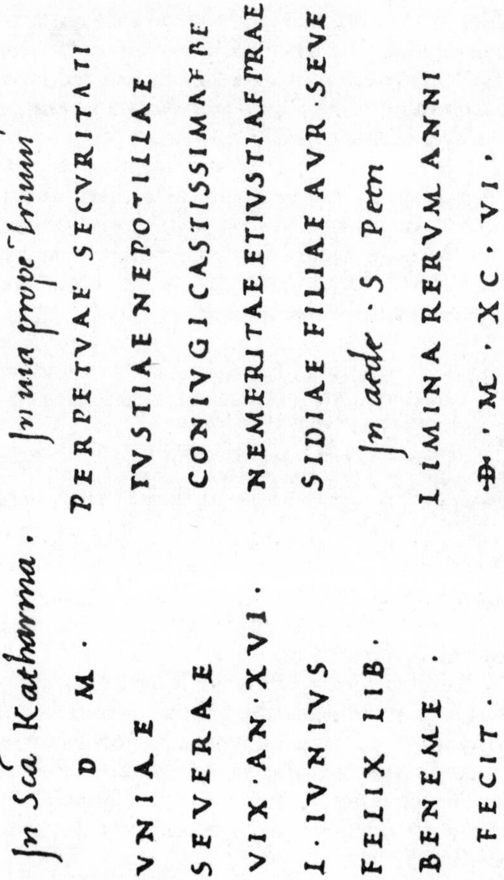

Jn Sca Katharina.

F VNIAE
SEVERAE
VIX·AN·XVI·
I·IVNIVS
FELIX LIB·
BENEME·
FECIT·

Jn uia prope truum

PERPETVAE SECVRITATI
FVSTIAE NEPOTILLAE
CONIVGI CASTISSIMAE RE
NEMERITAE ETIVSTIAE PRAE
SIDIAE FILIAE AVR·SEVE

Jn aede · S Petri

LIMINA RERVM ANNI
D·M·XC·VI·

FIG. 179.

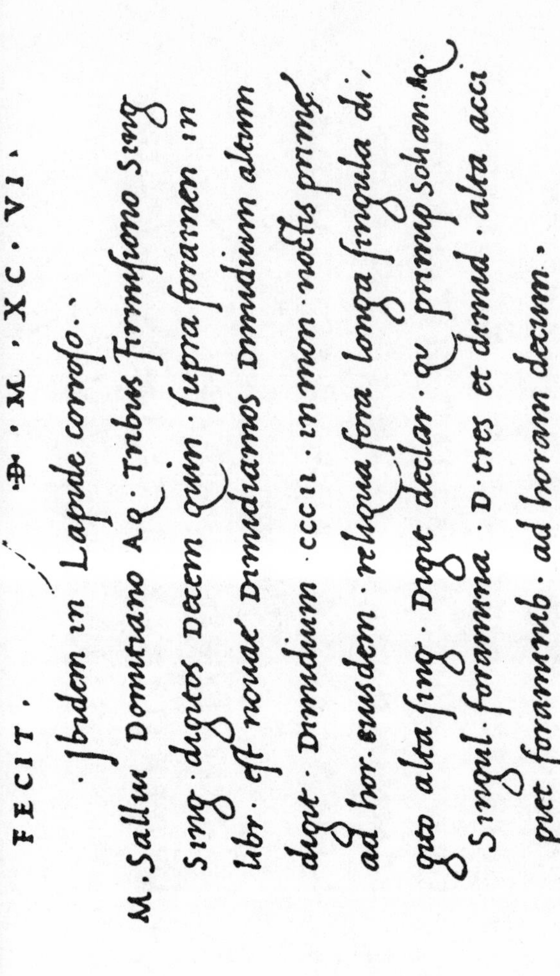

The Roman
Alphabet
& its
Derivatives

FECIT . Ð · M · XC · VI ·

Jbidem in Lapide corrofo.

M . Sallui Domitiano A.q . Tribus Firmiffimo S:oq

S:ing . digitos decem quin . fupra foramen in

libr. qt nouae Dimidiamos Dimidium alcum

digit . Dimidium . ccc ii . in non noctis primt

ad hor. eiusdem . reliqua fora longa fingula di .

quo alta fing . Digit declar . qu primp sohan ho

Singul . foramina . D . tres et dimid . alta acci

pict foraminib . ad horam decum .

FIG. 180.

283

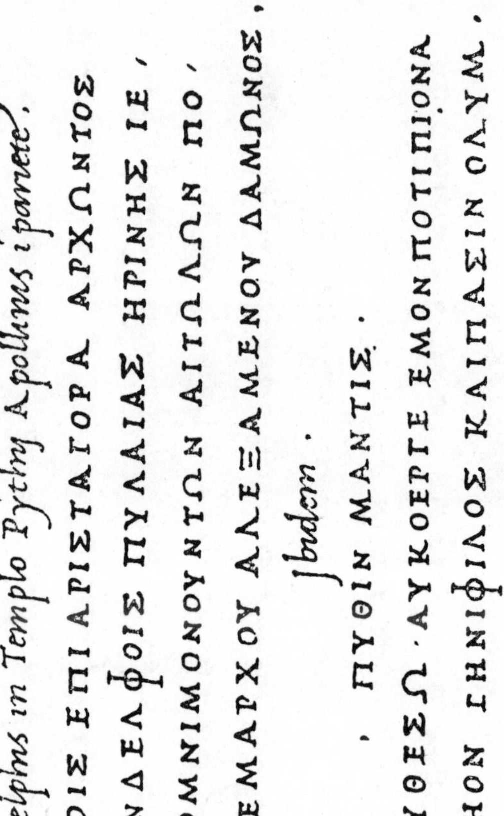

Delphis in Templo Pythiy Apollinis i ponete.

Θ ΕΟΙΣ ΕΠΙ ΑΡΙΣΤΑΓΟΡΑ ΑΡΧΩΝΤΟΣ

ΕΝ ΔΕΛΦΟΙΣ ΠΥΛΑΙΑΣ ΗΡΙΝΗΣ ΙΕ ,

ΡΟΜΝΙΜΟΝΟΥΝΤΩΝ ΑΙΤΩΛΩΝ ΠΟ ·

ΛΕΜΑΡΧΟΥ ΑΛΕΞΑΜΕΝΟΥ ΔΑΜΩΝΟΣ .

ʃbrdom .

, ΠΥΘΙΝ ΜΑΝΤΙΣ .

Ν ΑΥΘΕΣΩ · ΑΥΚΟΕΡΤΕ ΕΜΟΝ ΠΟΤΙ ΠΙΟΝΑ

ΝΗΟΝ ΓΗΝΙΦΙΛΟΣ ΚΑΙ ΠΑΣΙΝ ΟΛΥΜ ·

FIG. 181.

Construction.—The rapidity and uniformity of
this writing are largely due to an extremely easy
zigzag movement of the pen, such as is natural in
writing *m*, *n*, and *u*—the final upstroke usually running on into the next letter. Note particularly that
the *joined up* round letters, *c, d, e, g, o, q* begin with
a nearly straight down stroke—like the first part of

FIG. 182.

u—to which tops are *added* (see fig. 182). In the
case of *a*, the first stroke curves forward to meet
the second.

In the straight-stemmed capitals B, D, E, F, H, I, L, M, N, P, R, and T, the first stroke is made rather like an ⌐ (showing the tendency to a zigzag) the foot of which is generally crossed horizontally by a second stroke making a form resembling ⌐— on this as a base, the rest of the letter is formed (see fig. 182). This tends to preserve the uniformity of the letters: and gives a fine constructive effect, as, for example, in the letter N.

General Remarks.—The semi-formal nature of such a MS. would seem to permit of a good quill— not necessarily sharp—being used with the utmost freedom and all reasonable personal *sleight of hand;* of soft tinted inks—such as browns and brown-reds; of an *un*-ruled page (*a pattern page ruled dark, being laid under the writing paper, will, by showing through, keep the writing sufficiently straight*), and of a minimum of precision in the arrangement of the text. And in this freedom and informality lie the reasons for and against the use of such a hand. There is a danger of its becoming more informal and degenerating because it lacks the effect of the true pen in preserving form.[1] But, on the other hand, it combines great rapidity and freedom with beauty and legibility: few printed books could compete in charm with this old "catalogue," which took the scribe but little longer to write than we might take in *scribbling* it.

Many uses for such a hand will suggest themselves. Semi-formal documents which require to

---

[1] **Practising a more formal hand as a *corrective* would prevent this.**

be neatly written out, and Books and Records of which only one or two copies are required, and even Books which are worthy to be—but never are—printed, might, at a comparatively low cost, be preserved in this legible and beautiful form.

It suggests possibilities for an improvement in the ordinary present-day handwriting—a thing much to be desired, and one of the most practical benefits of the study of calligraphy. The practical scribe, at any rate, will prove the advantages of being a good all-round penman.

OF FORMAL WRITING GENERALLY

On Copying a Hand.—Our intentions being right (viz. to make our work essentially readable) and our actions being expedient (viz. to select and copy the simple forms which have remained essentially the same, leaving the complex forms which have passed out of use—see pp. 161–2), we need not vex ourselves with the question of "lawfulness."[1]

Where beautiful character is the natural product of a tool, any person may at any time give such character to a useful form, and as at this time a properly cut and handled pen will produce letters resembling those of the early MSS., we may take as models *such early, simple pen-forms as have remained essentially the same,*[2] and copy them as closely as we *can* while keeping them exact and formal.

Finally, *personal quality* is essential to perfect

---

[1] The Law fulfils itself: that which we must not copy is that which we *cannot* copy.

[2] *E.g.* the letters in the tenth-century English hand—Plate VIII.: excepting the archaic long f and round ꝯ (*b*, fig. 183).

workmanship, but that is the natural and gradual—
sometimes scarcely visible—departure from a model,
that comes of practice and time.

Forms of Letters: component pen-strokes.—In a good
hand the chief component strokes—stems, bows, and
serifs—are repeated again and again (see pp. 208,
218)—this is essential to the uniform character
and the quickness of the writing. When substituting a *new* for an *old* letter a naturally used pen
will produce such common pen-strokes, giving the
desired "family likeness" to the new letter[1] (*b*, fig.
183).

Proportion[2] *of Thick Strokes.*—The broader the
thick stroke is in proportion to the height of a
letter, the more the form of the letter is controlled
and affected by the pen (*c*, fig. 183). For training
and practice, therefore, the wide nib is the most
useful. A narrower nib (*d* or *e*) allows of more
freedom and variety, and there is a great charm in
slender lettering—this the trained scribe may essay
(see Plate XX., and p. 418).

Proportion[2] *of Stem Height.*—The character of a
writing depends very much on whether the stems
are *short*, *medium*, or *long*. The stems of b and p
may be as short as half the height of the bodies
(*f*, fig. 183); a *medium* stem for ordinary use might
be two-thirds of, or equal to, the height of the
body (*g*). Stems may be drawn out to almost any

---

[1] The propriety of the actual form of the new letter will
largely depend on the scribe's knowledge of the development of
that particular letter and its component parts: *conf.* the interesting development of g, sketched in figs. 3 & 183 (but
note correction of *example* 173 in *Addenda*, p. xxiv).

[2] The proportions of the *thick strokes, stem heights, &c.*, in a
given hand need not be exactly followed, but it should be
recognised that any alteration in these *will inevitably alter the
orms and the character of the letters* (fig. 183, and pp. 50 & xxiv).

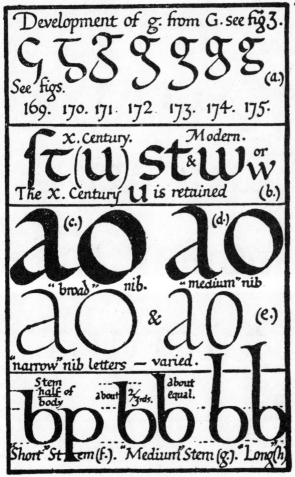

Development of g. from G. see fig 3.

See figs.
169. 170. 171. 172. 173. 174. 175. (a.)

X. Century. Modern.

The X. Century u is retained (b.)

(c.) (d.)

"broad" nib. "medium" nib.

& (e.)

"narrow" nib letters — varied.

Stem half of body . about 2/3rds. about equal.

"Short" Stem (f.). "Medium" Stem (g.). "Long"(h)

FIG. 183.

length, and may constitute a decorative feature of
the writing, as in the Anglo-Saxon[1] MS., Plate IX.
(See p. 295, and fig. 188.)

Distinct Lines of Writing.—The line—especially

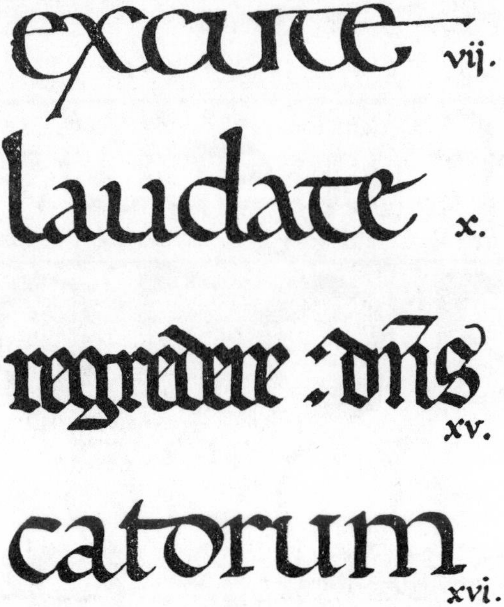

excute *vij.*

laudate *x.*

regrediar :dns *xv.*

catorum *xvi.*

FIG. 184.

in MS. books—is really a more important unit than

---

[1] In English so many *ascending* and *descending* letters are
used, that it might be the best and most natural treatment of
these to make them a marked feature of the writing (see also
"Fine Writing," pp. 225–27). Note, in this connection, that our
a b c has been developed as a Latin alphabet, and that the
evenness of Latin MS. is largely due to the infrequence of tailed
letters.

290

the page; and the whole question of the arrangement of Lettering hinges on the right treatment of the lines. One is particularly struck by the distinctness of the lines of writing in the old MSS., due mainly to—

(a) *The binding together of the letters in the line—commonly by strong serifs or heavy "shoulders" and "feet"* (see figs. 11, 184, and p. 376).

(b) *Packing the letters well together* (see pp. 43, 226).

(c) *Spacing the lines sufficiently apart* (see pp. 262–9).

It is a good rule (especially when practising) to space the lines fairly widely. Really fine writing shows generally to greater advantage if not too much crowded, and there is more danger of making reading hard by crowding the lines, than by crowding the words (see fig. 156).

Whatever mode of treatment be followed, each line should be written with as much freedom as possible, the simplest straightforward writing being preferable to that which is over-arranged.

DECORATIVE CONTRASTS

The decorative treatment of lettering generally involves contrasts of *size*, *weight*, *colour*, or *form*—that is, of large and small, heavy and light, variously coloured, or variously shaped letters. As a general rule, marked contrasts are best; a slight contrast may fail of its effect and yet be sufficiently noticeable to give an unpleasant appearance of irregularity.

Contrasts of Colour (see pp. 110, 146).—Note that, while it is convenient to distinguish "colour" —as *red*, *blue*, *green*, &c.—weight strictly involves

colour: built-up or heavy letters in black show extra
black beside lighter writing, while the latter appears
grey in comparison (see figs. 197, 186); in red
writing the heavy letters appear *red*, the lighter
letters, *pink* (see fig. 90).

Contrast of Size.—The simplest decorative contrast is that of LARGE[1] letters with SMALLER
letters (fig. 185); the strokes being of equal, or

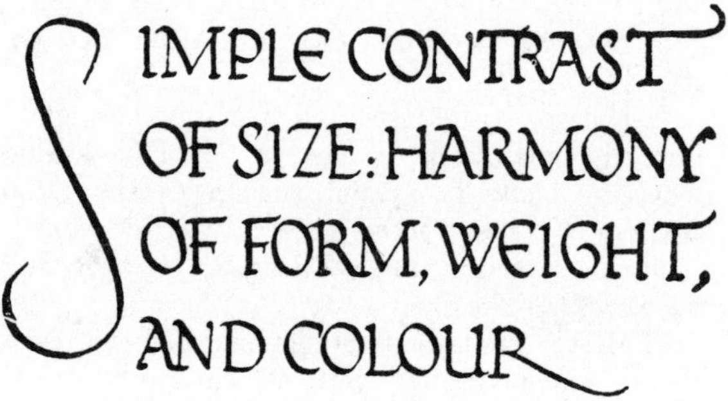

SIMPLE CONTRAST OF SIZE: HARMONY OF FORM, WEIGHT, AND COLOUR

FIG. 185.

nearly equal, weight, there is an harmonious evenness of tone throughout. Where the large letters
are very much larger, their parts are made somewhat
heavier to keep their *apparent* "weight" approximately equal (see p. 422). This is one of the most
effective treatments for inscriptions generally (see
p. 263, and Plates V. and XXIV.).

Contrasts of "weight" and size.—In simple writing these are obtained by using two sizes of pen—
the small, light letters being used for the bulk of the

---

[1] Where there is only a slight difference in size, the effect is
improved by using a different *form* or *colour* (see pp. 96, 309).

text, the larger heavier letters being used for occasional words or lines (or *vice versa*). This is a very effective simple treatment for MSS. (fig. 186).

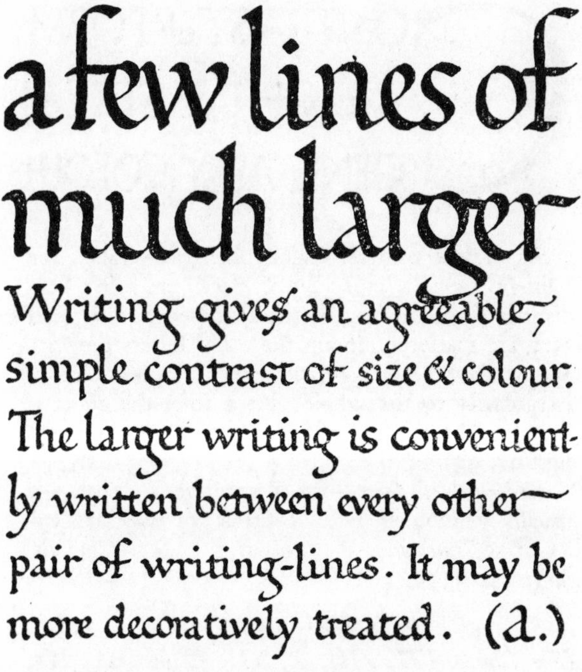

a few lines of
much larger
Writing gives an agreeable,
simple contrast of size & colour.
The larger writing is conveniently written between every other
pair of writing-lines. It may be
more decoratively treated. (a.)

FIG. 186.—(*See also fig.* 191.)

The occasional letters may be more decoratively treated (see *Responses and Rubrics*, p. 309) by introducing the further contrasts of *colour* (p. 110) or form (p. 300).

293

Contrasts of form, "weight," and size.—These
are generally obtained by the use of large built-up
Capitals, together with a simple-written (or
ordinarily printed) text (fig. 187).

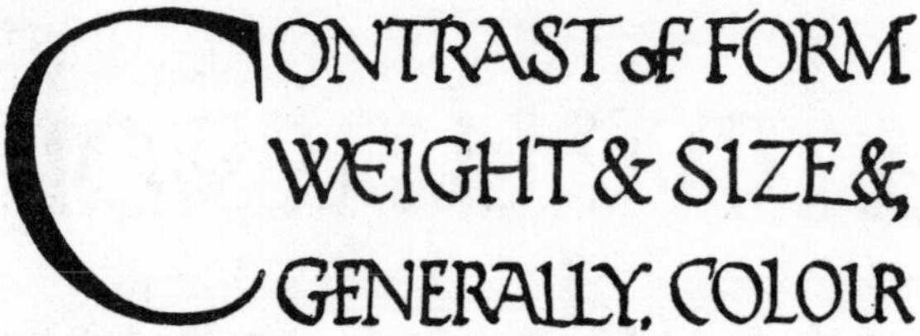

CONTRAST of FORM
WEIGHT & SIZE &
GENERALLY, COLOUR

FIG. 187.

A marked contrast usually being desirable, the
built-up capitals (especially if black) are safest kept
distinct from the rest of the text (see fig. 197): if
they are scattered among the other letters they are
apt to show like *blots* and give an appearance of
irregularity to the whole. As a rule, the effect is
improved by the use of red or another colour (see
figs. 91, 93).

Contrast of form—for decorative purposes—is
usually combined with contrast of weight (*e.g.*
"Gothic," *heavier*, p. 300) or size (*e.g.* Capitals,
larger, p. 335).

ORNAMENTAL LETTERS

(*See Chaps. VII, VIII, X, XII, & pp.* xxx, 215,
xxiv.)

To give ornament its true value we must *distinguish between ordinary occasions when simplicity and
directness are required, and special occasions when
elaboration is desirable or necessary.*

The best way to make ornamental letters is to
develop them from the simpler forms. Any plain

type may be decoratively treated for special purposes —some part or parts of the letters usually being rationally "exaggerated" (p. 216). Free *stems*, "*branches*," tails, &c., may be drawn out, and terminals or serifs may be decorated or flourished (fig. 203).

Built-Up Forms.—Even greater license (see fig. 161) is allowed in Built-Up Letters—as they are less under the control of the tool (p. 256)—and their natural decorative development tends to produce a subordinate simple line decoration beside or *upon* their thicker parts (fig. 189 & p. xxiv). In MSS. the typical built-up, ornamental form is the "Versal" (see Chap. VII.), which developed—or degenerated —into the "Lombardic" (fig. 1). Here again it is preferable to keep to the simpler form and to develop a natural decorative treatment of it for ourselves.

"*Black Letter*" *or* "*Gothic*," still in use as an ornamental letter (fig. 190), is descended from the fifteenth-century writing of Northern Europe (Plate XVII.). A better model may be found in the earlier and more lively forms of twelfth and thirteenth century writing (fig. 191).

Rightly made, and used, it is one of the most picturesque forms of lettering—and therefore of ornament—and besides its ornamental value, there is still in the popular fancy a halo of romance about "black letter," which may fairly be taken into account. Its comparative illegibility, however,— due mainly to the substitution of straight for curved strokes—debars it from ordinary use.[1] Though its

---

[1] Compare **monotone** and monotone. For general purposes, therefore, and particularly for forming a good hand, the earlier scripts are to be preferred (or the late *Italian*): even twelfth-century "Gothic" writing is hardly readable enough for "practical" purposes.

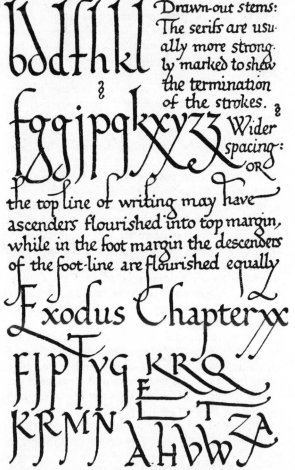

Drawn-out stems:
The serifs are usu-
ally more strong-
ly marked to shew
the termination
of the strokes.

Wider
spacing:
OR

the top line of writing may have
ascenders flourished into top margin,
while in the foot margin the descenders
of the foot-line are flourished equally

Exodus Chapter xx

FIG. 188.—(See also figs. 125 and 150.)

296

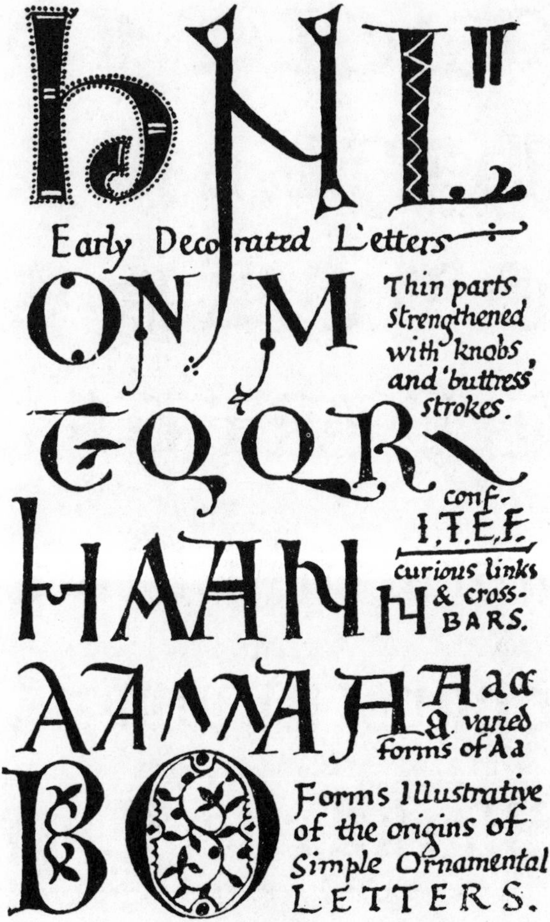

Early Decorated Letters

Thin parts
strengthened
with knobs,
and 'buttress'
strokes.

conf.
I.T.E.F.
curious links
& cross-
BARS.

varied
forms of Aa

Forms Illustrative
of the origins of
Simple Ornamental
LETTERS.

FIG. 189.—(*See also Plates VI, XI, XXII,
figs. 79 and 84, and p. 382.*)

297

ABCDEFG

HIJKLMN

OPQRST

UVWXYZ or Z

abcdefghijklmn

opqrstuvwxyzA

BlackLetterType

FIG. 190.—*Ordinary Modern " Black Letter" Type (see p. 295).*

Note: the lines have been dotted in parts, so that they may shew in the 'block.' (conf. fig.186)

FIG. 191.—MS. written by an English scribe, in 1269, at Mons, in Hainault—Part of Colophon in large text. (B. M. Egerton, MS. 2569. Reduced five-sixths Scale.)

distinction in form and *colour* (p. 291) from ordinary small lettering, make it useful in arresting attention; as in a legal document, where the clauses are marked by

whereas &c.

Its most effective use, however, is as pure ornament—when it does not matter whether the words are easily read or not. For mottoes, &c., painted or carved on walls or furniture, and for ornamental borders round tapestry hangings, tombs, bookcovers, bowls, flagons, plates, &c., bands of such ornamental lettering are extremely decorative (see *footnote* (2), p. 219, & also p. 328).

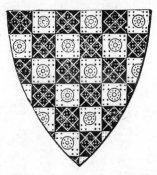

FIG. 191 *a.—Shield of Arms of Earl de Warrenne, Castle Acre Priory, Norfolk (Gold and blue chequers, diapered—see p. 181): reproduced, by permission, from Boutell's " English Heraldry," No.* 68.

APPENDIX A

CHAPTER XVI

SPECIAL SUBJECTS

Divers Uses of Lettering—MS. Books, &c.—Binding
MSS. (*with Note by Douglas Cockerell*)—Broadsides, Wall Inscriptions, &c.—Illuminated Addresses, &c.—Monograms & Devices—Title Pages
—Lettering for Reproduction—Printing—Inscriptions on Metal, Stone, Wood, &c.—Of Inscriptions
Generally—Bibliography, &c.

DIVERS USES OF LETTERING

The following list of some of the uses of hand-made lettering, though necessarily very brief, will perhaps suggest possibilities both to the student and the craftsman:—

Special
Subjects

MS. BOOKS, &c.:   (see pp. 64, 305, & *Author's Preface*).

Fine Literature:
(1) Preferably "the best."
(2) That which is worthy of calli-graphy.
(3) That which is the "favour-ite" of the owner of the book.
Poetry is differently treated from prose (see pp. 61, 227, 335, 104), and should have extra wide *side* margins when possible (p. 419).

301

Special
Subjects

Single Poems, &c.: { Poems, cards, hymns, &c. (see pp. 103-5, & *Poetry*, above), preferably in the form of small *books*.

Tracts or Treatises: { Copies might be preserved (p. 287) in good writing (*instead of Typewriting*).

Church Services: { Prayers, Communion, Marriage, &c. (pp. 106, 110, 309).

Gospels & Psalters: { Note.—The Psalms, &c., may be treated as poetry (as in the "Revised Version") or as prose (as in the "Authorised Version"), see *Fine Literature* above.

Almanacks: { These may be very varied; containing vacations, terms, sessions; public, church, or family festivals, personal memoranda or topical quotations. They offer great opportunities for heraldic or symbolic ornament (such as coats-of-arms, astronomical signs, &c.).

Dedications, &c. in Books: (*Lettering on Architects' Plans: see* MAPS & PLANS, p. 303) { These may be on a parchment leaf inserted and securely glued into the beginning (preferably bound up with book), or be written on a fly-leaf. Annotations, extracts, &c., may be written in colour in printed books (p. 110).

"Copy-Books": (see below).

BROADSIDES: { Sheets printed (or written) on one side: see p. 314.

Notices: (Posters, Placards, Hand-bills, &c.).

Quotations: (Texts, Mottoes, &c.) (see p. 300).

Church Texts, &c.: (The Creed, Commandments, &c.).

Family Trees & Pedigrees: { These may be very decorative—in plain black and red, or with coats-of-arms or other ornament. They might also be made in book form.

302

WALL INSCRIP-} Carved or painted: see pp. 314,
TIONS: see also p. 304} 339–349, & Chapter XVII.

Public Notices:⎫ Note: on walls, plastered, or un-
Lettering in Churches,⎮ suited for carving, *sgraffito* might
&c.:⎮ be used with fine effect.
⎮ Letters may also be painted upon
Lettering in & upon⎮ tiles, which (after baking) are
public buildings:⎭ cemented into the wall (p. 341).

(ILLUMINATED)⎫
ADDRESSES, &c.:⎬ (Petitions, &c.) (see p. 317).

MONOGRAMS &⎫ (see p. 325. These are frequently
DEVICES:⎬ designed for stencilling or other
⎭ mechanical reproduction).

LETTERING FOR⎫ ⎧ See also
REPRODUC-⎬ (see p. 329). ⎨ BROADSIDES,
TION:⎭ ⎩ above.

Printer's types and⎫ (in woodcut and metal: pp. 329,
Ornamental letters:⎭ 331).

Title Pages: (see p. 327).

Paper and other Book⎫ (Magazines, Newspaper-Headings,
covers:⎭ Music, Catalogues, &c.).

Maps & Plans: ⎰ good, clear lettering may be used
⎱ in these with fine effect.

Book Plates: ⎧ (preferably simple, with Arms,
⎨ Crest, or Symbol, and suitable
⎩ lettering).

Letter-paper Head-⎱ (preferably in copper-plate "Ro-
ings, Cards, &c.:⎰ man" and "Italic").

Bill Heads, Receipt⎱ (preferably in copper-plate or type:
Forms, &c.:⎰ see p. 329).

Certificates: ⎰ (Testimonials, &c.). The plainer
⎱ these are made, the better.

Programmes, Menus,⎱ (Christmas cards, &c.).
Cards, &c.:⎰

Almanacks: (see above)

303

Special Subjects		
MS. Books and "copy-books":	Possibly might be reproduced by copper-plate if written well enough (p. 331).
Advertisements, &c.:	Better lettering in these would not only mitigate many eyesores, but would probably attract by its novelty (see p. 316).
ENGRAVING, &c.:	(see pp. 328, 329, 339).
Brasses, &c.:	("Brasses," Name-plates, Door-plates, &c.).
Punches:	(for naming, numbering, &c. *e.g.* Bookbinders' *Finishing Tools*).
Utensils:	(Bowls, flagons, plates, &c.).
Ornaments:	(Jewellery, &c.).
Die Sinking:	(for coins, medals, &c., and for embossed paper headings, &c.).
INSCRIPTIONS IN STONE & WOOD:	(see pp. 339–349, & Chap. XVII).
On Monuments & Buildings:	Also on mile-stones, boundary stones, bridges, &c.
Tombstones:	
Foundation Stones:	
Memorial Tablets:	
Street Names:	
"SIGN WRITING":	(see pp. 314, 340).
Signs:	(for stations, inns, shops, &c.).
Shop Fascias, &c.:	
Names, &c.:	(on doors & on carts, *coaches*, &c.).
Notice Boards:	
"Ticket Writing":	
EMBROIDERY, &c.:	see remarks on *built-up forms*, p. 256: and Chapter XII [on Lettering, &c.] of "Embroidery and Tapestry Weaving," by Mrs. A. H. Christie, in this Series.

Decoration for hangings, (p. 300): *Marking clothes, &c.*

304

All the arts employ lettering directly or indirectly, in fine decoration or for simple service.

The following list of ancient uses is interesting:[1]—

"I. TITULI

1. Dedicatory and Votive Inscriptions (*Tituli Sacri*).
2. Sepulchral Inscriptions (*Tituli Sepulchrales*).
3. Honorary Inscriptions (*Tituli Honorarii*).
4. Inscriptions on Public Works (*Tituli Operum Publicorum*).
5. Inscriptions on Movable Objects (*Instrumentum*).

II. INSTRUMENTA

1. Laws (*Leges et Plebi Scita*).
2. Decrees of the Senate (*Senatus Consulta*).
3. Imperial Documents (*Instrumenta Imperatorum*).
4. Decrees of Magistrates (*Decreta Magistratuum*).
5. Sacred and Public Documents (*Acta Sacra et Publica*).
6. Private Documents (*Acta Privata*).
7. Wall Inscriptions (*Inscriptiones Parietariae*).
8. Consular Diptychs (*Diptycha Consularia*)."

MS. BOOKS, &c.

Books in the making—as compared with ordinary inscriptions—are capable of great compression or expansion, and may be said to have a quality of *elasticity*. Nearly all other ordinary inscriptions are *set inscriptions* (p. 314), requiring a given number of words to be set out in a given space. But in books, while it is convenient that the treatment of the text should conform generally to a chosen size of page (p. 69), the contents of the page may vary according to the letter-form and the spacing (pp. 73, 226), and the number of the pages is not definitely limited, so that another page, or a number

---

[1] p. 224, J. C. Egbert's "Introduction to the Study of Latin Inscriptions,"—1896.

of additional pages, may always be taken to complete the text.

The size of page, margin, and writing having been settled (see Chap. VI)—and the pages ruled —the penman writes out the text with the utmost freedom, not stopping to make fine calculations, but leaving such spaces and lines, for Initials, Headings, &c., as his fancy and common sense dictate, and letting the text—or its divisions—smoothly flow on from page to page till a natural termination is reached. And if the terminal page has only one or two lines on it, it is not necessary to attempt a balance with the previous page—the book or chapter[1] ends just there, for the good reason *that there is no more of it.*

Colophons, Tail-pieces, &c. (see p. 108), make a pleasant finish, and may complete the page or not as convenient.

Planning: Sections and Pages.—Calculations of the amount of text, of the number of sections or pages required, and so on, are useful, and planning the pages may be convenient—for example, one or more of the verses of a poem, or a given number of words, may be allotted to the page—provided always that the scribe preserves his freedom, and treats each case on its merits. If he think it most suitable to devote a complete page to each paragraph, he may do so in spite of its resulting in the pages all being of different lengths.

The one general limitation which it is proper to

---

[1] If there is sufficient room left on the terminal page *for a clearly marked beginning* (such as a decorative initial), the *next* chapter may begin there, and so fill the page—but generally there is no objection to leaving blank what the text has failed to fill.

observe is that of the *Writing-line*—its length[1] and spacing—and to this may be added the desirability of beginning the text of every page on the first or *head* line.[2] For most of us it is not practically possible to do without the *aid* of the writing-lines —which really lead, through uniformity, to greater freedom—though a book written without them[3] might be as beautiful as any ruled manuscript.

Marginal Lines.—These, the terminals of the writing-lines, are frequently made double, with about ¼ inch between (see Plates XX and XV). On the left this space is utilised for marginal capitals, or is left blank; on the right the *first* line acts as a warning mark and the normal termination of the text, the *second* as a barrier beyond which the writing should not go. The double lines, in being more obvious than single lines, are also more effective in "straightening" the page (p. 75): presumably for this reason the two upper and two lower *writing-lines* were often ruled from edge to edge of the page (see Plate XI).

Ruling.—Marginal and writing-lines, once ruled, are to be left intact, and may be regarded as actual component parts of the finished pages. They are best made with a hard blunt point (p. 74)—the *furrows* so made give an interesting character, almost a "texture," to the smooth surface of the page. But they may be ruled with a fine lead pencil, or with a fine pen and faint black or coloured inks.

---

[1] The line need not always be *filled* by the writing (p. 411).

[2] It would not be necessary for the first page of a chapter to have the ordinary *dropped head* and blank upper space if a fine initial or decorative heading were used to mark it.

[3] Some of the books *engraved* by William Blake suggest possibilities of such *un*-conventional treatment, of both writing and "illumination" (see also p. xix).

Inked or coloured lines, however, are not generally written *upon* (see *footnote*, p. 269), but *between* (see Plates XIII, XVII, XX, &c.).

Correcting Mistakes.—A neatly made rather small letter above and a *caret* (∧) below (as in ordinary writing) may be used for an omission (fig. 192). A superfluous letter may be neatly struck out. Erasures

makeing

cofrections

FIG. 192.

are usually unsatisfactory, and a simple, unostentatious correction, besides disarming criticism, is in accordance with the proper freedom of the craft (p. 140). In an important Manuscript the page is better re-written.

Annotations, *&c.*, preferably in smaller *coloured* writing, are very decorative in the broader margins (pp. 110, 279).

Special Books.—A MS. book is necessarily unique, and some special or personal interest—of either the craftsman (see p. 108) or his "client"—inevitably attaches to it. This may affect its size and form, the treatment of the text, and the decoration and construction generally (see p. 66). Every legitimate opportunity of adding to its individual character should be taken by the scribe and illuminator.

Fig. 175 and Plate XX are both taken from
private prayer books or psalters; in each the name
of the owner (e.g. *"Euanzelista famulo tuo,"* Plate
XX) is frequently inserted. Plates XV and XXII
are also taken from specially commissioned MSS.,
and many evidences of their ownership, such as portraits or coats-of-arms, form part of the decoration
of such books.

Church Services, &c.—(For a special church or
person.) Church uses are so varied, that it is most
important to ascertain the custom, use, or taste of
the persons concerned—especially as to the order
of, and the introduction or omission of, certain
words, paragraphs, or parts, the colours used in the
text, the notation of the music—and the manner
in which the book will be used.

A service book for the use of a priest gives
prominence to the parts in which he is concerned
—the responses[1] may be smaller, and different in
form or colour. The rubrics—in red (see pp. 106,
110)—are kept quite distinct, and may form a very
decorative feature. For a private person the other
parts—such as are said by the congregation—might
be specially marked. In either case a certain amount
of planning—*e.g.* completing prayers, &c., in an
opening, to avoid turning over—may be justified by
its convenience to the reader. Should very careful
planning ever be required, a *pattern-book* may be
made, having the contents of each page roughly
indicated in it.

Wedding Service Books, &c.—The interest and

---

[1] The distinction in the Prayer Book between "Amen" and
"Amen"—used as a response—is best marked by the sign ℞
(for Responsum) in red, placed before the *latter*, as: ℞ Amen
(see pp. 110, xxiii).

value is enhanced if the book is specially prepared
—containing the proper names and dates, and only
the special psalms, hymns, prayers, homilies, &c.,
which will be used. Dated pages may be provided
at the end of the book for the signatures of the
"friends and neighbours" of the principals.

BINDING MSS.

MSS. should be bound without delay in order to
complete and protect them.

To bind books in stiff boards, in leather, requires
considerable practice and skill, but a very effective
limp vellum cover can be made by the scribe himself,
who, in binding his own books, will learn to think
of the binding *as a part of the book*, and to allow for
it in the writing and planning (see p. 72).

The following note[1] on covering books in limp
vellum is specially contributed by Mr. Douglas
Cockerell:—

"*How to cover a book in a limp vellum cover without
using special appliances.*

"Cut four strips of stiff vellum $\frac{3}{8}$ inch wide and about
four inches long. On these slips you will sew the sections
of your book.

"Add to your book a plain section at either end;[2]
vellum for a vellum book, paper for a paper book.
Knock up the backs of the sections squarely, keeping
the heads level, and across the back mark with a soft
pencil guided by a square, lines to show the position of
the slips. The positions of the four slips should leave
the space between the slips the same as that between the

---

[1] Figs. 195 and 196 are from Mr. Cockerell's "Bookbinding
and the Care of Books," in this Series.
[2] These form the fly-leaves (p. 77).

top slip and the head of the book; the space between the bottom slip and the tail should be a little longer than the spaces between the slips. At about ½ inch from either end make an additional line across the back for the 'kettle' or catch stitch. These lines will show as dots on the back of single sections. Each individual section should now have at the back a dot at either end for the kettle stitches, and four pairs of dots ⅜ inch apart to show the position of the slips, ten dots in all.

"To sew the book, fold the vellum slips about 1½ inch from one end and bend to a right angle. Place your front end-paper outside downwards, with the back even with the edge of a table or board, and place your folded slips with their shorter ends under it. Then insert your needle from the outside, at the head 'kettle stitch' mark, into the centre of the section and bring it out at the first band mark; put the slip in position and reinsert your needle at the mark on the other side of the slip, and so on to the end of the section, coming out at the tail kettle stitch. This should leave your section with a thread,[1] passing alternately along the centre fold inside and across the slips outside, with a loose end hanging from the kettle stitch mark where you began, and a thread with the needle hanging from the other kettle stitch mark (fig 193).

_Head
Kettle
Stitch_

_Tail
Kettle
Stitch_

Fig. 193.

---

[1] _Thread_ should be unbleached. Silk of the best quality is better than thread.

311

"Lay on your next section and sew it in the same way but in the reverse direction, tying up with the first loose end when you come to it. Sew the whole book in the same way, tying on a new needleful of thread as each is exhausted, making practically a continuous thread going backwards and forwards inside the sections and across the slips from end to end of the book. Each succeeding kettle stitch should be caught up by a loop (fig. 194),

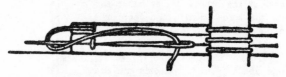

FIG. 194.

and it is well to catch together the loose threads crossing the slips.

"When the book is sewn, the back may be covered with thin glue and lined with a piece of leather, but as this is a little difficult to manage neatly, and as the book will hold together without it, for a temporary binding the sections may be left without glue.

"For the cover cut a piece of covering vellum[1] (vellum with a surface) large enough to cover the book and to leave a margin of $1\frac{1}{2}$ inches all round. Mark this with a *folder* on the underside, as shown at A, fig. 195. Spaces (1) and (2) are the size of the sides of the book with the surrounding 'squares,'[2] space (3) is the width of the back, and space (4) the width for the overlaps on the foredge.[3] Cut the corners as shown at (5), and fold the edges over as at B, and then fold over the overlaps and

---

[1] *Forrel* may be used as a cheap substitute for vellum.
[2] *"Squares"* = "*the portion of the boards projecting beyond the edges of the book.*"
[3] *"Foredge"* = "(fore edge) *the front edge of the leaves.*"

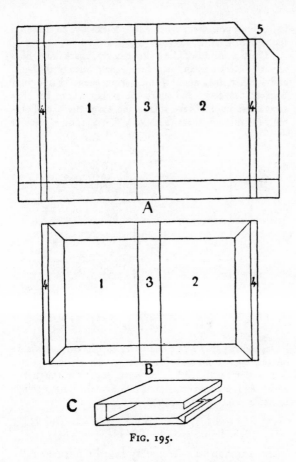

FIG. 195.

back as at C.   Be sure to make all folds sharp and
true.

"To avoid mistakes it is well to make a cover of stiff

313

paper first, and then, when that fits exactly, to make up
the vellum from it.

"On the inside of the vellum cover, mark faint lines
about ¾ inch from, and parallel to, the creases of the back,
and further lines about ¼ inch from these. Place your
book in the cover and mark the places where the slips
cross these lines. Make slits in the cover there, and lace
the slips through them (fig. 196), first putting a piece of

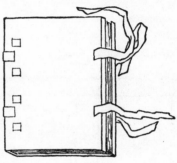

FIG. 196.

loose, toned paper inside the cover to prevent any marks
on the book from showing through the vellum. Then
lace pieces of silk ribbon of good quality[1] through the
cover and end-papers, leaving the ends long enough
to tie."

BROADSIDES, WALL INSCRIPTIONS, &C.

Set Inscriptions.—Ordinary inscriptions generally
consist of a given number of words to be set out in

---

[1] A good, rather dark green ribbon looks well—such as that
known as "Church lace," used for the "tyres" in some of the
Kelmscott books. Very good ribbons may be obtained from a
bookbinder, at 6d. to 1s. 6d. a yard.

a given space. Careful planning may sometimes be required to fit in the words suitably, or to adapt the lettering to the space. But setting-out (p. 222) becomes much simpler after a little practice, and the good craftsman avoids over-planning.

The Place of the Inscription.—The actual space for a wall inscription is commonly suggested by an architectural feature—a stone, a panel, or a niche —of the wall; but in choosing a suitable space for a given inscription, or suitable lettering for a given space, we must take into account—

1. *The office of the inscription.*
2. *How it is to be read—*
    (*a*) *"At a glance," or*
    (*b*) *by close inspection.*
3. *The distance from the reader.*
4. *The lighting of the space.*
5. *The character of the surroundings.*
6. *Any special features.*

The Size of the Letters.—The all-important question of readableness may be settled thus: the inscription having been planned suitably to fill the space, one or two words are written or painted (the exact size) on paper—smoked or otherwise coloured if necessary to resemble the background. This is stuck upon the chosen part of the wall, and then viewed from the ordinary position of a reader. When the inscription is high up, the *thin* parts—especially the horizontals of the letters—must be made extra thick to be seen properly from below.

Margins.—*Wide margins are only required for comparatively small lettering which demands the close*

315

attention of the reader,[1] and generally a set inscription looks best if the lettering be comparatively large—covering most of the given surface, and leaving comparatively narrow margins. The frame or moulding, or the natural *edge* or environment of the circumscribed space, is very often sufficient "margin" (see Plate XXIV).

The margins vary, however, according to circumstances; especially the foot margin, which may be very narrow if all the space is required for the lettering (see fig. 211), or very large[2] if there is plenty of space (see fig. 210). And, as in special pages or *terminal pages* of books, so in *single sheets, panels,* &c., the "foot margin" may show—as it really is—as *the space which did not require to be filled,* and was therefore "*left over.*"

Number of Different Types.—While in a book of many pages considerable diversity is allowed, it is essential to the strength and dignity of a single sheet or set inscription to limit the number of types employed in it. Three or four ordinary types will generally give sufficient variety, and if it be necessary—as in notices and placards— that IMPORTANT WORDS be put in *special* types to catch the eye, let two—or at most three—special types suffice, and let the remainder of the text be as quiet and reserved as possible. "Display Types" commonly defeat their object by being *overdone.* A simple contrast is the most effective (fig. 197).

---

[1] *E.g.* all ordinary written and printed matter intended to be read *at a short distance* (see pp. 69–72), *and generally held in the hand.*
[2] As much as two-thirds, or more, of the whole space.

316

CAPITALS

in the head-line, large and spaced wide, are
contrasted with a mass of smaller lettering
below (see p. 294).   NOTE.—Generally a
finer—though less striking—effect is obtained
by keeping large capitals rather slender—contrasting *size* rather than *weight* (p. 292).

FIG. 197.

ILLUMINATED ADDRESSES, &C.

Forms of Addresses, &c.—The writer should be
prepared to advise his "clients" on the form which
the address may take, on special features in its writing
and illuminating, and on its general treatment.

Ordinarily an Illuminated Address is prepared
either as a *Framed Parchment* (p. 320), a *Parchment
Scroll*, or sheet (p. 320), or a *small bound MS. (i.e.*
in book form: p. 321).[1]

The wording commonly consists of three parts:
the HEADING (usually the name of the addressee),
the TEXT (usually divided into paragraphs), the
SIGNATURES (or a list of names) of the subscribers.

An address is commonly in the 1st or 3rd person,
and in case of any confusion of these, any slip of
the pen, or other oversight in the draft, the penman

---

[1] The addressee's taste and convenience ought to be considered: *e.g.* to one the framed inscription might be an embarrass-
ment, while by another it might be preferred.

should, if possible, call attention to it before the document is put into permanent form.

A very convenient and agreeable style of "address" is a formal letter, beginning "*Dear Mr. A—B—*," and ending in the ordinary way. This is a form which may be drawn up more simply, and which reads more naturally, than the ordinary 1st or 3rd personal statement.

An "address" is sometimes in the form of a resolution passed by a public or private body or committee. For municipal or other important corporations, such an extract from their minutes, neatly and "clerkly" written out on parchment, and duly attested by the signatures of their "head" and their secretary, and without ornament save their seal—on a dependent ribbon—or their coat-of-arms, or badge, would not only be the most natural, but possibly the most dignified and effective shape which might be given to the formal presentation of their compliments.

An "address" accompanying a present is frequently little more than a list of names with a brief complimentary or explanatory statement. If possible such an inscription should be written or engraved on the article itself, or be specially designed to accompany it. In some cases this is very simple: when a volume, or set of volumes, is given, the inscription may be written in the first volume—or on a parchment which may be inserted—or it may be prepared in book form, in a binding to match. A silver statuette or "ornament" may have a little drawer provided to hold a narrow scroll of names. A portrait may have an inscription on the frame—or even in a corner of the picture—or be accompanied by a simple, framed parchment.

Signatures.—A neatly written out list of subscribers—especially when their number is large—is very convenient: it does not require individual personal appointments, nor involve risks of damage to the address. The actual signatures of subscribers, however, are of greater interest and sentimental value, and on such grounds are preferable to a mere list of names.

To avoid risks (or with a view to incorporating the signatures in the decorative scheme) the decoration, gilding, &c., may sometimes be deferred until *after the signing of the address.*

When the exact number and the names of the subscribers are known beforehand, lines may be provided for their signatures, marked with letters in alphabetical order (the proper number of lines under each). This method solves any difficulty in regard to *precedence* in signing.

Note.—Ordinary signatures require about ½ inch by 3 inches space each. If there are many they may be conveniently arranged in two or more columns, according to the space available.

Directions for Signing[1]—

Edges of parchment not to project beyond desk or table, lest they be creased.

Paper to be provided to cover the address, with flaps *to raise when signing.*

When lines for signatures are grooved (p. 74), signatories to face the light (this makes the lines more evident).

Ink of one colour to be used if possible.

Clean, ordinary *pens to be provided, and scraps of the vellum or parchment for trying them on.*

---

[1] To be given (with *scraps*) to the person in charge of the address.

Framed Parchments.—The written parchment
may, with care, be pasted upon a stout card—a piece
of plain parchment on the back of the card will
check warping. Or, the written parchment may be
damped, by laying it for a few seconds on damp blotting paper, and then be stuck to a board *carefully
glued round the edges:* in either case press under a
heavy weight for twelve hours. Or—extra margin
being allowed—the edges of the parchment may be
cut into tags, folded over an ordinary canvas stretcher,
and well tacked at the back with small brads. The
wedges are carefully adjusted till the parchment lies
flat.

A parchment mounted first is simplest, but it has
a less natural surface, and is not so easily managed
by the penman as the plain, flexible parchment.

Frames should be gold, black, or white; very
plain, and generally without mounts. The parchment, however, must be so framed (*e.g.* with a concealed slip of wood behind the glass) that there is
no danger of any part of it coming into contact
with the glass (as that, being damp, would lead to
cockling).

Parchment Scroll.—The foot edge of the parchment may be folded over twice,[1] a strong, silk ribbon
(see *footnote*, p. 314) is laced along through slits in
the folded part (*a*, fig. 198), so that the two ends
come out again at the centre—where they may be
knotted together—and are ready to tie round the
scroll when it is rolled up (*b*). A rather narrow,
"*upright*" parchment is most convenient (*c*). An
"*oblong*" parchment may be very effectively arranged

---

[1] The original intention of this fold, in deeds, was to provide
for the attachment of the seal, and, perhaps, to prevent any
addition being made. If the folded part be fairly wide, say
¾ to 1 inch, little or no foot margin need be allowed.

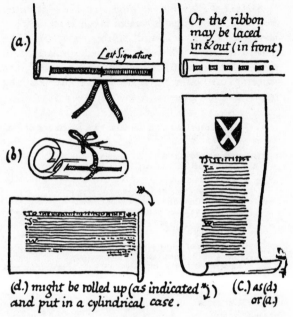

(a.)

Last Signature

*Or the ribbon
may be laced
in & out (in front)*

(b)

(d.) might be rolled up (as indicated ↘)
and put in a cylindrical case.

(C.) as (d)
or (a.)

FIG. 198.

in long lines of writing (*d*) if the lines are kept strong
and spaced well apart.

If a casket or case is not provided, a neat japanned
tin case may be obtained for a few shillings.

A small Bound MS. is certainly the most easily
handled form in which an address may be prepared
—its convenience to the penman, the signatories,
the reader, and the addressee, is strongly in its
favour. A lengthy address, or a very large number
of names, may be contained in a comparatively
small book.

Method of Planning out Addresses, &c.—If in the
book form, the address is treated much as an ordinary
book (see Chap. VI, and *Binding,* p. 310). The
framed or *scroll* address is planned similarly to a
single sheet (p. 56). The following notes of a
working method were made during the planning
out of an address:—

(1) Decide approximately the general *form,* shape, and decorative treatment of address.

(2) Count words in TEXT (leaving out
    HEADINGS and SIGNATURES) ═ 130

       Count paragraphs .   .   .   ═ 3

       (Decide whether first or last paragraph
       is to be in a different form or colour.)

       Decide approximate width .   .   . ═ 12 inches.

       Decide approximate side margins (2½
       inches each) .   .   .   . ═ 5 „

       Hence *length of writing-line* .   . ═ 7 „
       Allow ¼ inch lines, and approximately
       eight words to the line.

(3) 130 words TEXT, approx. .   16 lines ═ 8 in. deep.

       Allow extra (on account para-
       graphs) .   .   .   .   1 line ═ ¼ „ „

       (Roughly sketch out HEAD-
       ING on lines each ½ inch
       by 7 inches.) Allow for
       HEADING .   .   .   6 lines ═ 3 „ „

       Allow for two SIGNATURES,
       &c. .   .   .   .   3 lines ═ 1½ „ „

       Total depth of Writing, &c. .   26 lines ═ 13 inches.

       Allow for Top margin .   .   .   .   2 „

       Allow for Foot margin .   .   .   3 „

       (NOTE.—*This was a "scroll," and the foot
       margin was folded up to within an inch of
       the SIGNATURES. A plain sheet
       would have required about 4 inches foot
       margin.*)

       Length of Parchment .   .   18 inches.

(4) Cut a paper pattern, 12 inches by 18 inches. Rule (in pencil) *Side margins* (2½ inches and 2½ inches), and *Top margin* (2 inches), and 26 (½ inch) lines. On this write out the address in ordinary handwriting, using ordinary black and red (or coloured) inks: make approximately eight words to the line, and *write as fast as possible;* this helps to keep the spacing uniform.

This written pattern should not take more than twenty minutes for its entire preparation: it is intended to be used as a check on the previous calculation (not as an exact *plan*), and as a *copy*, it being easier to copy from your own, than from another's, handwriting.

If the original draft is typewritten, it is hardly necessary to make such a pattern.

(5) Check this *copy* very carefully with the original to see that the words, &c., are correct.

(6) Cut, rule, and pounce the *parchment* (pp. 307, 140).

(7) On some *scraps* of parchment, ruled with a few similar lines, and *similarly* pounced, try one or two lines of writing, both in vermilion and black, to see that all goes well.

This enables you to get the pens and inks into working order, and will very likely save the carefully prepared *parchment* from being spoilt.

(8) Write out the address, leaving suitable gaps for *gold* or special letters.

(9) Put in special letters, decorative capitals, and any other decoration.

(10) Check the finished *address* very carefully with the original draft (see (5) above) and look it over for mistakes, dotting i's, and putting in commas, &c., if left out. It is important that such a formal document should be accurate.

General Remarks.—The above simple mode of planning out can be further simplified in custom and practice. By the penman *keeping to regular shapes, proportions,*[1] *and modes of treatment for regular*

---

[1] *E.g.* to keep to ½ inch writing line spaces (except for extra small addresses, or small books). This being approximately the right space for ordinary SIGNATURES, results in further simplification of ruling and arrangement.

occasions, the addresses, &c., will practically "plan themselves" (p. 67), and better workmanship is the natural result.

Generally the simpler the form and the treatment of an Illuminated Address, the better the effect. The most effective decoration is the plain coloured or gold capital, and the finest ornament is a coat-of-arms (see "*Heraldry*," below; and for general,

Diagram shewing the arrangement of the charges in the earliest form of the English Coat of Arms: Rd. I. to Ed. III.

FIG. 199.

324

simple Illumination, see Chapters VII to XIII).
A symbolical mark, such as a crest, badge, monogram, cypher, or other device (p. 326), boldly and
decoratively treated, may be used in place of a coat-
of-arms.

There is too much "Illumination" in the conventional "Address," which looks like a *"piece of
decoration" with a little writing*. A really reasonable
and effective Illuminated Address is *a piece of writing
suitably decorated*.

.   .   .   .

Heraldry.—A reliable handbook must be con-
sulted, for accurate *"blazoning"* is essential. Early
examples should be studied (see p. 351). The diagram, fig. 199, is given as an example of how a charge
was evenly arranged on the shield (see *balanced* background, p. 381). Another example—showing a
diapered chequer—is given on p. 300.

Shields in *Illuminated* borders may be coloured
before the border, lest the brilliant mass of colour
of the shield clash with the border. The shield, if
large, may with advantage set the tone of the whole
colour scheme.

MONOGRAMS & DEVICES

A *Monogram* consists of two or more letters
combined in one form, as the diphthong Æ, and
the ampersand[1] & for ℰℐ : its legibility may
be helped by compound colouring. A *Cypher* consists of linked or interlaced letters, as ○○ , and

---

[1] In the common form &. the letters ℯ ℧ (see Plate
VI) are now barely traceable.

may be repeated and reversed if desired (see fig. 200).

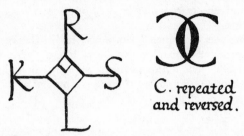

C. repeated
and reversed.

Device used by Charles the Great:
KAROLVS.

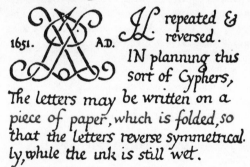

1651. A.D. repeated &
reversed.

IN planning this
sort of Cyphers,
The letters may be written on a
piece of paper, which is folded, so
that the letters reverse symmetrical-
ly, while the ink is still wet.

FIG. 200.

Monograms and cyphers may be very decoratively employed as ornaments, and may be used to
mark a man's goods, or as a *signature* on his work:
something easily recognised—either very legible or
characteristic—is therefore desirable. The two
modes may be combined, and there is no limit to

the effective devices and ornaments which may be composed of letters. Simple and straightforward devices, however, are generally preferable to very ornate or intricate designs.

Chronograms.—A chronogram consists of a word or words in which the numerical letters indicate a date. The following is from a very fine memorial inscription at Rye (see fig. 207):—

Ioannes ThreeLe MeDIo Lætæ ætatIs fLore obIIt.

It expresses the date I + L + M + D + I + L + I + L + I + I (or I + 50 + 1000 + 500 + I + 50 + I + 50 + I + I) = 1655. As every letter having a numerical value (*i.e.* C, D, I, (J), L, M, (U), V, (W), (X) may be counted, a proper chronogram is not easily composed.

The letter-craftsman will discover many ways of "playing" with letters, and of expressing—or concealing—names and numbers in other words, and he may take every liberty he chooses in his private pleasure, provided it does not clash with public convenience.

TITLE PAGES

If large capitals be used, the *Name of the Book*, *the Author*, &c., above; the *Name of the Publisher*, *the Date*, &c., below,[1] may together fill the page. Ordinary capitals (as used in the text) leave a space in the centre (see Title Page of this book): often pleasantly filled by a small woodcut—a symbolical device, monogram, or printer's mark.

Generally, the fewer and simpler the types, the

---

[1] Other particulars may be put in the colophon (p. 108).

better: though contrasts of size, form, or colour
(see p. 291)—such as printing one or two words in
large CAPITALS, or in 𝕭𝖑𝖆𝖈𝖐 𝕷𝖊𝖙𝖙𝖊𝖗 (p.
295), or part in red—may sometimes be used with
good effect. When the types are rather varied, single
or double *framing lines* (called "*rules*") placed round
the page have the effect of binding the whole together. The page may also be divided into parts by
transverse "rules"—these further solidify it. Black
rules are preferable to red (p. 110): if they are
double, the outer line may be thicker than the
inner.[1]

Relation of Title Pages, &c., to the Text.—Generally the practical part of the book is to be considered and settled before the ornamental and the
decorated Title page conforms to the treatment of
the text pages, and should be clearly related to them
by the character of its letters or its ornaments. Its
margins (especially the top margin) should be approximately the same as those of the text pages, though
framing borders may occupy part of, or nearly all,
the marginal space. Without doubt the artless,
ordinarily printed title page is preferable to those
specially designed "title pages" that have little or
no relation to the rest of the book.

Wood Engraving (see pp. 329, 335).—Of all the
"processes," wood engraving agrees best with printing. The splendid effect of Title and Initial pages
engraved in wood may be seen in the books of the
Kelmscott Press. In early printing, woodcut ornaments or borders were commonly used to decorate

---

[1] The use of "rules," though quite legitimate, will be found
misleading if it be depended on to "doctor" and "pull together" any weak arrangement of lettering.

328

the printed title page. An example of this combined method—of which unfortunately the greater part of the borders have to be left out—is shown in fig. 201 (from a 16th century book).[1]

Initial Pages and Openings.—The claim of these to decorative treatment should be considered (p. 94). We generally look at the outside of a book for the *title*—which should be clearly stamped on the cover. But inside the book we look rather for its *actual beginning* than for its name, and, while something in the nature of the "sub-title" might be used, it would be quite reasonable to revive the ancient fashion—especially in the case of MS. Books —of making the actual beginning the most decorative part of the book. Or a very fine effect may be obtained by the decoration of the entire *initial opening*—the title on the *verso* (left page), the beginning of the first chapter on the *recto* (right page).

LETTERING FOR REPRODUCTION

Where it is possible, it is generally best to make use of ordinary typography. A good fount of type and a natural *setting-up* or arrangement of it, are more effective than many special designs (see pp. 328, 231).

Wood and Metal Engraving.—If special forms or arrangements of letters are required, for which type is lacking or unsuited, they are best cut in wood or

---

[1] More, Sir Thomas: "*Utopia, et Mori et Erasmi Epigrammata*": 4to, Froben, Basle, 1518. Woodcut borders and Title pages by Holbein. (The reproduction is from the title page to the Epigrams.) NOTE.—The exceptionally fine type of capitals (see p. 337) here shown is used throughout the book for headings, &c.

329

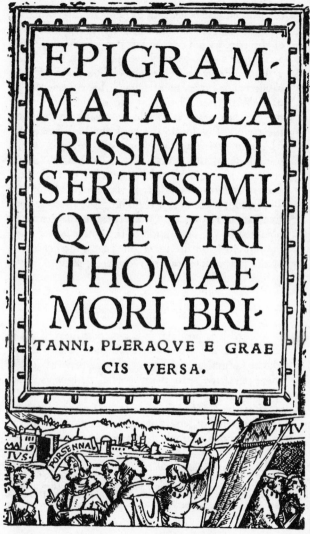

**EPIGRAM-
MATA CLA
RISSIMI DI
SERTISSIMI-
QVE VIRI
THOMAE
MORI BRI-**
TANNI, PLERAQVE E GRAE
CIS VERSA.

FIG. 201 *(see footnote, p. 329).*

metal. The engraver leaves the mark of his tool
and hand upon, and so gives character to, such lettering; while, if he has some knowledge of letters, he may give fresh beauty to their forms.

The Zincotype Process reproduces, either in *fac-simile* or on a reduced scale, the "design" made by the craftsman in "black and white." This it does more or less exactly according to the pains taken by the zincographer, the quality of the paper employed, &c. The literalness and facility of this process, however, seem to have had a prejudicial effect on the work of the designer. Unless he conscientiously determines that his design shall stand without "touching-up," the knowledge that he may blot out or trim a faulty line with white, that he may fill out or finish a deficient stroke with black, that he may work *large* and zincograph *small*, is apt to result in carelessness combined with over-finishing—or a sort of *perfection without character*.

If zincography be used, a strong, rather type-like letter, or a built-up letter—arranged to give a general effect of richness of mass, would appear more natural than the doubtful "reproduction" of delicate writing or fine pen-lettering.[1]

Etching.—Calligraphy might be reproduced with very fine effect, retaining its natural delicacy and on a plane surface, if a process of etching *writing* in facsimile were possible.

PRINTING

The general question of fine printing and its relation to calligraphy can only be briefly referred

---

[1] *Doubtful*, because, unless unusual care be taken, its delicate quality may be lost in the process, and also because of the type-like impress of the block on the paper.

to here. A proper study of the art of typography necessitates practice with a printing press, and probably the help of a trained assistant.

To would-be printers, printers, and all interested in typography, the easily acquired art of writing may be commended as a practical introduction to a better knowledge of letter forms and their decorative possibilities.

In this connection I have quoted in the preface (p. xi) some remarks on *Calligraphy* by Mr. Cobden-Sanderson, who, again, referring to typography, says—[1]

"The passage from the Written Book to the Printed Book was sudden and complete. Nor is it wonderful that the earliest productions of the printing press are the most beautiful, and that the history of its subsequent career is but the history of its decadence. The Printer carried on into Type the tradition of the Calligrapher and of the Calligrapher at his best. As this tradition died out in the distance, the craft of the Printer declined. It is the function of the Calligrapher to revive and restore the craft of the Printer to its original purity of intention and accomplishment. The Printer must at the same time be a Calligrapher, or in touch with him, and there must be in association with the Printing Press a Scriptorium where beautiful writing may be practised and the art of letter-designing kept alive. And there is this further evidence of the dependence of printing upon writing: the great revival in printing which is taking place under our own eyes, is the work of a Printer who before he was a Printer was a Calligrapher and an Illuminator, WILLIAM MORRIS.

"The whole duty of Typography, as of Calligraphy, is to communicate to the imagination, without loss by the

---

[1] *"Ecce Mundus (The Book Beautiful),"* 1902.

way, the thought or image intended to be communicated by the Author. And the whole duty of beautiful typography is not to substitute for the beauty or interest of the thing thought and intended to be conveyed by the symbol, a beauty or interest of its own, but, on the one hand, to win access for that communication by the clearness and beauty of the vehicle, and on the other hand, to take advantage of every pause or stage in that communication to interpose some characteristic and restful beauty in its own art."

Early Printing was in some points inferior in technical excellence to the best modern typography. But the best early printers used finer founts of type and better proportions in the arrangement and spacing of their printed pages; and it is now generally agreed that early printed books are the most beautiful. It would repay a modern printer to endeavour to find out the real grounds for this opinion, *the underlying principles* of the early work, and, where possible, to put them into practice.

Freedom.—The treatment or "planning" of early printing—and generally of all pieces of lettering which are most pleasing—is strongly marked by *freedom*. This freedom of former times is frequently referred to now as "spontaneity"—sometimes it would seem to be implied that there was a lawless irresponsibility in the early craftsman, incompatible with modern conditions. True spontaneity, however, seems to come from *working by rule, but not being bound by it*.

For example, the old Herbal from which figs. 135 to 141 are taken contains many woodcuts of plants, &c., devoting a complete page to each. When a long explanation of a cut is required, *a smaller type is used* (comp. figs. 135 & 138); when the explanation

333

is very short, *it does not fill the page.* This is a
free and natural treatment of the greatest convenience to the reader, for illustration and text are always
in juxtaposition. And though the size of the type
and the amount of the text are varied, yet the uniform
top margins, and the uniform treatment and arrangement of the woodcuts, harmonise the pages, and give
to the whole book an agreeable effect of freedom
combined with method.

An old way of treating a text and its commentary
is indicated by the diagram (fig. 202). The text is

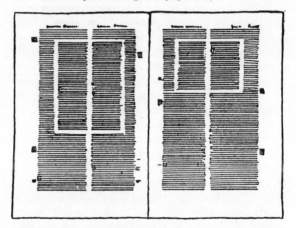

Diagram shewing arrangement of pages (about ⅓ size).
Note· Inner columns of Commentary narrow (Text cols. equal)

FIG. 202.

printed in large type, the commentary, in smaller
type, surrounds it; such portion of the text being
printed on each page as will allow sufficient surrounding space for the accompanying commentary

334

on that portion. The proportions and treatment of every page are uniform (note, particularly, the uniformity of the upper parts of the pages, five lines of commentary being allowed to enclose the text, or bound it above, on every page) with the exception that the height of the text-column varies—one page having as few as three lines of text to the column, another having fifty-nine lines. This free treatment of the text gives a charming variety to the pages.

Poetry.—A broader and freer treatment is desirable in the printing of poetry. The original lines and the arrangement of the verses should be more generally preserved. And though the opening lines of a poem may sometimes be magnified by printing them in capitals—which necessitate their division—to sacrifice the naturally varying line to the "even page" is questionable, and to destroy the form of a poem *in order to compress it* is a "typographical impertinence" (see p. 61).

DECORATION OF PRINT ✠ MUCH MAY BE DONE BY ARRANGING IMPORTANT TEXT IN "ITS OWN" CAPITALS; OR BY THE OCCASIONAL USE OF EXTRA LARGE CAPITALS.

For special letters or ornaments, woodcuts are best (see p. 328). The early printers generally had little, simple blocks of ornamental devices which might be used separately, or be built up into a frame border for a whole page—a simple method and effective, if used reasonably.

335

The judicious use of colour, especially of *red* (see pp. 93, 110), is very effective. The extra printings required for additional colours may make it worth while (in the case of limited editions) to put in simple initials, paragraph marks, notes, &c., *by hand* (see pp. 160, 79). The earliest printed books, being modelled on the MS. books, employed such rubrication freely, in spaces specially left in the text or in the margins. There are still great possibilities in the hand decoration of printed books.

. . . .

The following note on printing, reproduced here by the permission of Mr. Emery Walker, appeared in the *Introductory Notes* of the Catalogue of·the first exhibition of *The Arts and Crafts Exhibition Society*, in 1888.

"PRINTING

"Printing, in the only sense with which we are at present concerned, differs from most if not from all the arts and crafts represented in the Exhibition in being comparatively modern. For although the Chinese took impressions from wood blocks engraved in relief for centuries before the wood-cutters of the Netherlands, by a similar process, produced the block books, which were the immediate predecessors of the true printed book, the invention of movable metal letters in the middle of the fifteenth century may justly be considered as the invention of the art of printing. And it is worth mention in passing that, as an example of fine typography, the earliest dated [1] book, the Gutenberg Bible of 1455, has never

---

[*It was dated* 1456 *by a rubricator, not by the printer.—E.W.*]

been surpassed. Printing, then, for our purpose, may be considered as the art of making books by means of movable types. Now, as all books not primarily intended as picture-books consist principally of types composed to form letterpress, it is of the first importance that the letter used should be fine in form; especially, as no more time is occupied, or cost incurred, in casting, setting, or printing beautiful letters, than in the same operations with ugly ones. So we find the fifteenth and early sixteenth century printers, who were generally their own typefounders, gave great attention to the forms of their types. The designers of the letters used in the earliest books were probably the scribes whose manuscripts the fifteenth-century printed books so much resemble. Aldus of Venice employed Francisco Francia of Bologna, goldsmith and painter, to cut the punches for his celebrated italic letter. Froben, the great Basle printer, got Holbein to design ornaments for his press, and it is not unreasonable to suppose that the painter may have drawn the models for the noble Roman types we find in Froben's books. With the decadence in handwriting which became marked in the sixteenth century, a corresponding change took place in the types; the designers, no longer having beautiful writing as a model and reference, introduced variations arbitrarily. The types of the Elzevirs are regular and neat, and in this respect modern, but they altogether lack the spirit and originality that distinguish the early Roman founts of Italy and Germany: Gothic characteristics inherited from their mediæval predecessors. In the seventeenth century type-founding began to be carried on as a craft apart from that of the printer, and although in this and the succeeding century many attempts were made to improve the "face" (as the printing surface of type is called), such examples as a rule reflect only too clearly the growing debasement of the crafts of design. Notable among these attempts were the founts cut by William Caslon, who started in business in London as a letter-founder in 1720, taking for his models the Elzevir types. From this time until the end of the century he and his successors turned out many founts relatively admirable. But at the end of the eighteenth century a revolution was made, and the founders entirely abandoned the traditional forms of their predecessors, and evolved the tasteless letters with which nearly all the books published during the first sixty years of the present century are printed, and which are still almost universally used for newspapers and for Government publications. Particularly objectionable forms are in everyday use in all continental countries requiring Roman letter. (The last two sentences are set in a type of this character.)

"In 1844 the Chiswick Press printed for Messrs. Longmans 'The Diary of Lady Willoughby,' and revived for this purpose one of Caslon's founts. This was an important step in the right direction, and its success induced Messrs. Miller & Richard of Edinburgh to engrave a series of 'old style' founts, with one of which this catalogue is printed. Most other type-founders now cast similar type, and without doubt if their customers, the printers, demanded it, they would expend some of the energy and talent which now goes in cutting Japanese-American and sham seventeenth-century monstrosities in endeavouring to produce once more the restrained and beautiful forms of the early printers, until the day when the current handwriting may be elegant enough to be again used as a model for the type-punch engraver.

"Next in importance to the type are the ornaments, initial letters, and other decorations which can be printed along with it. These, it is obvious, should always be designed and engraved so as to harmonise with the printed page regarded as a whole. Hence, illustrations drawn only with reference to purely pictorial effects are entirely out of place in a book, that is, if we desire seriously to make it beautiful.

EMERY WALKER."

338

As the material naturally modifies the shapes of
the letters cut or formed on its surface, and as the
object bearing the inscription affects their arrangement, it is essential that the inscription cutter make
himself familiar with various stones, metals, woods,
&c., with the various chisels and gravers which are
properly employed on them, and with fine inscriptions or examples of good pieces of lettering (see
pp. 352, 201).

A knowledge of penmanship will be found useful,
and the pen may be appealed to to decide questions
of abstract form in regard to letters which have come
from pen forms (*e.g.* Roman Small-Letters, Italics,
&c.). And in this connection it may be noted again
that the "slanted-pen forms" (pp. 269, 9) are
generally the most practical.

Engraving on Metal.—Letters incised in metal
may most nearly approach pen forms, as the fine
grain of the metal and the comparatively small scale
of the work allow of fine "thin strokes." The
engraver, however, while following generally the
"thicks" and "thins" of the penman, allows the
metal and the tool and, to a large extent, his own
hand, to decide and characterise the precise forms
and their proportions.

Inscriptions in Stone (see Chap. XVII, Plates I,
II, and XXIV, and pp. 256, 2).—The grain
of stone does not generally allow of very fine thin
strokes, and the "thicks" and "thins" therefore
tend to differ much less than in pen-work. Their
origin, moreover, is much less easily traced to the
tool—*i.e.* the chisel—and the difference was less in
the early inscriptions (see Plate II) than we are now

339

accustomed to (see Plate XXIV): perhaps it may
be explained as a fashion set by penmanship (see
p. 205).

Inscriptions on Wood are frequently in relief (see
raised letters, p. 341), matching the carved ornament. Incised letters may be painted or gilded to
make them show more clearly.

Sign-Writing and Brush-Work.—Inscriptions,
such as shop signs, notices, &c., painted on wood or
stone, require—besides a practical knowledge of
materials—a considerable facility with the brush or
"pencil." Directness and freedom of workmanship
are most desirable.[1]

A suitable brush will make letters closely resembling pen letters. But the pen *automatically* makes
letters with a uniform precision, which it is neither
desirable nor possible for the brush to *imitate:* and
greater skill is required to control the brush, which
in the hand of a good "Writer" will be permitted
to give its own distinct character to the lettering
(see also p. 256, and fig. 164).

The brush is properly used for temporary inscriptions, especially on the surface of painted wood or
stone, but, for more important work, *incising* or
carving (painted if desired) are to be preferred as
being more permanent[2] and preserving the original
form[3] of the lettering.

---

[1] This is recognised in the Sign-writing profession where,
I understand, an applicant for work is sometimes given a blackboard or a piece of American cloth, on which he writes out a
short inscription in "sharp white." It is not necessary to
watch the writer; good, direct workmanship shows itself, and
also every hesitating stroke or fault, every patch or "touching-
up" or "going over," is made evident.

[2] Brush lettering may be used very effectively on Tiles and
China, &c. (see p. 303), when it is of course rendered permanent
by baking.

[3] The original form of a painted inscription (not carved) is
inevitably spoilt by re-painting.

(See also Chapter XII, and pp. 314–317)

Alphabets.—For practical purposes the best letters are the *Roman Capitals, Roman Small-Letters, and Italics.* These are susceptible of very decorative treatment without loss of legibility. And there are many varieties of the pure Roman Capital (see figs. 203–207), besides the "Gothicised" Roman and the simple "Gothic" Capitals, which are all essentially readable.

Different Sizes of Capitals in inscriptions in wood, stone, metal, &c., are generally kept approximately equal in "weight" (see p. 292). NOTE.—A downward decrease in height of the letters is common in early inscriptions (p. 372).

Incising is generally the most simple, and therefore the most natural, method for making an ordinary inscription. The letters should be large rather than small, and be deeply cut. Note, however, an *incised* stamp or die produces an impression in *relief* on clay, &c. This may be seen in the lettering on Roman pottery.

Raised Letters.—From the earliest times letters in relief (or *litteræ prominentes*) have been used for special purposes. They are generally rather more legible than the incised letters, and the difference between "thicks" and "thins" tends to disappear. It is quite possible to make a beautiful and characteristic alphabet of equal-stroke letters, on the lines of the so-called "Block Letter" but properly proportioned and finished (such letters may be *Raised*, or *Incised* or *Painted:* see *incised form*, p. 355).

Raised letters, if exposed to wear or damage, may be protected by being on a sunk panel or having a raised frame or ornament. The background also

341

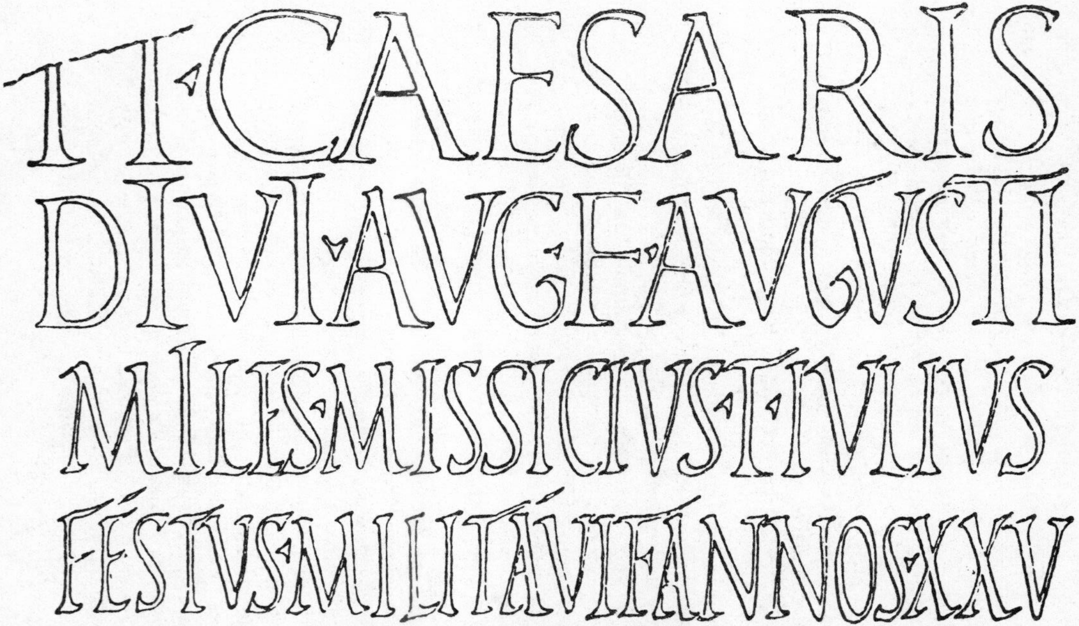

TI·CAESARIS

DIVI·AVG·FAVGSTI

MIUSMISSICVSISMVVS

FESTVSMILITAVITANNOSXXV

342

FIG. 203.—Hubner's *Exempla*, No. 187 (⅓ scale of inscription), "*Rustic Capitals*" (see p. 261) *between* A.D. 14–37

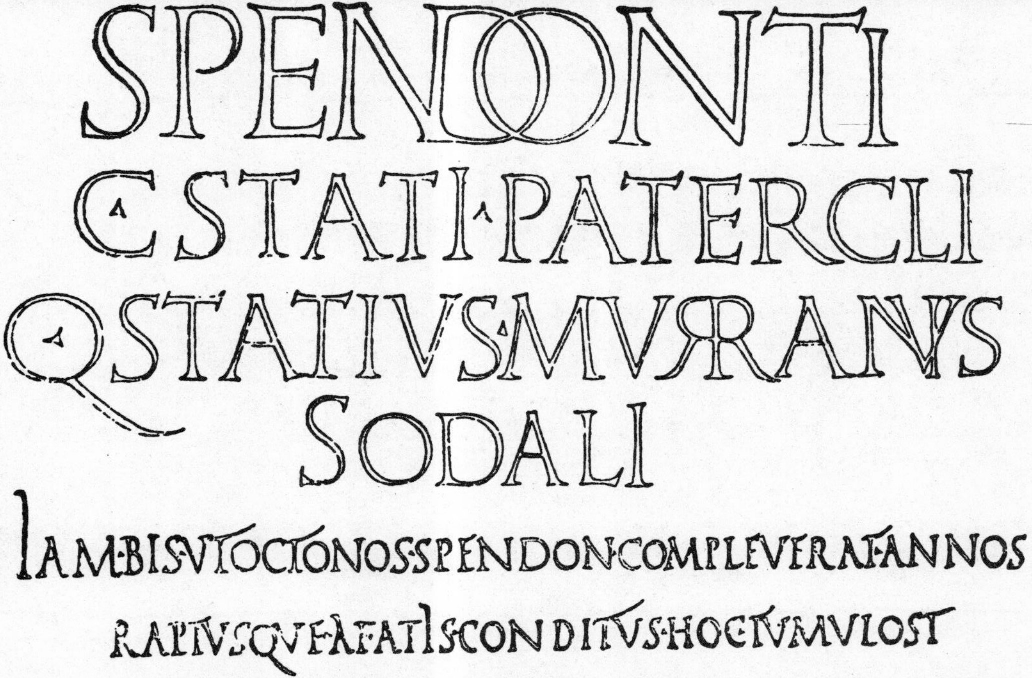

SPENDONTI
C·STATI·PATERCLI
Q·STATIVS·MVRRANVS
SODALI
I·AMBIS·VIOCION·OSS·P·ENDON·COMPLEVERA·ANNOS
RA·IVSQVE·FATIS·CONDITVS·HOC·CVMVLOST

Fig. 204.—Hubner's *Exempla*, No. 384 (one-fifth scale of inscription). 1st or 2nd Century, A.D.

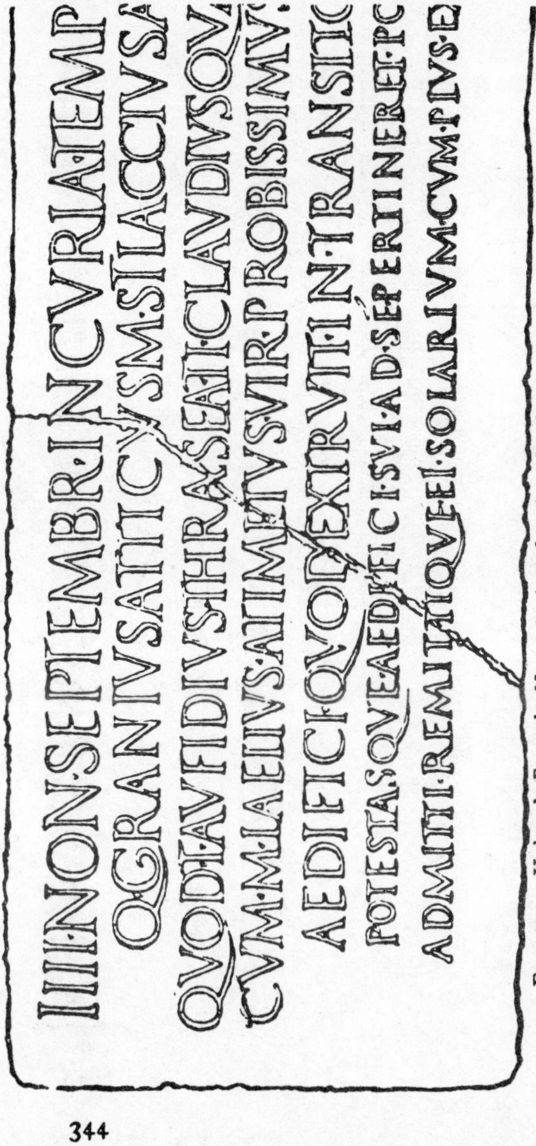

FIG. 205.—Hubner's *Exempla*, No. 1084 (one-fourth scale of inscription). 2nd Century, A.D.

FIG. 206.—(*Two portions.*) From a Rubbing of a Florentine marble dated MCCCCLXVII., slightly reduced (scale twelve-thirteenths). Note the interlinear spaces are 1⅛ inch.

FIG. 207.—From a Rubbing of a Slate at Rye, dated 1655 (see p. 327). Exact size.

Fig. 208.—From a Rubbing of a Stone at Oxford (by A. E. R. Gill. 1905.) Reduced, two-thirds scale.

347

may be left in raised strips flush with the letters, between the lines of the inscription.

Punctuation.—In early inscriptions the words were separated by points; in the more ancient they are square shaped ▬, ■, ▬, in the more elaborate, triangular ▶, ▲, ◀, sometimes with curved-in sides ➤ (Plate I). These developed later into the ivy leaf ☙ ☙, or "*hereræ distinguentes.*" Such points may be used occasionally in modern work with fine effect, but should seldom be used between every word, unless the words are *necessarily* so close that distinguishing marks are required.

Phrasing and Arrangement.—An inscription may be arranged in sentences or phrases, and occasionally, by the use of larger letters, greater prominence is given to a word or phrase (see figs. 197, 204, 211). This method is particularly adapted to the nature of a *set inscription* (p. 228), and may help both its readableness and its appearance, but it must be borne in mind that to lay stress on any one statement or work may pervert its meaning or attract too much attention to it.

Any confusion of sense, or accidental word (p. 223) or phrase, *appearing in the setting-out* is avoided, if possible, by a slight rearrangement of the part, or, if necessary, of the whole inscription. Great care is taken that the spelling is accurate: a pocket dictionary should be carried.

Reading is further facilitated by avoiding, where possible, the dividing of words at the ends of lines. It may be observed that in the more ancient inscriptions words were generally kept *entire*.

Exercises in letter form and arrangement, more
profitable than mere paper "designing," might be
devised by the craftsman. Inscriptions might be cut
—on a small scale—in gesso or chalk, or inscriptions
might be variously spaced and arranged on a properly
coloured surface—such as a drawing-board covered
with light or dark cloth—in letters cut out of sheet-
lead or card.

BIBLIOGRAPHY, &c.

The few books and pamphlets given below are
generally practical or useful. They are roughly
classed under Writing, Illumination, Books, &c.;
Heraldry, and Lettering; but examples of most
of these subjects occur under nearly all the headings.
Some of the books are now out of print. They are
all illustrated, except those marked with an asterisk.

WRITING, &c.

The Story of the Alphabet: Edward Clodd.
5s.

Handbook of Greek and Latin Palæography: Sir E. M. Thompson. (*See
extracts here*, pp. 2, 7, 380, &c.)

The Journal of the Royal Society of Arts,
No. 2726, Feb. 17, 1905; Papers on
Calligraphy and Illumination: Edward
Johnston and Graily Hewitt. 3s.

Manuscript & Inscription Letters: Edward
Johnston & A. E. R. Gill. 5s. (16 Pl.)

Fac-similés de Manuscrits Grecs, Latins et
Français du Vᵉ au XIVᵉ Siècle exposés
dans la Galerie Mazarine: Bibliothèque
Nationale, Département des Manuscrit,
Paris.

A Guide to the Manuscripts, Part III:
the British Museum. 9d.

Bible Illustrations: *Oxford Univ. Press*,
1896.

ILLUMINATION, &c.

Illuminated Letters and Borders: John W.
Bradley, 1901 (19 plates).

Illuminated Manuscripts: John W. Bradley,
first published 1905 (21 plates).

British Museum: Reproductions from
Illuminated MSS. Series I, II, III, 6s.
each; Series IV, 7s. 6d. (*each 50 Plates*).

English Illuminated Manuscripts: Sir E. M.
Thompson, 1895. (*Out of print.*)

* The Journal of the Royal Soc. of Arts, No.
2368, Ap. 8, 1898; a Paper on *English
Art in Illuminated Manuscripts:* Sir E. M.
Thompson. 4s.

* The Book of the Art of Cennino Cennini
(a contemporary practical treatise on 14th-
century Italian painting): Translated by
Christiana J. Herringham, 1899. 6s.

* Some Hints on Pattern-Designing: (lecture,
1881), William Morris, 3s.

BOOKS — MANUSCRIPT & PRINTING.

Books in Manuscript: Falconer Madan.
5s. (*Frontispiece drawn from this by
permission.*)

The Story of Books: G. B. Rawlings, 1901.

The Old Service-Books of the English
Church: Christopher Wordsworth and
Henry Littlehales, 1904. 5s.

Early Illustrated Books: Alfred W. Pollard.
5s.

Facsimiles [in colour] from Early Printed Books in the British Museum, 1897.

A Guide to the Exhibition in the King's Library (illustrating the History of Printing, Music Printing, and Bookbinding): British Museum (36 illustrations).

"Arts and Crafts Essays by Members of the Arts and Crafts Exhibition Society" —*Printing:* William Morris and Emery Walker—(1st pub. 1893), 1899.

* "Ecce Mundus," containing *The Book Beautiful:* T. J. Cobden-Sanderson, 1902.

Printing (a technological handbook): Chas. T. Jacobi, 4th (revised) edition, 1908.

Bookbinding and the Care of Books (*The Artistic Crafts Series of Technical Handbooks*), 4th ed. Douglas Cockerell. 7s. 6d.

HERALDRY, SYMBOLISM, &c.

The Journal of the Royal Society of Arts, No. 2309, Feb. 19, 1897; A Paper on The Artistic Treatment of Heraldry: by W. H. St. John Hope.

English Heraldry: Charles Boutell, 7s. 6d.

The Stall Plates of the Knights of the Garter, 1348–1485: Sir W. H. St. John Hope (90 coloured plates, Imp. 8vo).

Heraldry for Craftsmen & Designers: Sir W. H. St. John Hope. (Numerous illustrations & 8 coloured plates.) 12s. 6d. (*The Artistic Crafts Series.*) Out of stock.

Didron's Christian Iconography (or the History of Christian Art in the Middle Ages): 2 vols.

LETTERING, &c.

Lettering in Ornament: Lewis F. Day, 1902.

Alphabets: Edward F. Strange (1895). 7s. 6d.

The Palæographical Society's Publications (out of print), containing hundreds of facsimiles (chiefly of MSS.), are of great interest. They may of course be seen in the British Museum Library. *The New Palæographical Society* publishes a selection of facsimiles annually.

Hübner's *Exempla Scripturae Epigraphicae Latinae a Caesaris dictatoris morte ad aetatem Justiniani* (Berlin, 1885), contains many fine outline drawings of ancient Roman inscriptions (see figs. 203–5). It is kept with the books of reference in the Reading Room at the British Museum.

Photographs of fine pieces of lettering may be obtained at the Book Stall in the Victoria & Albert Museum, South Kensington (see *footnote*, p. 371).

Original MSS. or Inscriptions—from which we can learn much more than from photographs or drawings—may be found in most parts of the country, and in London especially in the British Museum, the Victoria & Albert Museum (see p. 355), the Record Office (*Rolls Chapel*, see p. viii), and Westminster Abbey (MSS. in the Chapter-House).

APPENDIX B

CHAPTER XVII

INSCRIPTIONS IN STONE

(By A. E. R. Gill)

Arrangement—The Three Alphabets—Size & Spacing—
The Material—Setting Out—Tools—A Right Use
of the Chisel—Incised Letters & Letters in Relief—
The Sections of Letters—Working *in situ*.

ARRANGEMENT

Inscriptions are carved in stone for many uses:
for Foundation Stones and Public Inscriptions, for
Tombstones and Memorial Inscriptions, for Mottos
and Texts, for Names and Advertisements, and each
subject suggests its own treatment.

Colour and Gold may be used both for the beauty
of them and, in places where there is little light, to
increase legibility.

Arrangement.—There are two methods of arranging Inscriptions: the "*Massed*" and the "*Symmetrical.*" In the former the lines are very close

Inscriptions
in Stone

353

together, and approximately equal in length, and form a mass (see fig. 205). Absolute equality is quite unnecessary. Where the lines are very long it is easy to make them equal; but with lines of few words it is very difficult, besides being derogatory to the appearance of the Inscription. In the "*Symmetrical*" Inscription the length of the lines may vary considerably, and each line (often comprising a distinct phrase or statement) is placed in the centre of the Inscription space (see fig. 204).

Short Inscriptions, such as those usually on Tombstones or Foundation Stones, may well be arranged in the "*Symmetrical*" way, but long Inscriptions are better arranged in the "*Massed*" way, though, sometimes, the two methods may be combined in the same Inscription.

THE THREE ALPHABETS

The Roman Alphabet, the alphabet chiefly in use to-day, reached its highest development in Inscriptions incised in stone (see Plate I).

Besides ROMAN CAPITALS, it is necessary that the letter-cutter should know how to carve Roman small-letters[1] (or "Lower case") and *Italics*, either of which may be more suitable than Capitals for some Inscriptions.

Where great magnificence combined with great legibility[2] is desired, use large Roman Capitals,

---

[1] With which we may include Arabic numerals.

[2] It should be clearly understood that legibility by no means excludes either beauty or ornament. The ugly form of "*Block*" *letter* so much in use is no more legible than the beautiful Roman lettering on the Trajan Column (see Plates I, II).

Incised or in Relief, with plenty of space between the letters and the lines.

Where great legibility but less magnificence is desired, use "Roman Small-Letters" or "Italics."

All three Alphabets may be used together, as, for instance, on a Tombstone, one might carve the Name in Capitals and the rest of the Inscription in Small-Letters, using Italics for difference.

Beauty of Form may safely be left to a right use of the chisel, combined with a well-advised study of the best examples of Inscriptions: such as that on the Trajan Column (see Plates I, II) and other Roman Inscriptions in the Victoria and Albert and British Museums, for Roman CAPITALS; and sixteenth and seventeenth century tombstones, for Roman small-letters and *Italics*.[1] If the simple

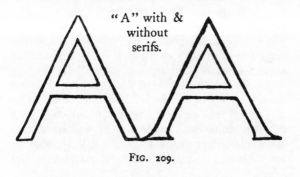

" A " with & without serifs.

FIG. 209.

---

[1] Roman small-letters and Italics, being originally pen letters, are still better understood if the carver knows how to use a pen, or, at least, has studied good examples of manuscripts in which those letters are used.

elementary form of the letter be cut firmly and directly, it will be found that the chisel will suggest how that form may be ornamented. This may be shown, for example, by an attempt to carve a quite simple Incised letter with no Serifs and with all the strokes equally thick. In making the ends of the strokes nice and clean it will be found that there is a tendency to spread them into Serifs, and the letter is at once, in some sort, ornamented (see fig. 209).

SIZE & SPACING

Drawing out.—Take paper and pencil, or what you will, and write out the words of the Inscription in Capitals, or small-letters (or both), without any regard to scale or the shape of the space the Inscription is to go in. The carver will then see easily of what letters and words his Inscription is composed. Next draw the shape of the Inscription space (say to 1 inch or 1½ inch scale), and in that space set out the Inscription, either "*Massed*" or "*Symmetrical*," as has been decided. The drawing should be neither scribbled nor elaborated. The carver will thus be able, after a little experience, to calculate quite easily what size he will be able to carve his letters, what space he will be able to leave between the lines, and what margins he can afford.[1]

---

[1] Some advice from the letter-cutter might be useful to the client as to *the number of words* and *the space they will occupy* in cases where it is possible to adapt the one to the other.

The Size of Lettering depends on where it is to go (*i.e.* outdoors or indoors, far away or near), the material to be used, and the space at the carver's disposal.

Out of Doors capital letters should, as a rule, be not less than 1¼ inch high, more if possible.[1]

Indoors smaller lettering may be carved, but even then 1 inch is quite small enough, and that only in marble, slate, or the finest stones.

In such stones as *Ancaster* or *Ham-Hill* it is not possible to carve good letters less than 3 inches high.

More than one size of letter may be used in the same Inscription to give emphasis to certain words, thus: on a Foundation Stone the Date (see fig. 210),

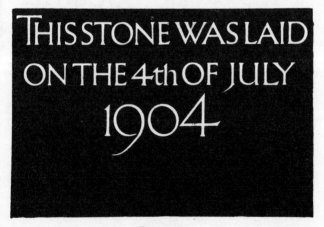

FIG. 210.

---

[1] Small lettering is less convenient to read out of doors, and is apt to get filled with dirt or moss.

and on a Tombstone the Name (see fig. 211), may
be made larger than the rest.

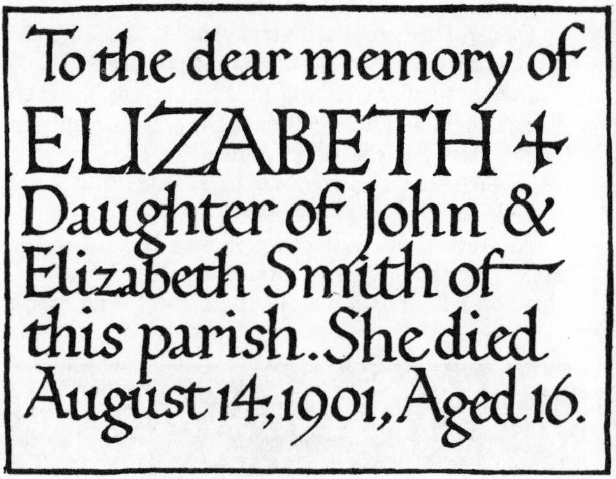

To the dear memory of
ELIZABETH ✝
Daughter of John &
Elizabeth Smith of—
this parish.. She died
August 14, 1901, Aged 16.

FIG. 211.

Spacing.—Proper spacing is essential to a good
Inscription. As a general rule, Roman letters should
not be crowded together. Space should be left
between each, varying according to the letters—a
narrower space between two O's, for example, and,
generally, a wider space between two straight letters.
The lines may be about the height of the lettering
apart (see Plate I) or pretty close together (see
Plate XXIV).

Margins.—If the Inscription is to be carved in a
panel, the surrounding mouldings take the place of
margins, and the lettering may fill the panel (see
fig. 211). If any space be left, let it come, as it

358

naturally will, at the bottom. If the lettering is not to be in a panel, the margins depend primarily on what the carver can afford, and where the Inscription is to go. Every case must be treated on its own merits, but as a general rule one may say that the bottom margin should be the widest and the top margin the narrowest.

THE MATERIAL

The best quality a stone can have, from a letter-cutter's point of view, is fineness or closeness of texture, combined with freedom from holes and flints or occasional shells, and the letter-cutter will do well to choose the stone himself, if possible, having regard to this quality.

The following is a list of a few of the best stones for outdoor and indoor use:—

Outdoors or Indoors.	*Indoors* only.
Portland.—Good for lettering: excellent weathering qualities: becomes quite white if exposed to wind and rain, thus showing very clearly any differences of light and shade.	Clunch Chalk { Very fine and delicate work may be done in these.
	Bath.—A cheap stone, and easily carved; but unsuitable for small lettering.
Hopton-wood Slate { Especially good for lettering: fine and hard: good weathering qualities. Great delicacy may be attained in these.	Marbles and Alabasters.—Excellent for inscriptions indoors, but much colour or veining tends to confuse lettering.
Ancaster Ham-Hill Ketton { Only suitable for large lettering.	

The stone being ready for the setting out, *i.e.*
smoothed and cleaned, lines are ruled on it for
the lines of lettering and margins with a pencil or
point.

The carver should rule and set out one line and
carve that before ruling another, as pencil marks are
liable to be rubbed off by the hand in carving.[1]

In "*Setting Out*," the spacing of the letters is
thought of rather than their forms. And though
the beginner may find careful drawing helpful, the
forms which may best be produced with the
chisel are found only by practice and experience
(p. 363).

TOOLS

The chisels needed for simple work are flat chisels
of the following sizes:—

$\frac{1}{16}$ inch, $\frac{1}{4}$ inch, $\frac{3}{8}$ inch, $\frac{1}{2}$ inch, 1 inch.

The shanks should be about 7 inches long.

It will be found useful to keep a few "*Bull-
nosed*" chisels (see 7, fig. 212) for use in cutting
curves, and a few "*skewed*" chisels (8, fig. 212) for
use in cutting the background of Raised letters,
as a chisel of that shape is more easily used in a
corner.

The chisels are either *Hammer-headed or Mallet-
headed*, or they may have wooden handles (see fig.

---

[1] Whenever it is possible the carver should not be bound
to follow a drawing strictly, but should do his work in the
straightforward manner described above. Unfortunately he
is often obliged to set out the whole Inscription exactly before
carving it, and in such a case it is usual to carve the bottom
line of letters first and to work upwards cutting the first line
last.

212, and pp. *365–6*). The Hammer-headed are the Inscriptions
most used, and a good number should be procured. in Stone

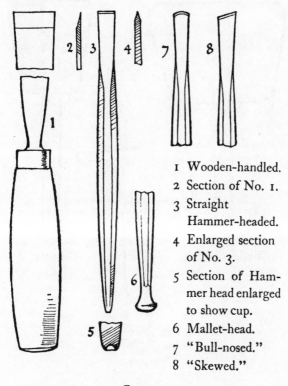

1 Wooden-handled.

2 Section of No. 1.

3 Straight
  Hammer-headed.

4 Enlarged section
  of No. 3.

5 Section of Ham-
  mer head enlarged
  to show cup.

6 Mallet-head.

7 "Bull-nosed."

8 "Skewed."

FIG. 212.

The best are made with *cupped* ends, to prevent them
from slipping on the hammer (see 5, fig. 212).

Temper and Sharpness.—Above all things the
chisels must be of the right temper, and sharp.[1]

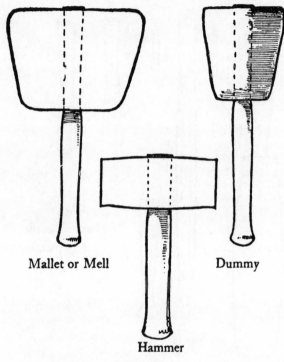

Mallet or Mell   Dummy

Hammer

Fɪɢ. 213.

They are tempered by a smith or tool-maker—
if the craftsman can do it for himself, so much the

[1] Really sharp, *i.e.* sharp enough to cut a piece of paper
without tearing it.

better. They are sharpened on a piece of *Grit-stone*
(hard York stone, for instance) with water. The Temper of a chisel may be seen by the colour (blue shows a soft or low temper, straw colour a hard or high temper), and felt by the way it rubs on the Grit-stone (a hard tool will slide easily over the stone, while a soft one will seem to stick or cling).

Mallets.—A wooden mallet or *Mell*, a Zinc mallet or *Dummy*, and an iron or steel hammer are required (fig. 213).

The Mell is made wholly of wood, and should, for letter cutting, be about 5½ inches in diameter.

The Dummy has a head of zinc and a wooden handle. It should be about 2½ inches in diameter.

The hammer should be about the same size and weight as the Dummy.

A RIGHT USE OF THE CHISEL

The workman must find out, for himself, how best to use his tools. In the ordinary way, it is best to hold the chisel at an angle of about 45° with the surface of the stone—in the manner shown in fig. 214—in cutting both straight stems and curves. The chisel is held firmly (usually in the left hand, with the little finger about an inch from the cutting end of the chisel), tapped rather than banged, and lightly rather than heavily.

The best way to cut an ordinary letter is to start at the left-hand side at the bottom, and, working upwards, to cut the left side of the stem first. Similarly cut the right side of the stem, and then cut the serifs (see fig. 218).

When cutting a curve, cut the inside first (fig. 214), and start as near the narrowest part of the curve as possible.

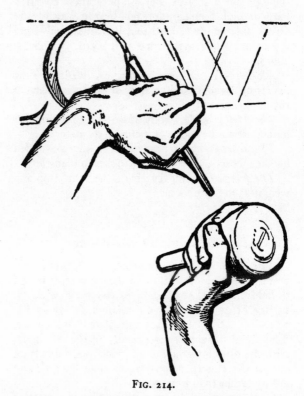

FIG. 214.

In Incised letters unnecessary junctions of the parts may be avoided (see fig. 215). Where they are necessary, as in a capital E, or in a small y, cut

away from the junction or down on to it, rather
than towards it.

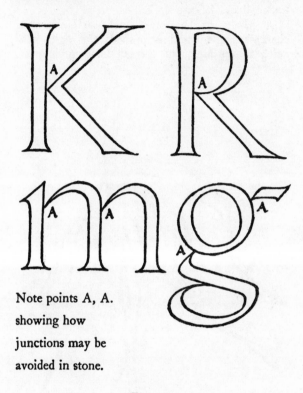

Note points A, A.
showing how
junctions may be
avoided in stone.

FIG. 215.

The Mallet-headed and wooden-handled chisels
are used with the Mell for large work and for
cutting surfaces.

The Hammer-headed chisels are used with the hammer for ordinary work, and with the Dummy for small and delicate work.

A Mallet or Dummy is not used in carving chalk, but the chisel is pushed; the right hand doing the pushing, and the left hand guiding and

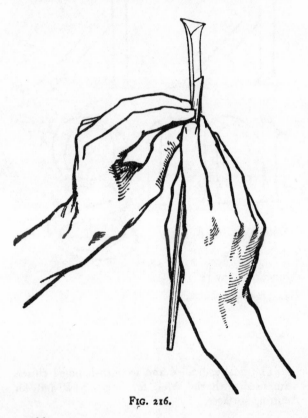

FIG. 216.

steadying the chisel (see fig. 216). If the chisel were struck, the surface of the chalk would flake off.

In cutting an Incised Inscription with the ordinary "V" section (see fig. 217), use one size of chisel throughout. The width of the chisel should generally be about the width of the letter stem required. More elaborate sections necessitate the use of several sizes of chisels.

INCISED LETTERS & LETTERS IN RELIEF

Inscriptions may be *Incised* or in *Relief*, that is, sunk or raised.[1] The *modus operandi* and the time spent in carving the actual letters are the same in either case, but whereas when the Incised letter is carved there is nothing more to be done, after the carving of the Raised letter there is still the stone surrounding it (*i.e.* the background) to be dealt with, and this should simply be carved smooth.[2]

Other things being equal, it becomes a question of economy which form of lettering one will carve, as the necessity of dealing with the background of a Raised Inscription, while more than doubling the opportunities of the carver, at least doubles the time spent in carving.

Raised lettering will show out more clearly than Incised lettering where there is little light.

---

[1] In learning to cut Inscriptions one would naturally begin with Incised letters.
[2] Where the ground between the letters is left plain, an absolute flatness and evenness is not necessary. The common method of jabbing or "pecking" the background is objectionable.

Roman Capitals are more adapted for carving in Relief than are Roman small-letters or Italics, which are directly derived from the pen.

Raised lettering is more allied to ordinary carving, while Incised lettering may be thought of as writing in stone.

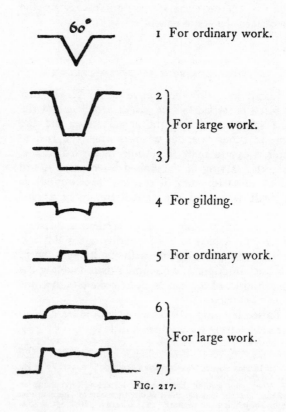

1 For ordinary work.

2
⎫
⎬ For large work.
⎭
3

4 For gilding.

5 For ordinary work.

6
⎫
⎬ For large work.
⎭
7

FIG. 217.

For Incised letters, a "V" section (1, fig. 217) of about 60° is best for regular use; deeper rather than shallower. The letters may with advantage be cut a little deeper towards the Serifs (see fig. 218).

Although the simple "V" section is the most useful, other sections may be used for large letters (*i.e.* letters more than 6 inches high), or letters in a very fine material (2 & 3, fig. 217).

FIG. 218.

If the lettering is to be gilded, and the stone will permit of it, Section 4 (fig. 217) is a good one to use. Only the curved part is to be Gilded, and not the small bevelled sides.

For Raised letters, the best and most useful section is No. 5; the slightly bevelled sides tell as part of the letter. Experience, and the weathering conditions, will suggest the amount of Relief to be given. For letters $1\frac{1}{2}$ inch high, out of doors, $\frac{3}{16}$ inch of relief is ample, and if there be good light $\frac{1}{8}$ inch is enough. Excessive relief looks clumsy.

Sections Nos. 6 and 7 are suitable only for large letters; and elaborate sections should as a rule be used only for letters standing alone.

WORKING *IN SITU*

If possible the carver should work *in situ.* When that is impracticable,[1] he should consider most carefully where his Inscription is to go.

---

[1] *E.g.* Tombstones and Memorial Slabs are not usually fixed until finished.

In an Inscription which is much above the eye level, the letters may be narrower in proportion to their height, and the horizontal strokes extra thick to allow for foreshortening. (See also pp. 315, 234.)

The advantages of working *in situ* are great, for by so doing the carver sees his work under the same conditions of light and environment that it will finally be seen under.

(NOTE.—*In order to make the illustrations [whether of facsimiles or enlargements] as large and as full as possible, I have sacrificed "appearance" to use and allowed most of the plates, and many of the diagrams in the book, to encroach on the margins. —E. J.*)

GENERAL NOTE.—All the plates are in *facsimile* as to size (or *nearly so*, allowing for errors in reproduction) except I, II, XXII, and XXIV, which had to be *reduced*, and, therefore only *portions* of the MSS. can be shown. NOTE.—All the MSS. are on "Vellum" (see p. 139). In order to get a better impression of the size and general proportion of a MS., the student might reconstruct it—or at least mark off the margins, text, &c.—on paper, from the measurements given. Or a sheet of paper might be cut to the size of the given page or *opening*, with an aperture (in its proper place) through which the plate might be viewed.

The plates are arranged in chronological order as nearly as possible. They are intended briefly to illustrate *the Development of the Formal Book Hands from the Roman Capital* and *the General Development of the Illuminated MS.*: I hope, moreover, that, fragmentary as they are, they will prove usefully suggestive in regard to *the Arrangement of Text and Lettering and Ornament*. The wonderful effect of the *colouring* cannot be given here, but, in any case, the illuminator should look at some original MSS. Several of the MSS. from which the plates are taken are exhibited in the British Museum.

PLATE I.—Portion of Inscription on base of Trajan Column,[1] *Rome, circa* A.D. 114 *Scale approx. ⅛th linear.*

THE STONE (within the internal line of the moulding): 3 feet 9 inches high, and 9 feet ¾ inch long.

---

[1] There is a cast (No. 1864–128) in the Victoria and Albert Museum, South Kensington, where also the photograph of the inscription is obtainable, from portions of which Plates I and II are reproduced.

THE BORDERS.—The lettering practically fills the panel (see p. 316): the surrounding moulding is approx. 4 inches wide.

THE LETTERS (*for their forms see note on Pl. II*).

Approximate heights
$\begin{cases} \text{First two lines:} & 4\frac{1}{2} \text{ inches high.} \\ \text{Second two lines:} & 4\frac{3}{8} \text{ ,, \quad ,,} \\ \text{Fifth line:} & 4\frac{1}{8} \text{ ,, \quad ,,} \\ \text{Last line:} & 3\frac{7}{8} \text{ ,, \quad ,,} \end{cases}$

THE SPACES (between Lines) decrease from 3 inches to $2\frac{3}{4}$ inches. A decrease in the height of the letters from the top to the foot line is common in early inscriptions (see figs. 203–205). Several reasons for this suggest themselves: (*a*) (Sometimes the beginning words, being farther from the reader, may require to be larger). (*b*) The architectural beauty of a large heading (comp. *stem heads*, p. 252). (*c*) The importance of *beginnings* generally (there is very often a marked difference between the upper lines containing important words and the rest of the inscription: comp. figs. 197, 91).

NOTE.—The WORDS are separated by triangular points (p. 348).

PLATE II.—Alphabet from Trajan Inscription. (*Circa* A.D. 114). *Scale approx. ⅙th linear.* (See note above.)

THE "TRAJAN" ALPHABET.—Very fine letters for inscriptions in stone: possibly painted before incision (see p. 256); see also remarks on Roman Capitals, pp. 232-260, and note:—

SERIFS.—Small and carefully curved.

THIN PARTS about half the width of the *thick stems* (pp. 339, 249).

A (M and N), *pointed* (p. 244).
B—a very beautiful form, with large lower *bow* (p. 242).
C, G, and (D)—Upper parts rather straight (p. 245).
E and F—*mid arm* slightly shorter than upper arm.
E and L—*lower serif* pointed out (p. 246).

LO (shown sideways in plate) and LT show L's *arm* projecting under next letter.

M—*pointed:* slightly spread (p. 248), distance apart of points above equal to *inside* distance of stems below.

N—*pointed:* practically no difference in thickness of vertical and oblique parts (p. 249).

O—very beautiful: *width slightly less than height* (p. 234): slightly *tilted* (as are all the other curved letters: see p. 249).

P—*Bow* not joined to stem below (first P rounder topped).

Q—*tail* carried under **v** (**u**).

R—large *bow:* straight *tail,* with finishing-curve (p. 255).

S—leans forward slightly (p. 250).

Proportions of widths to heights (comp. with pp. 233–237)		
OCDGMNQ	width slightly *less* than height.
ARTV	width approx. ¼th *less* than height.
BX	width rather more than *half* height.
P	width approx. equal half height.
LS	width slightly *less* than half height.
EF	width approx. ¾ths of height.

H, (J), K, (U), W, Y, Z are not present in the inscription. A rough diagram (fig. 219) is given below showing approximately suitable forms for these (*Re junction of* u *in stone;* see p. 364, & fig. 215).

FIG. 219.

*PLATE III.—Written Roman Capitals, Fourth or Fifth
Century. (Virgil's "Æneid".)*

(From a facsimile in the Palæographical Society's
Publications, 1st Series, Vol. II, Pl. 208, of a MS.
in the library of S. Gall, Switzerland. See also "Greek
and Latin Palæography," p. 185.)

LETTERS.—Simple-written (slanted-pen) Roman
"Square Capitals."

WORDS in early MSS. were not separated (p. 78).

LINES ruled with a hard point (p. 307). The letters
appear to have been written between every alternate pair
(p. 263), but slightly over the line.

A very handsome writing which might still be used for
special MSS. (see pp. 268, 264, 263).

*PLATE IV.—Uncial Writing, probably Italian Sixth or
Seventh Century. (Latin Gospels.) Brit. Museum,
Harl. MS. 1775.*

(Shown in Brit. Mus. Department of MSS., Case G,
No. 11.)

THE VOLUME contains 468 leaves (7 inches by
$4\frac{3}{4}$ inches).

MARGINS, Approx.: *Inner* $\frac{5}{8}$ inch, *Head* $\frac{7}{8}$ inch,
Side $\frac{9}{8}$ inch, *Foot* $\frac{8}{8}$ inch. (They may have been cut
down by the binder.)

WRITING.—A fine *round* Uncial MS. (pp. 4, 266),
arranged in long and short lines.

NOTE.—On many of the letters there are fine hair-line
curved *tails* and flourishes, which are scarcely visible in
the photograph. (These tails were also used in the
earlier Uncial shown in fig. 5—see also *Addenda*, p. xxi.)

SECTIONS.—Marked by built-up letters of an Uncial
type, and numbered, mʀ cxxiiii to mʀ cxxvi (with references
to "Harmonics"). The passage is S. Mark xi. 21–25.

PLATE V.—Uncial Writing, probably Continental Seventh Century. (Gospel of S. John). Ex libris Stonyhurst College. (See also enlargement, fig. 169.)

(From a facsimile in the Palæographical Society's Publications, 1st Series, Vol. II, Pl. 17.)

THE VOLUME contains 90 leaves, approx. $5\frac{3}{8}$ inches by $3\frac{5}{8}$ inches. The *Inner margin* is approximately $\frac{1}{2}$ inch wide.

WRITING.—A very beautiful pointed (slanted-pen) Uncial. The "pointed" character of the letters, which yet retain their typical roundness, give this writing a peculiar charm. Note the top of the P has a marked angle, and the M and H, and even the O, have this slightly or strongly.

RULING.—Single lines, rather wide (p. 269).

ARRANGEMENT.—Certain of the lines are *indented* one letter (p. 228).

LARGE LETTERS.—On *verso* Col marking a "Chapter" is built-up in *red*, on *recto* the three large letters (marking sections) are simply written with the text pen (p. 263). (The passage is S. John xi. 46–56.)

PLATE VI.—Half-Uncial (Irish), Seventh Century "Book of Kells" (Latin Gospels). Ex libris Trinity College, Dublin.

(From a facsimile—part of Pl. XLVII—in "Celtic Ornaments from the Book of Kells," by the Rev. Dr. T. K. Abbott.)

THE LEAVES—which are cut down and much damaged—measure 13 inches by 10 inches.

WRITING.—A beautiful and highly finished (approx. straight pen) Half-Uncial (pp. 6, 268), tending to ornamental and fanciful forms whenever opportunity offered. (Note the treatment of ɪɴde.)

ARRANGEMENT.—Long and short lines: wide spacing.

THE LETTERS combine extreme gracefulnes[s] with an unusual appearance of strength. This is mainly due to the ends of *all* the strokes being finished ; the thick strokes have large, triangular heads (p. 291) on the left, and bases broadened by an additional stroke below on the right (thus *'/,*). And the horizontal thin strokes are either finished with a triangular terminal (p. 210), or run on into the next letter—*joining the letters together*.

The extreme *roundness* of the letters is contributed to by their being written between DOUBLE LINES (pp. 268, 54), the upper line of which tends to flatten the tops.

The pen not being quite "straight" (see *footnote*, p. 268) together with a tendency to *pull* the left hand curves, gives a characteristic shape to the letters

α.c.δ.e.q.τ.

THE ILLUMINATION throughout the book is most elaborate and beautiful. Each division has an entire Initial page occupied with the first few letters. The COLOURS were "*paled green, red, violet, and yellow, intense black, and white, but no gold*": see description of Celtic MSS., p. 40, Bradley's "Illuminated Letters and Borders," and also the Palæographical Society's 1st Series, Vol. II, Pl. 55–58, 88, 89.

This notable book may be taken as an example of the marvellous possibilities of pen-work and complex colour-work (see p. 180).

In considering the value of the writing as a model, it may be noted that its highly finished nature demands practised skill on the part of the copyist, and that though modern *Irish writing* (for which it would be an excellent model) still employs ▲.δ.ꝼ.ꝫ.ı.ꞃ.τ. these letters would be apt to look peculiar in English. The Kells MS. α, c.e.ħ.m.ŋ.o.p.q.ꞃ.s'.u, however, might be used, and a very beautiful ornamental hand (p. 268) might be founded on this writing.

376

PLATE VII.—Half-Uncial (English), circa A.D. 700
   *"Durham Book" (Latin Gospels). Brit. Mus.,
   Cotton MSS. Nero D. IV.*

THE VOLUME contains 258 leaves (13½ inches
by 9⅞ inches).

THE WRITING is an English—or rather *Anglo-
Irish*—Half-Uncial, written at Lindisfarne (*Holy I.*)
under Irish influence (p. 6). ARRANGEMENT
—two columns of 24 lines—long and short—to the page
(note how eis is got into the fifth line): wide spacing.

The writing bears a strong resemblance to that of the
"Book of Kells," but is generally much plainer; it is
also less graceful, being *heavier* and *wider* in proportion.
The "Book of Kells" O is a *circle*, while the "Durham
Book" O is considerably wider than its height, and all the
other letters are correspondingly wide. The RULING
in both books consists of double lines, ruled with a hard
point *on both sides of each leaf.*

THE ILLUMINATION also resembles that of the
"Book of Kells" (see *opposite*), but a small amount of
gold is employed in it. (See also Palæographical Society's
1st Series, Vol. II, Pl. 3–6, 22.)

NOTE.—The "Gloss," or interlinear translation, is in
the Northumbrian dialect, and was put in in the tenth
century, more than 200 years after the book was written.

A hand founded to some extent on the "Durham
Book" hand is given in Chap. IV as an easy copy: see
figs. 49, 50.

*PLATE VIII.—English Tenth-century Writing.(Psalter.)
   Brit. Mus., Harl. MS. 2904. (See enlargement, fig.
   172.)* (Shown B. M. Grenville Lib. Case 1, No. 9.)

THE VOLUME contains 214 leaves (13¼ inches by
10 inches), 18 lines to the page; probably written at
Winchester in late tenth century. (*Pl. reduced scale* ⅝*ths.*)

WRITING.—An extremely good, formal, "slanted-
pen" writing, having great freedom (note the very slight
slope forward) and simplicity. This type of letter may

377

be regarded as a link between the Half-Uncial and the
Roman Small-Letter (see p. 274).

THE RULING: *single* lines (see *footnote*, p. 269).

THE LETTERS show very strongly the effects of
the "slanted pen" (see pp. 7, 269). Note the heavy
shoulders and feet in **n, b,** &c., and the thick horizontals
in r**C**. The curved tops or *arches* are flattish and strong:
the thick strokes end abruptly in points, in d, (h), i, m,
n, u forming small (and in l, **G** LARGE) heavy *hooks* below.
The thin stroke scarcely appears, except as a *finish*, *e.g.* in
a, or an *accidental*. Note generally the tendency to *internal
angles* and *external roundness* (examples **f** and **o**).

Note particularly the junctions and accidental crossings
of the strokes (seen best in the enlargement, fig. 172) as
bearing on the mode of construction of the letters (see
p. 50).

Note the fine shape of the *ampersand* (&: 3rd line).

THE ILLUMINATION (see *Characteristics of
Winchester Illumination, or "Opus Anglicum,"* pp. 48, 49,
Bradley: "Illuminated Letters and Borders"). *All* the
CAPITALS beginning the verses are in raised, burnished
gold, in the margin. The titles are in *red* in fancy "Rustic
Capitals" (p. 261). The Line-Fillings consist of groups
of red dots, in threes (∴ ∴ ∴).

This extremely legible MS. would form an almost
perfect model for a modern formal hand (s being substituted for long f, and the straight t for the curved **C** (see
fig. 183): the removal of the e *Tongue* would also help
readableness). And though it is somewhat large and
heavy for ordinary use, it is good for practising, and
might be developed into a form resembling any of the
more difficult later forms (*e.g.* Plates IX, X, XX).

PLATE IX.—English Writing, dated 1018. *Two
portions of a Charter of CNUT. Brit. Museum. (See
also enlargement, fig.* 173.) [*Pl. reduced scale* $\frac{1}{12}$*ths.*]
(Shown in Brit. Mus., Department of MSS., Case V.,
No. 3.)

THE WRITING resembles that in Plate VIII

(see above), but is more slender and rounder—the pen
being a little less slanted, and the *arches* more curved,
and showing more of the *thin* stroke. The ascenders
and descenders are longer, the heads are more marked,
and there is a general elegance and distinction, due perhaps to the MS. being a charter. Charter-hands are
generally more showy and less legible than Book-hands,
but in this hand there is great legibility, and a very few
changes (similar to those suggested above) would make it
quite suitable for modern use. Its relation to the Roman
Small-Letter is obvious.

NOTES.—The (black) ✠ V and u were probably built-
up with the writing pen.

The forms of a, e, g, (h), r, may be noted as differing
considerably from the tenth-century hand.

The combined ra (in the 4th line) is curious; and the
r in *Anglorum*—this r (which represents the Bow and
Tail of R) commonly follows the round letters b, o, p,
in "Gothic" writing: there is another curious form in
the linked rt in *cartula* (last line).

The word CNUT and several other names are in
ornamental "Rustic" Capitals (see p. 261).

The two lines of English from another part of the
charter have very long stems and ornamental serifs, giving
a very decorative effect (see *footnote*, p. 290).

*PLATE X.—Italian (first half of) Twelfth-century
Writing. (Homilies and Lessons.) Brit. Mus.,
Harl. MS. 7183. (See also enlargement, g. 174.)*

(Shown in Brit. Mus., Department of MSS., Case C
[lower part], No. 101.)

THE VOLUME.—Homilies and Lessons for Sun-
days and Festivals from Advent to Easter Eve—contains
317 leaves (approximately $21\frac{1}{2}$ inches by 15 inches);
two columns, each of 50 lines, to the page. The
MARGINS are, approximately, *Inner* $1\frac{1}{4}$ inch, *Head*

$1\frac{1}{4}$ inch, *Side* $3\frac{1}{4}$ inches, *Foot* $4\frac{1}{4}$ inches (*between columns* $1\frac{1}{8}$ inch: see Plate). The portion of a page, shown in Plate X., consists of the last eleven lines, second column, of folio 78.

WRITING.—This has all the qualities of good writing (p. 203) in a marked degree, and I consider it, taken all round, the most perfect and satisfactory penmanship which I have seen.

Its simplicity and distinctiveness are very marked, so also are its character and freedom. There is an almost entire absence of artificial finish—the terminals are natural hooks, beaks and "feet" made with a fine sleight of hand (p. 275)—and its very great beauty of form is the natural outcome of good traditions and eminently satisfactory craftsmanship.

NOTES.—The letters are very wide, and the *inside shapes* differ considerably from those of the tenth-century MS. (above)—with which, however, there is a considerable affinity (see p. 378).

The ſ is longer than the f, the g has a very fine form with a *closed* loop, the r is sharpened, the t *straight*.

Small (Uncial) CAPITALS um follow the Versal; the serifs on the S and E are made with dexterous movements of the nib (p. 210), and resemble those on the Versal C. V and U are both used for the consonant (V).

There are very few VERSALS in this book: the C shown is in red (which has been smudged).

The large "ILLUMINATED INITIALS" in the book are in yellow, blue, and red, and appear to me to be comparatively poor, at least, to fall short of the perfection of the MS.

Of this writing, Sir Edward Maunde Thompson ("Greek and Latin Palæography," pp. 271–2) says:—

"The sense of grace of form which we perceive in the Lombardic writing of Italy is maintained in that country in the later writing of the new minuscule type, which assumes under the pens of the most expert Italian scribes a very beautiful and round even style. This style, though peculiarly Italian, extended its influence abroad, especially to the south of France, and became the model of Spanish writing at a later time. We select a specimen from a very handsome MS. of Homilies of the first half of the 12th century (*Pal. Soc.* ii. pl. 55), written in bold letters of the best type, to which we shall find the scribes of the fifteenth century reverting in order to obtain a model for their MSS. of the Renaissance. The exactness with which the writing is here executed is truly marvellous, and was only rivalled, not surpassed, by the finished handiwork of its later imitators.

"It will of course be understood that this was not the only style of hand that prevailed in Italy. Others of a much rougher cast were also employed. But as a typical book-hand, which was the parent of the hands in which the greater proportion of carefully written MSS. of succeeding periods were written in Italy, it is to be specially noticed."

(P. 284)—"we give a specimen of a hand of the Italian Renaissance, a revival of the style of the eleventh or twelfth century, and a very successful imitation of a MS. of that period. It was this practice, followed by the scribes of the Renaissance, of reverting to that fine period of Italian writing (see p. 272) to find models for the exquisitely finished MSS. which they were compelled to produce in order to satisfy the refined taste of their day, that influenced the early printers of Italy in the choice of their form of type."*

(P. 285)—"in the comparatively small number of extant literary MSS. of a later date than the close of the [fifteenth] century it is noticeable that a large proportion of them are written in the style of the book-hand of the Italian Renaissance —the style which eventually superseded all others in the printing press. The scribes of these late examples only followed the taste of the day in preferring those clear and simple characters to the rough letters of the native hands."

---

* The specimen hand given is of date 1466. Plate XVIII may here be taken as an example of the Renaissance revival; Plate XX and fig. 175 as examples of later MSS.

PLATE XI.—English (late) Twelfth-century Writing, with flourished Capitals. (Breviary.) Brit. Mus., Royal MS. 2. A.x.

(Shown in Brit. Mus., Department of MSS., Case D, No. 111.)

THE VOLUME—sometimes called the St. Albans or *Albanus* Breviary—contains 200 leaves (6$\frac{7}{8}$ inches by

$4\frac{7}{8}$ inches); twenty-seven lines to the page, some pages have two columns. MARGINS approximately, *Inner* $\frac{5}{8}$ inch, *Head* under $\frac{1}{2}$ inch (see Plate), *Side* $1\frac{1}{4}$ inch (part occupied by Versals), *Foot* $1\frac{1}{8}$ inch.

THE WRITING is fairly legible, but approaches Black Letter (p. 295) too nearly to be of use to us for ordinary purposes. Note the ornamental Semi-Rustic Capitals in text. Note the RULING of the two head lines and of the foot line is carried into the margin.

THE VERSALS.—The main interest lies in the varied forms of the Versals, which are most beautifully made in *red* and *green* alternately. There is one elaborate *gold* initial in the book, and several Versals in blue and white (*hollow*: see p. 174).

The five δ's—and the D in the text—on this page (folio 85b) by no means exhaust the varieties of D alone, and there are very many varieties of the forms of the other letters. On some pages each line begins with a small Versal, while the more important Initials are much larger, varying in size and ornament.

THE CONSTRUCTION of the Versals is unusually slender, curved, and gradated. A rather fine pen seems to have been used (p. 256), and though the letters are upright, the natural tendency to slant the pen can be detected in the thickening of the thin parts—*above*, on the right, and *below*, on the left—giving the suspicion of a *tilt* to the O.

The O-part of each δ was made first, and the *tail* \ added. This is very obvious in the D in the text, where a *stem* | was added to O to make D.

Note the *dots* inside the Versals, one above and one below. Originally these may have been intended to effect—or hide—the junction of the thin strokes, by a twirl of the pen at the end of the first stroke and the beginning of the second, thus ( ). Their use is very common in Versal forms (see fig. 189), and besides being

[*Continued on p.* 407

Plate I.—Portion of Inscription on base of Trajan Column, Rome, *circa* A.D. 114, Scale approx. ⅛th linear. (*See also Plate II.*)

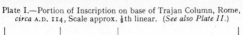

0	6 *in.*	1 *foot.*	2 *feet.*

Descriptive Note on p. 371.

Plate II.—Alphabet from Trajan Inscription (*circa* A.D. 114),
Scale approx. ⅛ linear. (*See also Plate I.*) *Note.—L and O are
shown sideways in the 2nd line.*

384

Descriptive Note on p. 372.

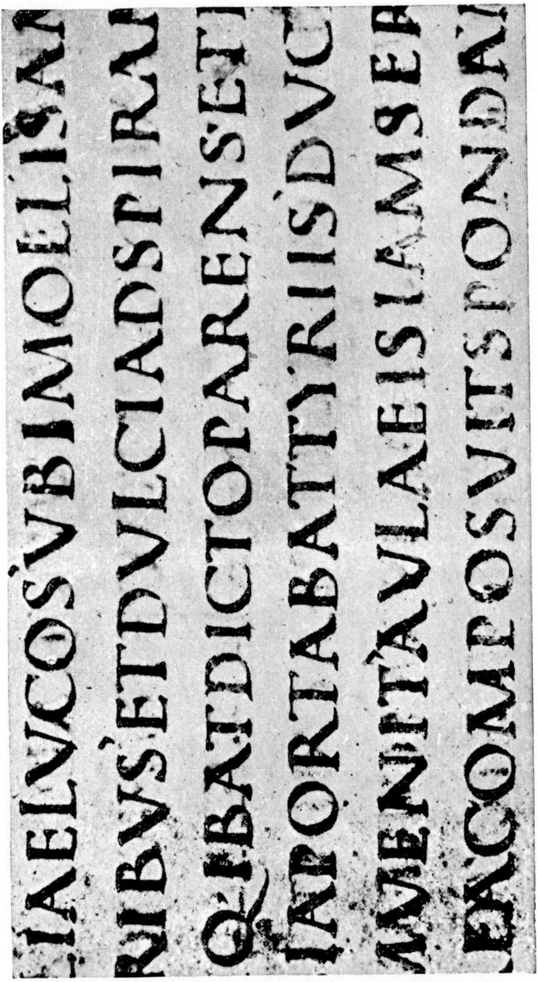

Plate III — Written Roman Capitals, Fourth or Fifth Century.
(Virgil's "Æneid".)

385

Descriptive Note on p. 374.

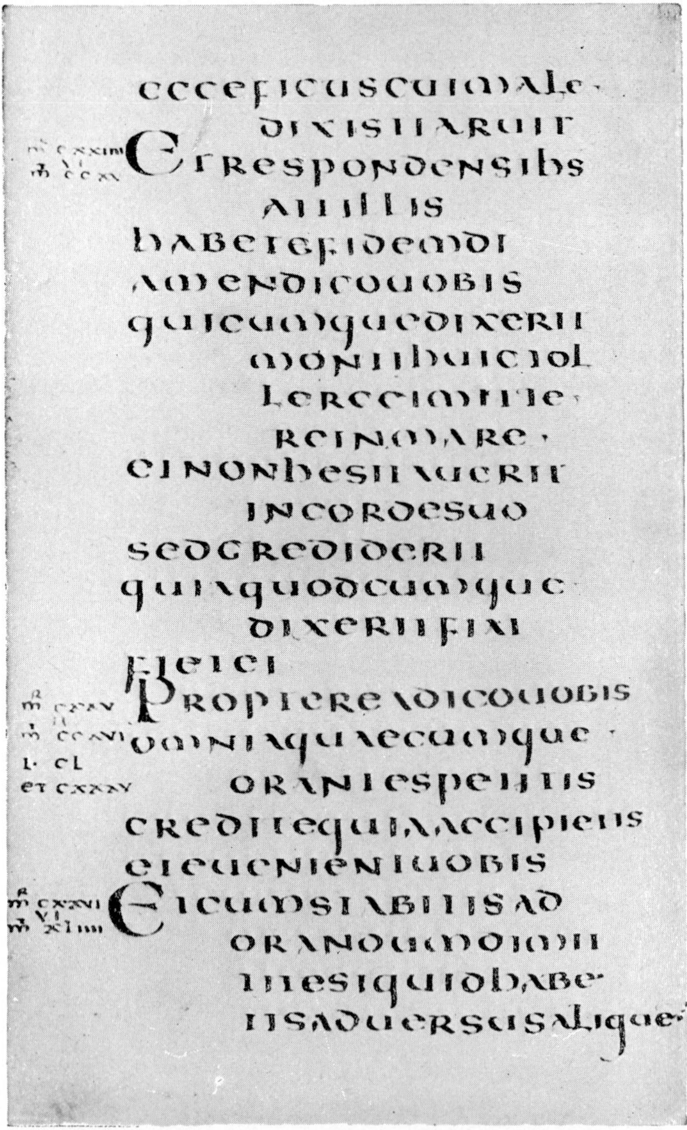

ecceficuscuimale
dixistiarguit
Et respondens ihs
ait illis
habete fidem di
amen dico uobis
quicumque dixerit
monti huic tol
lere et mitte
re in mare
et non hesitauerit
in corde suo
sed crediderit
quia quodcumque
dixerit fiat
fieiei
Propterea dico uobis
omnia quaecumque
orantes petitis
credite quia accipiens
et euenient uobis
Et cum stabitis ad
orandum dimitti
te si quid habe
tis aduersus aliqe

Plate IV.—Uncial Writing, probably Italian Sixth or Seventh Century.
(Latin Gospels.) Brit. Museum, Harl. MS. 1775.

386

Descriptive Note on p. 374.

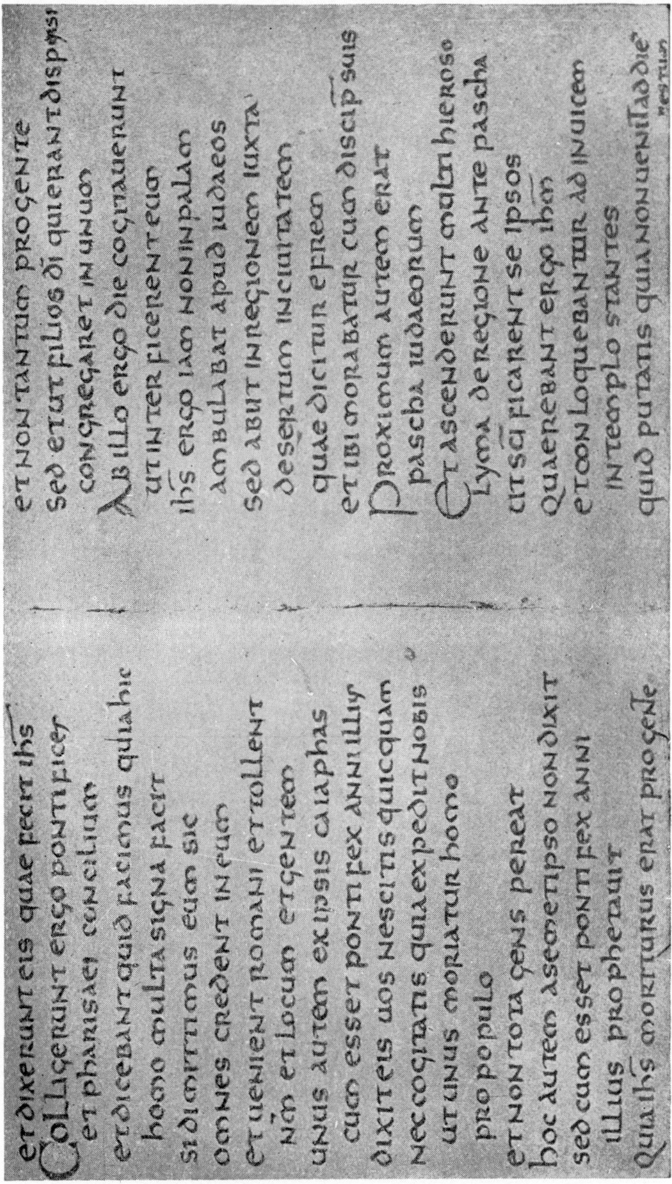

Plate V.—Uncial Writing, probably Continental Seventh Century. (Gospel of S. John.) Ex Libris Stonyhurst College. (See also enlargement, fig. 169.)

Descriptive Note on p. 375.

Plate VI.—Half Uncial (Irish), Seventh Century, "Book of Kells" (Latin Gospels). Ex Libris Trinity College, Dublin.

Descriptive Note on p. 375.

sicut ethnici faciunt
hia poenas fordon dado
putaut enim qui
in monig fald genóc hir
in multiloquio suo
bid gehened
exaudiantur
nallas ge donne fora gelic
Nolite ergo assimila[ri]
pat fordon fadon iunne
Scit enim pater uester
ordum deupp rietir iuh
quib: opus sit uobis
aen don
antequam
giebidde hine
petatis eum
yup don iuh giebiddo
Sic ergo uos orabitis
faden upon du and t[
Pater noster qui es
heo in heofnu sie gehalgud
ar in caelis scificetur
noma din
nomen tuum
to cymed sic dm
adueniat regnum tuu[m]

Descriptive Note on p. 377.

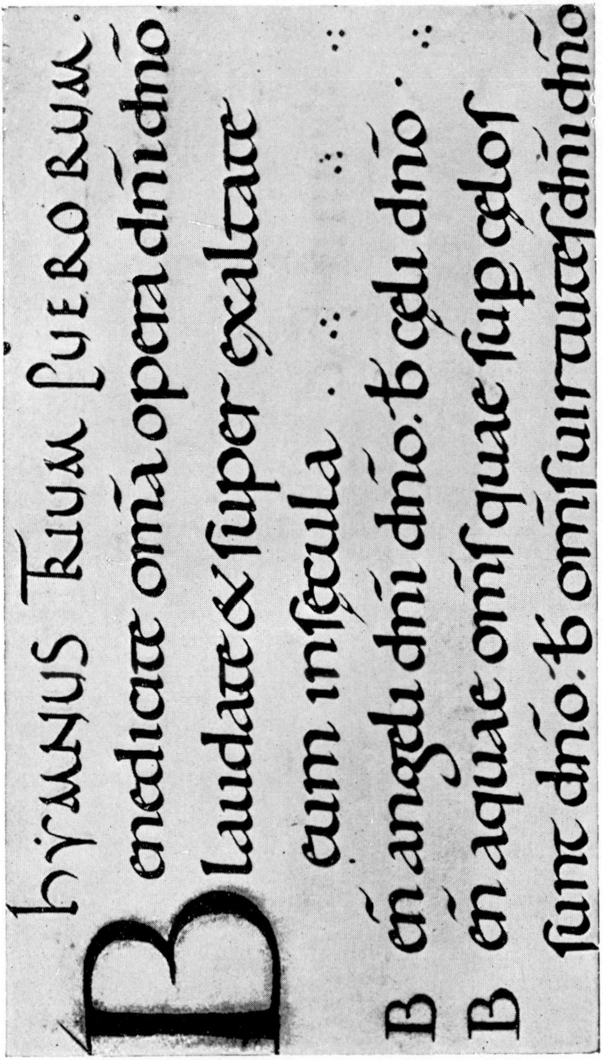

Plate VIII.—English Tenth-century Writing. (Psalter.) Brit. Mus.,
Hart. MS. 2904. (See enlargement, fig. 172.)

Descriptive Note on p. 377.

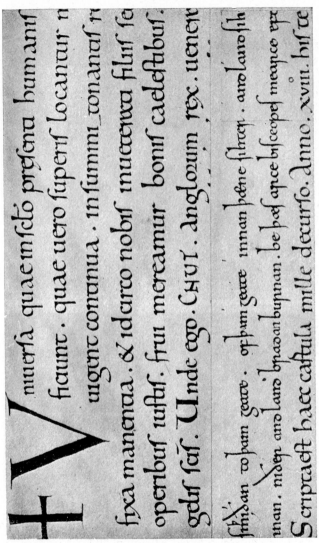

Plate IX.—English Writing, dated 1018. Two portions of a Charter of
CNUT. Brit. Museum. (See also enlargement, fig. 173.)

Descriptive Note on p. 378.

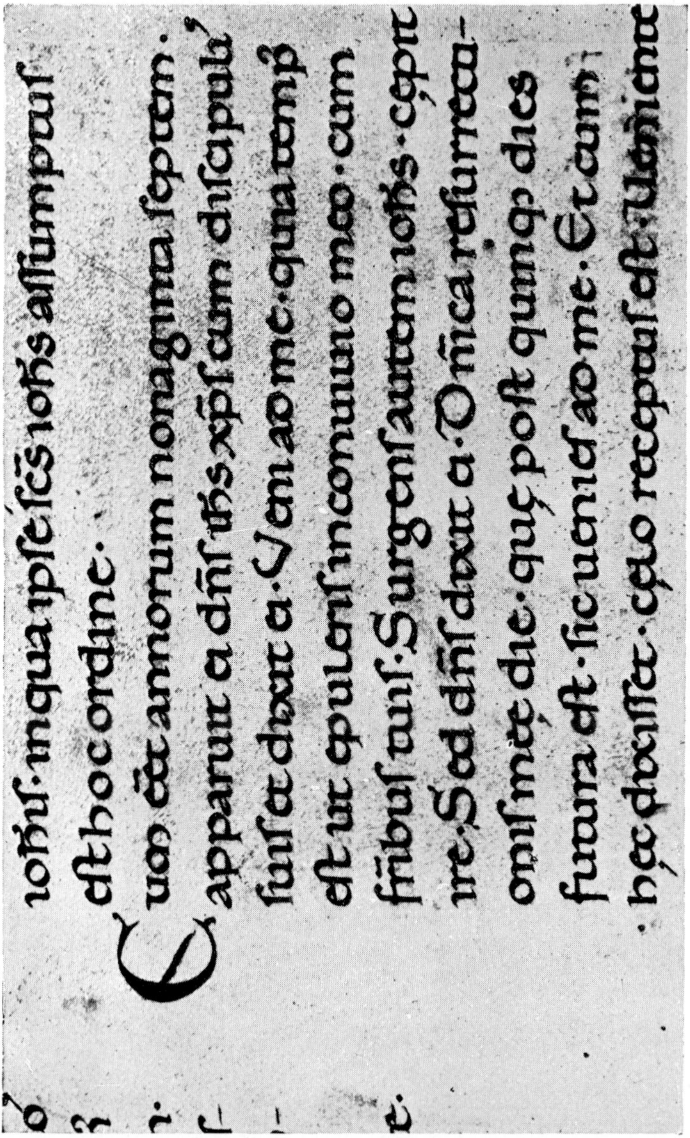

iohs · ingua ipse scs iohs assumptus
est hoc ordine ·

Cuos est annorum nonagima septem ·
apparuit a dns ihs xps cum discapuli
suis dixit a · Ueni ad me · quia tempus
est ut epulemini in convivio meo · cum
fribus tuis · Surgens autem iohs cepit
ire · Sed dns dixit a · Dnica resurreca-
onis mee die · que post quinqp dies
futura est · sic uenies ad me · Et cum
hec dixisset · ceto recepus est · Uenientque

Plate X.—Italian (first half of) Twelfth-century Writing. (Homilies and
Lessons.) Brit. Mus., Harl. MS. 7183. (See also enlargement, fig. 174.)

Descriptive Note on p. 379.

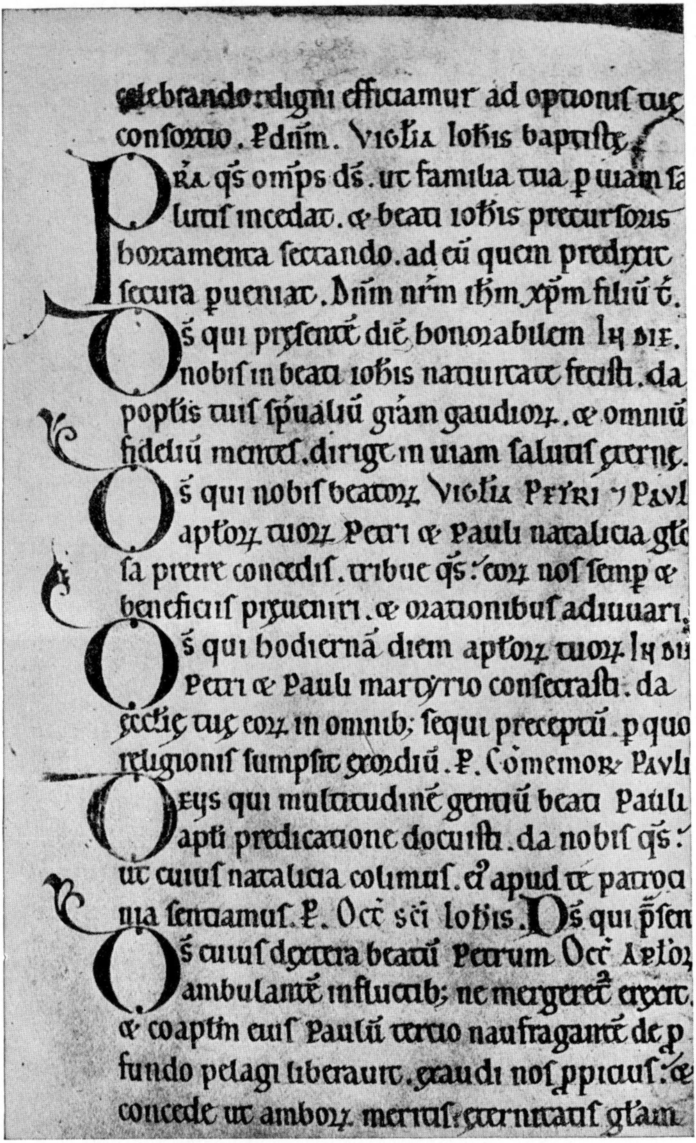

celebrando digni efficiamur ad optionis tue
consortio. Pdnm. Vigilia Johis baptiste

PRA qs omps ds. ut familia tua p uiam sa
lutis incedat. & beati Johis precursoris
hortamenta sectando. ad eu quem predixit
secura pueniat. Dnm nrm thm xpm filiu t.

OS qui psentm die honorabilem Ih die
nobis in beati Johis natiuitate fecisti. da
poptis tuis spualiu gram gaudioz. & omniu
fideliu mentes. dirige in uiam salutis eterne.

OS qui nobis beatoz Vigilia PETRI 7 PAVLI
aptoz tuoz Petri & Pauli natalicia gto
sa pcece concedis. tribue qs: coz nos semp &
beneficiis pxueniri. & orationibus adiuuari.

OS qui hodierna diem aptoz tuoz Ih di
Petri & Pauli martyrio consecrasti. da
ecclie tue coz in omnib; sequi preceptu. p quo
religionis sumpsit exordiu. P. Comemor Pauli

Oeys qui multitudine gentiu beati Pauli
apli predicatione docuisti. da nobis qs:
ut cuius natalicia colimus. & apud te patroci
nia sentiamus. P. Oct sci Johis. Ds qui psen

OS cuius dextera beatu Petrum Oct Aplox
ambulante influctib; ne mergeret erexit.
& coaptin eius Pauliu tertio naufragante de p
fundo pelagi liberauit. exaudi nos ppicius: &
concede ut amboz meritis eternitatis gram

Plate XI.—English (late) Twelfth-century Writing, with flourished
Capitals. (Breviary.) Brit. Mus., Royal MS. 2, A.X.

Descriptive Note on p. 381.　　　　393

Plate XII.—Illuminated Initial in a Flemish MS. A.D. 1148. (Latin Bible.) Brit. Museum, Addl. MS. 14790.

Descriptive Note on p. 407.

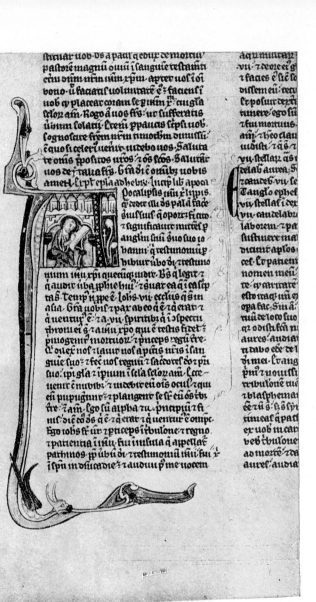

Plate XIII.—English (2nd half) Thirteenth-century Writing and Illumination.
(Latin Bible.) Ex Libris S. C. Cockerell.

Descriptive Note on p. 409.

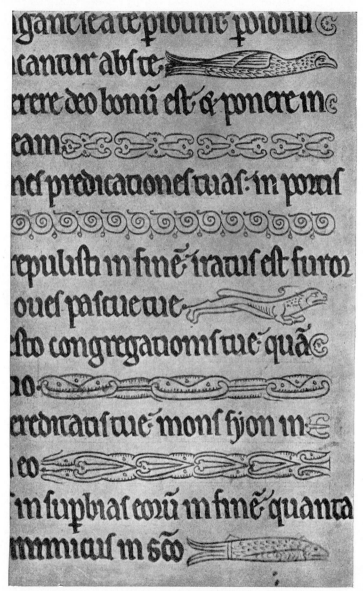

Plate XIV.—Thirteenth-century Line-finishings: Penwork. (Psalter.)
Brit. Museum, Royal MS. I, D.X.

Descriptive Note on p. 411.

Plate XV.—English Writing and Illumination, *circa* A.D. 1284. (Psalter.)
Brit. Museum, Addl. MS. 24686.

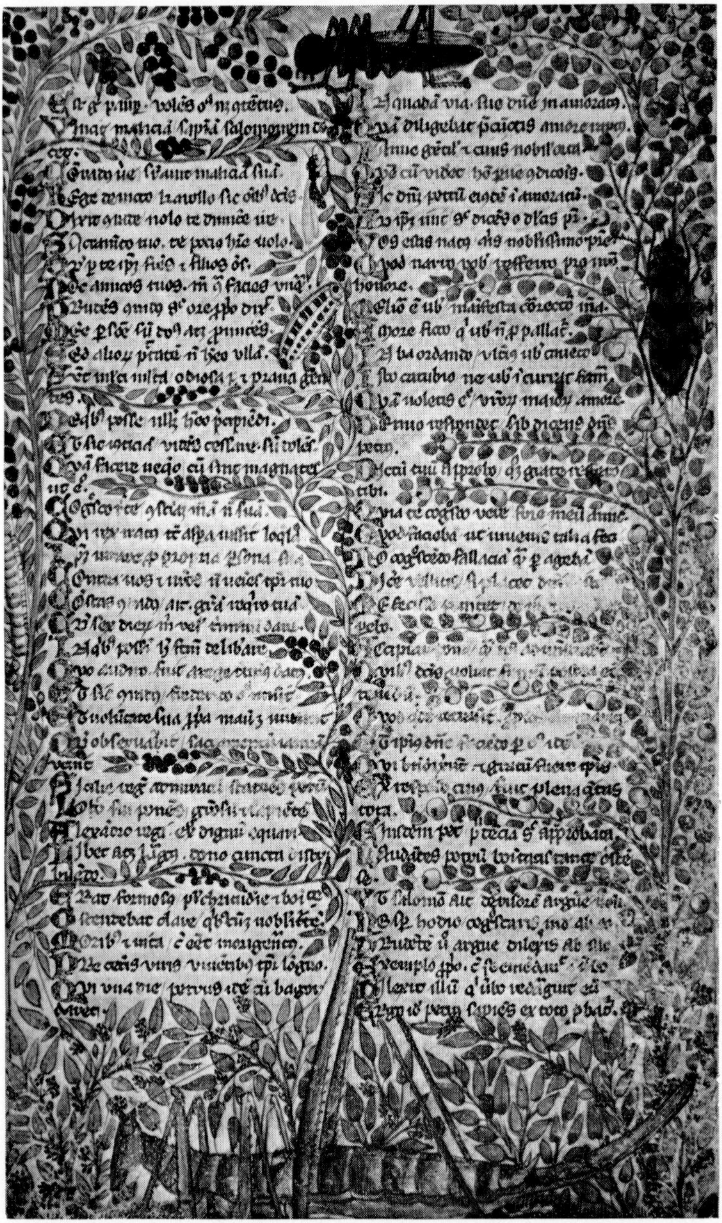

Plate XVI.—Italian Fourteenth-century MS., Brit. Mus., Addl. MS. 28841.

 Descriptive Note on p. 413.

Plate XVII.—French Fifteenth-century Writing, with
Illuminated Borders. Ex Libris E. Johnston.

399

Descriptive Note on p. 414.

Plate XVIII.—Italian Fifteenth-century Writing and Illumination (Perotti's translation of Polybius). Ex Libris H. Yates Thompson.

Descriptive Note on p. 415.

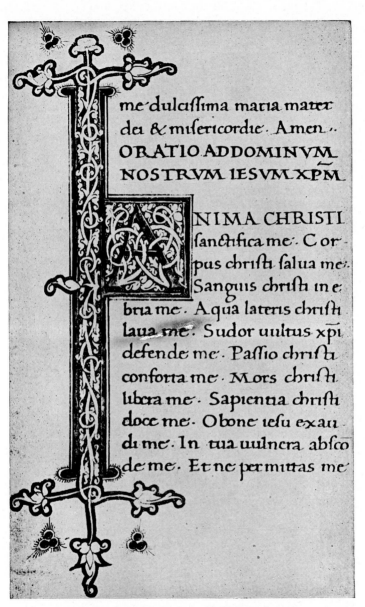

me dulcissima maria mater dei & misericordie. Amen. ORATIO ADDOMINVM NOSTRVM IESVM XPM.

ANIMA CHRISTI sanctifica me. Corpus christi salua me. Sanguis christi in ebria me. Aqua lateris christi laua me. Sudor uultus xpi defende me. Passio christi conforta me. Mors christi libera me. Sapientia christi doce me. O bone iesu exaudi me. In tua uulnera absco de me. Et ne permittas me

Plate XIX.—Italian MS., dated 1481. Ex Libris S. C. Cockerell.

Descriptive Note on p. 416.

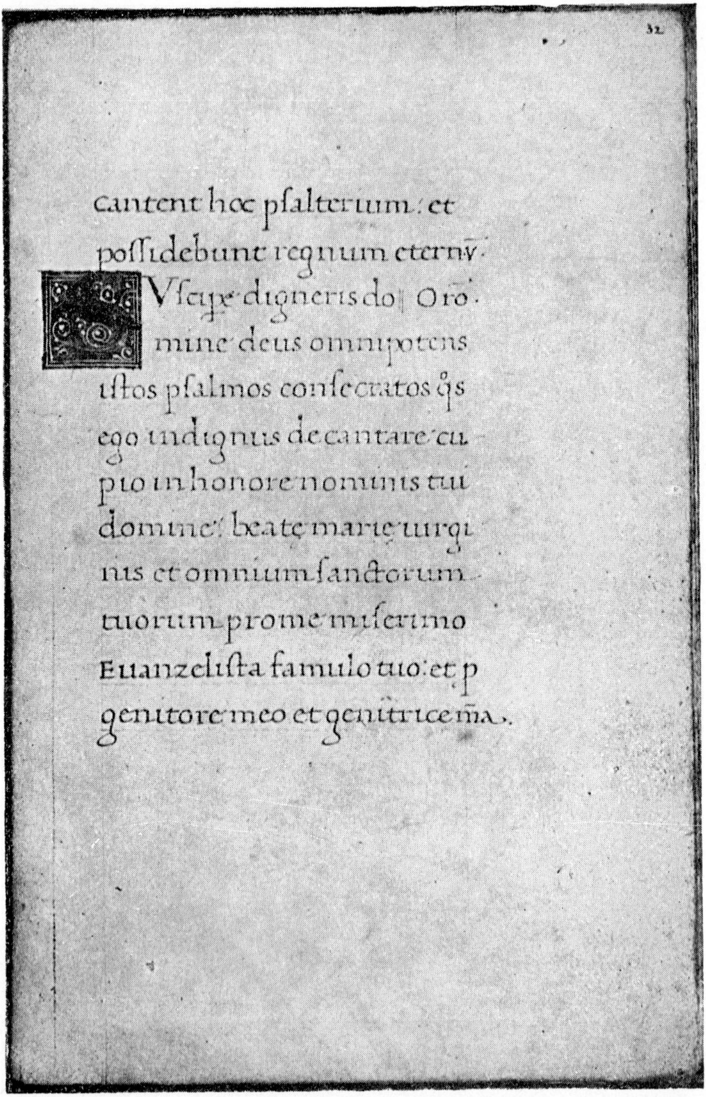

cantent hoc pfalterium : et
poffidebunt regnum eterny.
Vfcp digneris do Oro.
mine deus omnipotens
iftos pfalmos confecratos q̊s
ego indignus decantare cu-
pio in honore nominis tui
domine: beate marie uirgi
nis et omnium fanctorum
tuorum prome miferimo
Euanzelifta famulo tuo: et p
genitore meo et genitrice ma̅.

Plate XX.— One page of an Italian (late) Fifteenth-century MS.
Ex Libris S. C. Cockerell.

Descriptive Note on p. 417.

Per tutto, oue'l suo mar sospira et piagne,

Percosse in uista oltra l'usato offesa ;

Tal, ch'a noia et disdegno hebbi me steßo,

Et se non fuße che maggior paura

Freno l'ardir ; con morte acerba et dura,

A laqual fui molte fiate preßo ;

D'uscir d'affanno harei corta uia presa.

Hor chiamo ; et non so far altra difesa ;

Pur lui ; che l'ombra sua lasciando meco

Di me la uiua et miglior parte ha seco.

Che con l'altra restai morto in quel punto

Ch'io senti morir lui, che fu'l suo core ;

Ne son buon d'altro, che da tragger guai.

Tregua non uoglio hauer col mio dolore

In fin ch'io sia dal giorno ultimo giunto ;

Et tanto il piangero, quant'io l'amai.

Deh perche inanzi a lui non mi spogliai

La mortal gonna ; s'io men' uesti prima ?

S'al uiuer fui ueloce ; perche tardo

Sono al morir ? un dardo

Almen haueße et una steßa lima

Parimente ambo noi traffitto et roso ;

Che si come un uoler sempre ne tenne

Viuendo ; cosi spenti anchor n'haueße

Vn'hora, et un sepolcro ne chiudeße.

Et se questo al suo tempo, o quel non uenne ;

Descriptive Note on p. 419.

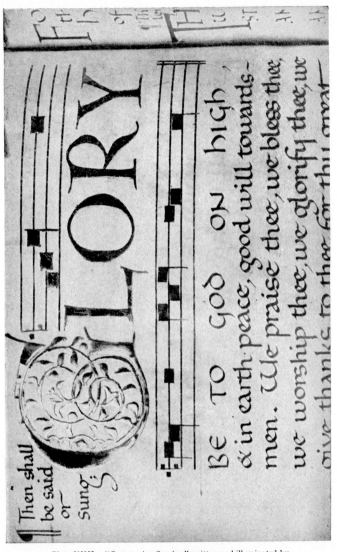

Plate XXII.—"Communion Service," written and illuminated by
E. Johnston, A.D. 1902. ("Office Book," Holy Trinity Church,
Hastings.) Reduced (nearly ¾ scale).

Descriptive Note on p. 420.

Plate XXIII.—The story of Aucassin and Nicolette, written and illuminated by W. H. Cowlishaw, A.D. 1898.

Descriptive Note on p. 421.

Plate XXIV.—Inscription cut in Stone by A. E. R. Gill, A.D. 1903.
Reduced ($\frac{3}{16}$ scale). *Note.*—To view these incised letters have the
light on the left of the plate (*or cover with thin tissue-paper*).

Descriptive Note on p. 422.

decorative in the ordinary sense, they may be said to strengthen the thin parts (much as the weakest part of the loop in an old key was thickened for strength).

Note the right-hand Bows of the ♦'s are made thinner, as though the Rubricator had been afraid of running into the text in making their last curves—such an expert, however, may well have had a better reason for it.

PLATE XII.—Illuminated Initial in a Flemish MS.
A.D. 1148. (*Latin Bible*). *Brit. Museum, Addl.*
MS. 14790.

(Shown in Brit. Museum, Department of MSS., Case C, No. 91.)

THE VOLUME—the *third*, and most interesting, of this MS. Bible (Numbered 14788-89-90)—contains 223 leaves (17 inches by 11⅞ inches). MARGINS, approximately, *Inner* 1⅛ inch, *Head* (*cut*) 1 inch, *Side* 2⅜ inches, *Foot* 3½ inches. (Between columns 1⁵⁄₁₆ inch.)

THE WRITING is a not very legible "Gothic." The *zigzag* tendency exhibited, especially by the word *niniuen* (Niniveh), second line, is unsuited for such *formal* writing (see p. 420). The rapid placing of the Heads of the letters is such that they appear broken and partly detached from the *stems*. The VERSALS are of a good type.

THE INITIAL is a monogrammatic ET. The arms of the round Є terminate in leaves folded back, its form is *hollow* and *inwoven* (p. 174), and gives rise to foliage, which fills the interior—passing over the fish and behind Jonah. Note also how the jaws of the fish are interlaced, and how compactly *all* the parts are put together.

The close application of the background to the *curves* adds to the general compactness, and, together with its spacing from the *straight* front, balances the masses (p. 410): it may be compared to the even spacing of curved and straight strokes (see fig. 53). There is an extension of the background to hold the fish's tail.

THE COLOURS—

Initial, Foliage, Fish:	red:	outlined		*Vellum*
Jonah:	black:	& lined		*left plain.*

Bands on Initial,
Hollows in Initial, ⎱ *gold*, outlined *red.*
Backs of folded leaves: ⎰

Outer background: *paled green.*

Dots on outer ground: *red.*

Inner background: *paled blue.*

We may not, I think, attempt to imitate the complex 12th-century decoration of this initial (see p. 162), but the treatment of the *elements* of form and colour is very suggestive, and the whole piece of lettering is characteristic of the grand style in which a book was at that time begun. The ARRANGEMENT of the letters themselves is very simple, and might be made good use of (fig. 220).

INCIPIT·JONAS͜-PPHĀ:
(propheta)

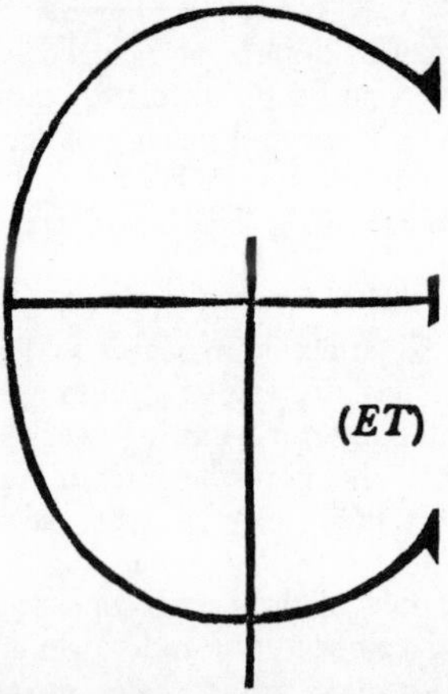

F
A
C
T
U
M.
E
S
T.

(ET)

verbum d(*omi*)ni ad jonam filiu(*m*) amathi dicens. Surge & vade in niniven civitatem magnam. & pr(*a*)edica in ea.

     FIG. 220.

*PLATE XIII.—English (2nd half) Thirteenth-century
Writing and Illumination. (Latin Bible.) Ex libris
S. C. Cockerell.*

THE VOLUME—probably written at York—contains 427 leaves (8 inches by $5\frac{1}{2}$ inches): two columns to the page: MARGINS, approx.: Inner $\frac{5}{8}$ inch, *Head* $\frac{5}{8}$ inch, *Side* $\frac{7}{8}$ inch, Foot $1\frac{7}{16}$ inch. (Between the columns $\frac{3}{8}$ inch.) The pages have been cut down.

THE WRITING is very small, and there are many contractions.[1] In the thirteenth and fourteenth centuries the whole Bible, written in this fashion, was often small enough to be carried in the pocket. Note the closed $\mathfrak{a}$ and the 7 form of &. The page is RULED with 50 lines; the 49 lines of writing lie between these, so that in each case the *ascenders* touch the line above, and the *descenders*, the line below. Note the double lines in the Foot margin (see p. 307).

VERSALS.—A very narrow type is used in the narrow margins: the example shown is in red, flourished blue; it begins the second chapter (*Et angelo ephesi, &c.*), which is also marked by coloured Roman Numerals at the side (II). The page heading is "APOCA" in small red and blue Versals.

THE ILLUMINATED INITIAL is "historiated"—*i.e.* it contains a picture illustrating the text, viz. a representation of S. John writing to the Seven Churches —purely conventional forms, or rather symbols, for the most part, are used and beautifully fitted into the available space. The greater size and more careful drawing of the human figure (the centre of interest) is characteristic of a fine convention. The slope of the vellum page on which S. John is writing, and even the manner in which the quill is held, are such as would naturally be employed by a scribe (see *frontispiece,* & p. 33).

---

[1] The Apocalypse here begins "APocalipfis iħu x¹" (for IĦU XP̄I, derived from the Greek and used as a mediæval Latin contraction for *Jesu Christi*).

The *capitals* of the pillars mark the position of the cross-bar of A. The top serif is carried up and forms a bud, which gives rise to leaf-like flourishes; the free thin stem runs down forming a grotesque, which gives out a leaf-like tongue In either case the object—in every sense *recreative*—is a renewal of interest in the designed, elongated, growth of the forms.

Note the curved thickening of A's left stem ends nearly level with the foot of the right stem. This gives balance to the letter (see R, fig. 81 & A, fig. 189), and preserves the *essential form*, which suffers no distortion by the thinner continuation below.

Note the balancing of the background mass on the *straight* and *curved* sides of the Initial (as in Plate XII, see above); also the extension and shape of the background accompanying the drawn out parts of the letter.

COLOURS of Initial—

Right stem:	*red* with *white* lines
Left stem and serif:	*blue* and patterns.
L. stem, lower half, & dragon:	*pale "lake."*
The back- ⌈ outer:	*pale "lake."*
ground ⟨ inner:	*blue.*
(*counter-* ⟨ lower extension:	*blue.*
charged) ⌊ final flourish:	*pale "lake."*
Band (dark) down left side, dragon's wings, 6 "berries," halo, seat, tops of pillar caps:	*burnished gold.*
Leaves (dark) & pillar caps:	*red.*
Small stems & leaves:	*green.*

Here again no natural work would come of a modern attempt to imitate so complex a "design"—natural and even inevitable 600 *years ago*. But the spirit of delicacy and fantasy, the ingenious contrivance, and the balancing and disposal of form and colour shown by the antique art, may well be matter for imitation by the modern draughtsman-illuminator, and even by the mere penman.

THE LINE-FINISHINGS (see p. 171), of which there are very many throughout the book, all in red or blue pen-work, are very varied. Nine kinds are shown in the plate (which represents about a quarter of a page), and three others from the same MS. are given in figs. 87 (*b*) and 126 (*f, g*).

The directions of the thick and thin strokes indicate a pen held at right angles to its usual position (almost "upside down," in fact: see fig. 126, *g*), and the penmanship exhibits great speed and lightness of hand—the rapidity and skill are indeed quite remarkable (*e.g.* in the Lion in the eighth line).

Note that, though the writing occasionally runs into the margin, the line-finishings stop at the marginal-line.

The photograph shows red *dark* and blue *light: e.g.* the Bird is red, the Lion and the Fish are blue. The fifth Line-finishing is a red filigree with blue "berries" —it can hardly be described as a "floral growth," as the "branching" is reversed: the rubricator gained speed and uniformity by the simple repetition of the whorls all along the line—the upper branches were probably put in afterwards, and the "berries" were added later when he was making the *blue* Line-finishings.

The more complex decoration (not shown in the plate) in this MS. is inferior to the penmanship: the small *background* Capitals with which the verses begin—presumably put in by a different hand—are more pretentious, and do not match the Line-finishings.

General Note.—When a space occurs at the end of a line of writing, it is often best to leave it, and in a plain MS., if it be "well and truly" written, there is no objection to varying lengths of line (see pp. 227, 335). But a book, such as a *Psalter*, divided into many short verses —in which the last line usually falls short of the marginal line—offers a fair field for such simple and effective

411

decoration. (See also pp. 414, 422, fig. 130, and Plate
XXIII.)

*PLATE XV.—English Writing and Illumination, circa
1284 A.D. (Psalter.) Brit. Museum, Addl. MS.
24686.*

THE WRITING is a fine, freely formed, "Gothic"
(p. 295). Note, the i's are "dotted." Note the double
MARGINAL LINES (p. 307).

THE SMALL INITIALS are of the "Lombardic"
type (p. 176), in which the Serifs are much thickened
and ornamented. Note the tails of the Q's are turned to
the left to clear the writing. The LINE-FILLINGS
match the small initials (p. 159).

THE LARGE INITIAL, &c.—The plate shows
the end of the fourteenth and beginning of the fifteenth

Psalm (**O** omine quis habitabit). Note "*Arabic*"
numerals (15) in margin.

The tail of the Initial **O** is formed of a dragon, the
head of which rests on the O-part: its wings project into
the inner margin (and these in the plate, which shows a
fragment of a *verso* page, run into the fold between the
pages): the tail (together with the background) descends
till a convenient point is reached from which the lower
scroll-work springs. The tail, wing, and claws above,
belong to a magpie which is perched on the initial.

THE DRAWING: see reference to this at p. 169,
and below.

Sir Edward Maunde Thompson (p. 39, "English
Illuminated MSS.") says of this—

"—the Additional MS. 24686 in the British Museum, known
as the Tenison Psalter, from its having once formed part of the
library of Archbishop Tenison. This psalter is one of the most
beautiful illuminated English manuscripts of its time, but unfortunately only in part, for it was not finished in the perfect

style in which it was begun . . . in the first quire of the text the ornamentation is of peculiar beauty. . . ."[1]

"—the progress of the art [since the earlier part of the thirteenth century] . . . is . . . manifest. There is more freedom in the drawing, the stiffness of the earlier examples is in great measure overcome; and the pendant has thrown out a branch which has already put forth leaves. A great variety of colours, blue, rose, vermilion, lake, green, brown, as well as burnished gold, is employed in the composition of the large initial and its accompanying pendant and border, and the small initials are of gold laid on a ground of blue or lake, and filled with lake or blue; while the ribbons which fill up the spaces at the ends of the verses are alternately of the same colours and are decorated with patterns in silver on the blue and in gold on the lake."

"The group of the dismounted knight despatching[2] a gryphon, which has proved too much for the horse, upon whose dying body the expectant raven has already perched, is tinted in lighter colours. It is an instance of the use to which marginal space was put, particularly by English artists, for the introduction of little scenes, such as episodes in romances or stories, games, grotesque combats, social scenes, &c., often drawn with a light free hand and most artistic touch. Without these little sketches, much of the manners and customs, dress, and daily life of our ancestors would have remained for ever unknown to us."

---

[1] It is supposed that the book was at first intended as a marriage gift for Alphonso, son of Edward I.

[2] The characteristic *over and under* arrangement of the gryphon's upper and lower bill, makes this doubtful.

PLATE XVI.—Italian Fourteenth-century MS., Brit. Mus., Addl. MS. 28841.

THE VOLUME: one of two (the other numbered 27695), a *Latin* treatise on the Virtues and Vices (The miniatures, drawings, &c., probably by "the Monk of Hyères," Genoa). The vellum leaves have been separated, and are now preserved in paper books. The leaf illustrated shows a margin of vellum of less than $\frac{3}{16}$ inch all round (the plate).

The decorative borders are much more naturalistic in

form and colouring than any other old illumination that I
have seen (see reference to Plate XVI, p. 169).

The foliage is a delicate green, the berries are dark
purple, the single fruits plain and pale orange-red; the two
beetles in *crimson* and *brown* are made darker and too
prominent in the photograph. The bands of small
"Lombardic" Capitals are in burnished gold.

Note how skilfully and naturally the upper corners of
the border are managed, and also the beautiful way in
which the branches run into and among the text (see
p. 179).

PLATE XVII.—*French Fifteenth-century Writing, with Illuminated Borders. Ex libris E. Johnston.*

THE PAGE $9\frac{1}{2}$ inches by $6\frac{1}{8}$ inches: MARGINS,
approx.: *Inner* $1\frac{1}{8}$ inch, *Head* $1\frac{3}{8}$ inch, *Side* $2\frac{3}{8}$ inches,
Foot $2\frac{7}{8}$ inches (the edges have been slightly cut down).
The marginal lines (from head to foot of the page) and
the writing lines are RULED in faint red.

THE WRITING is a late formal "Gothic"—the
thin strokes have evidently been added (p. 13). The
written Capitals are blotted with yellow (see p. 106).
The ILLUMINATED INITIAL Q is in blue, white
lined, on a gold ground, contains a blue flower and five
ornaments in "lake." The LINE-FILLINGS are in
blue and "lake," separated by a gold circle, triangle, or
lozenge.

THE FILIGREE ILLUMINATION springs from
the initial in the narrow margin, and from a *centre*
ornament (see "knot," fig. 127) in the wide side margin.
The side margins are treated similarly on either page
(see p. 179); the inner margins are generally plain.
This repetition gives to the pages a certain sameness—
which is a *characteristic* rather than a fault of the
treatment.

The border on the *recto* of the vellum leaf shows
through on the *verso* or back of the leaf. The main
lines of the first border, however, are freely traced and

414

followed on the *verso* (and so nearly hidden) by the
second border. This is also suggestive of the more rapid
methods of book production in the 15th century.

COLOURS—

Stems, tendrils, &c.:   *black.*

Leave $\begin{cases}\text{ivy-shaped}\\\text{lanceolate:}\end{cases}$ $\begin{cases}\textit{burnished gold}, \text{ out-}\\\text{lined black (p. 153).}\end{cases}$ $\begin{cases}\textit{plain.}\\\textit{furred.}\end{cases}$

Flowers, buds, centre
ornaments, &c.:
(See p. 148.) $\begin{cases}\textit{blue}, \text{ "}\textit{lake},\text{" or } \textit{green} \text{ tempered}\\\text{with white, and shaded with}\\\text{pure colour; white markings;}\\\text{the forms not outlined.}\end{cases}$

This type of illumination is discussed in pp. 163–8·
Its chief points are its simplicity and rapidity. A penman
or a novice in illuminating can, by taking a little pains,
beautify his MSS. easily and quickly; and he may perhaps
pass on from this to "higher" types of illumination.

*PLATE XVIII.—Italian Fifteenth-century Writing and
Illumination. (Perotti's translation of Polybius.) Ex
libris H. Yates Thompson.*

THE VOLUME consists of 174 leaves ($13\frac{1}{8}$ inches
by 9 inches); 35 lines to the page. The plate shows a
portion of the upper part of the Initial (*recto*) page.

THE WRITING.—The Capitals are simple-written,
slanted-pen "Roman"—slightly ornamental—forms.
They are freely copied on a large scale in fig. 168: see
p. 261. The Small-letters match the Capitals—they are
"Roman" forms with a slight "Gothic" tendency. Both
these and the Capitals would make very good models for
free Roman hands.

THE INITIAL is a "Roman" A in burnished gold.
Note the exceedingly graceful shaping of the limbs, the
ornamental, V-shaped cross-bar, and the absence of serifs
(see fig. 116).

415

The *"White Vine Pattern"* (see p. 168), most delicately and beautifully drawn, interlaces with the letter and itself, and covers the BACKGROUND very evenly. The interstices of the background are painted in blue, red, and green, and its edge is adapted to the slightly projecting flowers and leaves. There are groups (∴ and ⋯) of white dots on the blue parts of the background.

THE BORDER (of which a small part is shown) is approximately ½ inch wide in the narrow margin at the side of the text—it is separate from the Initial. It extends above and below the text, where its depth is greater, matching the greater depth of the margins. Its treatment is similar to, though perhaps a little simpler than, that of the Initial decoration.

PLATE XIX.—Italian MS., dated 1481. *Ex libris
S. C. Cockerell.*

"Part of a [verso] page from a book containing the Psalter of St. Jerome and various Prayers, written and decorated by Joachinus de Gigantibus of Rotenberg in 1481 for Pope Sixtus IV. Joachinus was employed at Naples by Ferdinand I., and there are other fine examples of his work at the British Museum and the Bibliothèque Nationale, Paris. In each of these, as well as in the present book, he states that he was both scribe and illuminator."—[S. C. C.]

THE VOLUME contains 31 leaves (6½ inches by 4¾ inches): MARGINS, approx.: *Inner* ⅞ inch, *Head* ⅞ inch, *Side* 1½ inch, *Foot* 1¾ inch. (The head margin, together with the edge of the book-cover, is shown in the plate.)

THE WRITING.—Very clear, slightly slanted-pen "Roman." Note the blending of **b** and **p** with **e** and **o** (see fig. 176, & p. 43). The CAPITALS are quite simple and plain, made (in *(A)NIMA CHRISTI* and in text) in black with the text pen. Note the long, waved

serifs (see p. 253). The two lines of capitals preceding
the prayer are made in burnished gold with a larger pen.

THE INITIAL A, its frame, the frame of the border,
and the "furred" *berries* (∴) are all in burnished gold,
outlined black. The "white vine pattern" is rather
simpler, and has a rather thicker stalk (in proportion)
than that in the previous plate (see above). Its treatment
is very similar, but it may be noted that the border is in
this case attached to the Initial, and the pattern has almost
an appearance of springing from the Initial. The pattern
—save one escaped leaf—is straitly confined, by gold
bars, throughout the length of the text, but at the ends
it is branched out and beautifully flourished in the free
margins above and below. These terminals of the pattern
having a broad blue outline (dotted white) may be said
to carry their background with them.

The (recto) page opposite that shown in the plate has
an initial D and a border similarly treated, and each one
of the Psalms and Prayers throughout the book is begun
in like manner.

*PLATE XX.—One page of an Italian (late) Fifteenth-
century MS. Ex libris S. C. Cockerell.*

"From a book containing the Penitential Psalms in
Italian, the Psalter of St. Jerome, and various prayers.
Written with great delicacy by Mark of Vicenza for
some one named Evangelista [see 11th line] in the last
quarter of the fifteenth century. Other works of this
accomplished scribe are known."—[S. C. C.]

THE VOLUME—of which a complete (recto) page
is shown—contains 60 leaves ($5\frac{1}{2}$ inches by $3\frac{3}{4}$ inches):
MARGINS, approx.: *Inner* $\frac{1}{2}$ inch, *Head* $\frac{7}{8}$ inch, *Side*
$1\frac{3}{16}$ inch, *Foot* $1\frac{13}{16}$ inch.

This very fine WRITING is typical of the practical
style and beautiful workmanship which should be the aim
of a modern scribe (see pp. 13, 274).

It is written with a very narrow nib, hence the pen-
forms are not so obvious as in some early formal hands;

417

and for this reason alone it would be better to practise such a hand as the tenth-century MS. (Plate VIII) before seriously attempting to model a hand on the above (see pp. 378, 275, 288, xxiv).

The use of a fine pen is apt to flatter the unskilled penman, and he finds it hard to distinguish between delicate penwork which has much character, and that which has little or none. And he will find, after some knowledge of penmanship gained in practice with a broad nib, that the copying of this fine Italian writing—while in reality made much more feasible—may even *appear* more difficult than before.

CONSTRUCTION.—The pen has a moderate slant —see thin stroke in **e**. The letters are very square, the tops flat (especially in **m, n,** and **r**), and the lower parts flat (as in **u**). This shows the same tendency that there is in the tenth century and other hands *to avoid thin or high arches in the letters.*

The feet in some of the letters (in **i**, for example) are in the nature of stroke-serifs, but the pen probably made these with an almost continuous movement—from the stem.

Note—the fine form of the **a**;

that **b** and **l** have an angle where the stem joins the lower part;

that **b,o,p,** *overlap* **o** and **e** ;

that **f** and long **ſ** were made something like **ı**'s, and then the upper parts were added ; this was a common mode—see fig. 180 ;

that **g**—a very graceful letter—has no terminal projection or *lug* ;

that **i, p, u** have *triangular heads,* and **m, n, r** *hooks;*

that the *ascenders* have triangular heads, and the *descenders* **p** and **q,** stroke-serifs;

that the ascending and descending stems are longer than the bodies, and the writing is in consequence fairly widely spaced.

418

Like most of the finest writings, this bears evidences
of considerable speed (see pp. 50, 275). Besides the
great uniformity of the letters, the *finishing strokes* are
occasionally carried into the succeeding letter, the *arches*
of b, h, m, n, p, r (and the *heads* of the ascenders) frequently are separated from the stems, and the o and b
occasionally fail to join below. These broken forms are
the *results of speed*, and are not to be imitated except as
to that which is both a cause and a result—their *uniformity
and freedom* (p. 218).

The RULING is in faint ink: there are *two* vertical marginal lines on the left and *one* on the right of
every page.

The DECORATION of the MS. is very simple. The
Initial (here shown) is in green and powder-gold, on a
lake ground, with white pattern: there is a very fine
brownish outline, probably drawn first. The two upper
lines of writing and ||oro are in red.

PLATE XXI. — *Italian* (*early*) *Sixteenth - century*
"*cursive*" or "*Italic*" *MS. Ex libris S. C. Cockerell.*
(*See enlargement, fig.* 178.)

"From the Poems of Cardinal Bembo, a fine example
of the cursive writing perfected in Italy in the first half
of the sixteenth century. The book measures 8½ by 5¼
inches, and contains 79 leaves."—[S. C. C.]

THE MARGINS of the page from which the plate
is taken are approximately: *Inner* ⅝ inch, *Head* ¾ inch,
Side 2 inches, *Foot* 1½ inch. *Note.*—The lines of writing
begin as usual at the left margin, but do not extend to the
(true) margin on the *right*, hence the latter (the *side*
margin on the recto, and the *inner* margin on the verso)
would appear unnaturally wide, but the effect is carried
off by the (true) side margins being already exceptionally
wide (and by the writing on the backs of the leaves
showing through the semi-transparent vellum and so
marking the true margins).

This mode is very suitable for a book of poems, in which the lengths of the lines of writing may vary considerably, because the *writing-line* being longer than the *ordinary* line of writing allows room for extraordinarily long lines, and any appearance of irregularity is carried off by the extra wide side margins.

THE WRITING is very beautiful, clear, and rapid —made with a "slanted pen" (see "Italics," p. 275, and fig. 178). Note the *slightness* of the slope of the letters (especially of the Capitals), and the length of the stems and the wide spacing.

Note, also, the flatness of the curves in *a c d e g o q* and the horizontal top stroke in *a d g q*, oblique in *e c* (giving angular tops). The branching away from the stem of the first part of the *arch* in *b h m n p r* (seen also reversed in *a d g q u*), and the pointed, almost angular, quality of the *arch*. This, which is apt to become a fault in a more formal upright hand (see note on Plate XXII) is helpful in a more rapid running hand, and gives *clearance* to the junctions of the strokes (*r r*)—see fig. 182.

The *heads*, simple or built-up, *hooks* tending to become triangular.

The letters in this MS. are rarely coupled.

The very graceful *g* has a large pear-shaped lower loop touching the upper part.

PLATE XXII.—*"Communion Service" written and illuminated by E. Johnston,* A.D. 1902. *("Office Book," Holy Trinity Church, Hastings.) Reduced (nearly ¾ scale).*

The MS. on 160 leaves (15 inches by 10 inches) of fine parchment ("Roman Vellum," see p. 139), contains the Communion Service and many collects, epistles, and gospels for special festivals, &c. MARGINS: *Inner* 1⅛ inch, *Head* 1¾ inch, *Side* 2¼ inches, *Foot* 3¾ inches.

THE WRITING—after tenth century model (see
Plate VIII)—has the fault (referred to at p. 407) of
showing too much *thin* line (running up obliquely), the
upper and lower parts of the letters are not flat enough.
The tail of the g is inadequate, and the lines of writing
are too near together. The writing is readable, however,
and fairly regular. The CAPITALS are Uncials (after
Plate V.) and occasional "Romans."

The RUBRIC ("¶ *Then shall be said or sung*") is in
red, fitted in beside the round initial and marking the top
left-hand corner of the page (see *footnote*, p. 177).

The word "GLORY" (and decoration)—and also
the F and T, showing in recto page—are in raised burnished gold, which, it will be seen, has cracked considerably in the G (see p. 130).

The STAVES are in red (p. 106), the *notes* above
GLORY in raised *gold*, those in the lower stave, *black*.

The BOOK was of a special nature (see pp. 308–9),
being intended for use in a certain church and on certain
special festivals: hence a considerable degree of ornament and a generally decorative treatment was permitted
(p. 294). The Prayer of Consecration, together with a
miniature, occupied a complete *opening*, the eight margins
of which were filled with solid, framing borders (p. 179)
in red, blue, green, and gold. Coats-of-arms and other
special symbols and devices were introduced on the Title
page and in other places.

*PLATE XXIII.—The Story of Aucassin and Nicolette,
    written and illuminated by W. H. Cowlishaw,
    A.D. 1898.*

THE VOLUME consists of 50 + leaves of "Roman
Vellum" (7½ inches by 5½ inches).

MARGINS, approx.: *Inner* ¾ inch, *Head* 1 5/16 inch,
Side 1⅜ inch, *Foot* 2 inches.

THE WRITING, very legible, rather "Gothic-
Roman."

THE CAPITALS are illuminated throughout the text in *gold* on blue and red grounds. The backgrounds are square, with edges pointed or indented, outlined *black*, and lined inside *white*. The INITIAL n is in gold on blue: the moon and stars are in white and gold and white.

THE LINE-FINISHINGS, mostly in black pen-work, consist of little groups (sometimes of sprays) of flowers, &c. Sprays from the border separate the "Song" from the "Tale."

THE MUSIC.—*Staves* black; *Clefs*, gold; *Notes*, red.

THE BORDERS (in the opening from which the plate is taken) frame the text on both pages—nearly filling the margins (see p. 179): the side and foot edges of the (verso) page are shown in the plate. The main pattern is a wild rose, flowers and all, outlined with a rather broad blue line: the stalks and leaves (lined white) are apple-green, the flowers are *painted* white with raised gold hearts, the thorns are red. Through the wild rose is twined *honeysuckle and woody nightshade:* stalks— (*h*) red, (*wn*) black; and flowers—(*h*) red with yellow spots, (*wn*) purplish red with gold centres.

The whole effect is very brilliant and charming. The freedom and naturalness of the "design" remind one of a country hedgerow (p. 179), and show that vital beauty which is the essence of true illumination.

PLATE XXIV.—Inscription cut in Stone by A. E. R. Gill, A.D. 1903. *Reduced* ($\frac{3}{16}$ *scale.*) Note.—*To view these incised letters have light on the left of plate (or cover with thin tissue-paper).*

The STONE—a slab of "Hopton Wood" (p. 359), 30 inches by 18 inches by 2 inches, is intended to go over a lintel. It has a simple moulding. Note how the INSCRIPTION occupies the space (pp. 316, 358): the LETTERS have approximately the same *apparent weight* (p. 292)—the large stems are more than twice the *height* of the small; they are only $\frac{1}{2}$ *wider*.

422

Note the strongly marked and elegantly curved serifs; the straight-tailed R; the I drawn out (marking the word IN); the *beaked* A, M, and N; the Capital form of u.

The letters DEO would be rather wide for ordinary use (p. 234), but as *special* letters, occupying a wide space,[1] are permissible.

Even in the plate, I think this inscription shows to what a high level modern inscription cutting might be raised by the use of good models and right and simple methods.

---

[1] Letters in early inscriptions separated as these are indicated *each* a word (contracted), as S. P. Q. R. (*Senatus Populus Que Romanus*).

APPENDIX C

COPY OF LETTER WRITTEN ON 5TH APRIL, 1933,
FROM EDWARD JOHNSTON TO COLONEL CROSLAND

Dear Sir,

Letter to
Colonel
Crosland

Your letter of the 3rd raises an interesting question—the treatment of the uncut quill. My experience is not great, but, as since the War it has been more difficult to buy good ready-cut quills, I have got the local poulterer to save a bunch of turkeys' pen feathers, and have succeeded in making quite satisfactory pens of these.

I hang up the bunch of feathers (as it is my fancy that they are better for some drying or shrinking—I think *Cocker* says something about *warm ashes*, but slow, "natural" processes are usually safest for the ignorant [and, perhaps, for the "cunning" as well]: I have not proved this fancy by contrary experiment). The quills have usually had about a year's drying, or more when I cut them.

1st   I cut off the unwanted length (p. 20);
2nd   I strip off the barbs (pp. 30–31)—*Note:* this is more easily done by holding them between the *blade* (edge) (touching) *and the thumb*—than between finger and thumb (as shown, Fig. 27);

424

3rd I scrape off the horny surface—almost like a skin—which appears to surround the quill and stick to it very closely. I have noticed that although the end of the pen feather may *look* quite clean and ready, unless this horny "skin"—or surface—is thoroughly scraped off—or at least well scraped—the pen will usually not split satisfactorily: in fact it is apt to show a ragged tear in this surface substance or skin, while the "slit" (beneath the surface) appears to be diverted or interrupted.

I assume the structure of the quill to consist of an inner longitudinally fissile substance, and an outer membrane or substance which has a binding effect (i.e. tending to prevent splitting)—comparable to a "wire-wound" gunbarrel (if that is the correct expression) or to the remarkable anticipation of that construction to be found in "Mons Meg" in Edinburgh Castle.

4th I cut off the end

and shape and make the slit exactly as shown in Figs. 17–21 (pp. 18–19) in the cutting of the *Cane* pen;

5th but, *before the final edge-cut* (Fig. 22) in both cane and quill I hollow out the sides of the tip to give this shape rather than  , making it approx.

parallel sided and

6th cut a long bevel

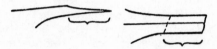

(compare (*b*) *Fig.* 36) and

7th finally cut the nibs-edge (vertically) getting
a shape which in side section might be
indicated (much magnified) thus

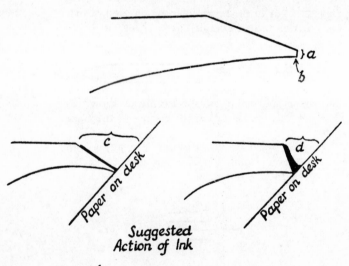

Suggested
Action of Ink

The *thickness* of the edge (*a*) is so slight that it "does not count" as long as the true edge (*b*) remains sharp (which sharpness is as necessary, and no more lasting in perfection, in a thicker nib).

The great advantage of this long bevel is that the ink which oozes out of the tip is kept well away from the paper (*c*) and is less likely to ink the thin strokes too heavily than the blunt-bevelled pen may (*d*).

It has another advantage, that being made by the long bevel very thin, the nibs-edge may be finally cut with great ease and little danger of distortion of the Quill (or Cane).

To revert to my 4th and the making of the slit (I think that you will not find much difficulty after good scraping) I make a short slit with a thin-edged knife—a surgical scalpel is good—and lengthen it, preferably by a jerk with a lever (Fig. 27), and sometimes by pressing up both sides with my fingers.

In any case it is best to make the split go back pretty far and cut away from the front part all of it in which the slit remains, or tends to remain open.

The best rule for length of slit is *as long as is compatible with strength* (i.e. as long as possible).

For the shaping of the pen a proper "pen-cutting

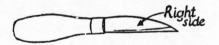

blade" is most desirable: this professional penknife is *quite* flat, or *even hollow-ground* (to keep it so) *on the "left" side*, and on the "right" side it has a

427

bevel (i.e. the cross-section somewhat resembles that of a joiner's chisel).

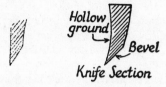

Let me know if you have any further difficulty: I am interested in improvements and in correcting my errors. Especially for those who hold my book in kindness.

Yours faithfully,
(Signed) EDWARD JOHNSTON.

Note. The diagrams in the above letter have been redrawn for purposes of reproduction.

INDEX

430

435

437